HAGGAI

Readings: A New Biblical Commentary

General Editor
John Jarick

HAGGAI

Tim Meadowcroft

SHEFFIELD PHOENIX PRESS

2006

Copyright © 2006 Sheffield Phoenix Press

Published by Sheffield Phoenix Press
Department of Biblical Studies, University of Sheffield
Sheffield S10 2TN

www.sheffieldphoenix.com

All rights reserved.
No part of this publication may be reproduced or transmitted in any form or by any means, electronic or mechanical, including photocopying, recording or any information storage or retrieval system, without the publishers' permission in writing.

A CIP catalogue record for this book
is available from the British Library

Typeset by Forthcoming Publications
Printed by the Lightning Source

Hardback ISBN 978-905048-59-5
Hardback ISBN 1-905048-59-9

Paperback ISBN 978-1-905048-60-1
Paperback ISBN 1-905048-60-2

To Lois and Andrew Young

With Thanks

CONTENTS

Preface	ix
Abbreviations	xi
Prolegomena: Reading Haggai as Scripture	1
Introduction: Haggai and Haggai's Readers	41
Haggai 1.1-2 (Section A, The First Oracle): **Setting the Scene**	88
Haggai 1.3-12 (Section B, The Second Oracle): **'Consider How You Have Fared'**	108
Haggai 1.13-15a (Section C, The Third Oracle): **'I Am with You'**	135
Haggai 1.15b-2.9 (Section D, The Fourth Oracle): **'The Latter Splendour'**	146
Haggai 2.10-19 (Section E, The Fifth Oracle): **A Proper Offering**	173
Haggai 2.20-23 (Section F, The Sixth Oracle): **The Signet Ring**	198
Conclusion: The Contemporary Relevance **of Haggai**	210
Appendices	243
Bibliography	249
Index of Authors	258

ABBREVIATIONS

AB	Anchor Bible
ABCS	Asia Bible Commentary Series
AOTC	Abingdon Old Testament Commentary
AV	Authorised Version
BHS	*Biblia Hebraica Stuttgartensia*
BI	*Biblical Interpretation*
BS	Biblical Seminar
BT	*Bible Translator*
CBQ	*Catholic Biblical Quarterly*
CSCD	Cambridge Studies in Christian Doctrine
FOTL	Forms of the Old Testament Literature
ICC	International Critical Commentary
JETS	*Journal of the Evangelical Theology Society*
JJS	*Journal of Jewish Studies*
JNES	*Journal of Near Eastern Studies*
JOTT	*Journal for Translation and Textlinguistics*
JSJSup	Supplements to the *Journal for the Study of Judaism*
JSOT	*Journal for the Study of the Old Testament*
JSOTSup	*Journal for the Study of the Old Testament* Supplements Series
LXX	Septuagint
MT	Masoretic Text
NICOT	New International Commentary on the Old Testament
NIV	New International Version
NRSV	New Revised Standard Version
NTS	*New Testament Studies*
OBT	Overtures to Biblical Theology
OTG	Old Testament Guides
OTL	Old Testament Library
P&B	Pragmatics and Beyond
RSV	Revised Standard Version
RTR	*Reformed Theological Review*
SBLDS	Society of Biblical Literature Dissertation Series
SBLEJL	Society of Biblical Literature Early Judaism and its Literature
SJT	*Scottish Journal of Theology*
SNTSMS	Society for New Testament Studies Monograph Series
SOFS	Symbolae Osloenses Fasc. Supplet
SPS	Sacra Pagina Series
STAR	Studies in Theology and Religion
STDJ	Studies on the Texts of the Deserts of Judah

TOTC	Tyndale Old Testament Commentary
TriJ	*Trinity Journal*
TynBul	*Tyndale Bulletin*
VT	*Vetus Testamentum*
VTSup	*Vetus Testamentum*, Supplements
WBC	Word Biblical Commentary

PROLEGOMENA:
READING HAGGAI AS SCRIPTURE

Haggai is a book that very few people can even find in a modern version of the Bible, let alone know quite what to do with when they get there. For the fledgling student of prophecy, poor Haggai stands as an example of a prophet who somehow made it into the canon despite the apparent non-fulfilment of his prophecy on Zerubbabel, thus immeasurably complicating the question of what constitutes true and false prophecy. As a result, at the level of popular preaching one of two things can happen. More often than not the problematic final reference to Zerubbabel as 'signet ring' is ignored in favour of the earlier part of the book with its more temporal focus on the rebuilding of the temple. Yet, even here a full-orbed appreciation of the message of Haggai is potentially sidelined in the rush to bring an equally temporal application to a local situation, such as a church building project. Alternatively, Zerubbabel is interpreted messianically with little acknowledgment either of the problems that this raises or of Zerubbabel's own Judean context.

Scholarly treatment of Haggai is equally uncertain. At one extreme, the commentator Wilhelm Rudolph states that the book of Haggai is 'without significance', and 'having been overtaken by Christian belief'.[1] In fairness to Rudolph, this view is moderated somewhat by his explanation that the irrelevance of Haggai arises from the subsequent fulfilment of the prophet's hopes in the person of Christ. Peter Ackroyd's description of the prophet as a 'lesser character' is not as bald an assessment as Rudolph's, but does seem to damn Haggai with faint

---

1. W. Rudolph, *Haggai–Sacharja 1–8–Sacharja 9–14–Maleachi* (Gütersloh: Gerd Mohn, 1976), p. 58: 'für uns Heutige ohne Belang', and 'für den christlichen Glauben überholt ist'.

praise.² He relegates the book of Haggai to the status of a minor player, operating in the shadows of such giants as the Isaianic corpus.

While we do well to heed Ackroyd's warning not to claim too much for Haggai, I note also his grudging admission that Haggai may have had 'a distinctive word to his own generation'.³ There are others who would claim still more. H.G. May urges his readers not 'to underestimate his importance'.⁴ And Hans Walter Wolff sets a tone from which this volume takes its cue:

> this little book is a model of effective proclamation in its dispute with a stubborn and dispirited people—a model in its questions and its admonitions, its encouragement and its activating promise.⁵

Haggai, with his fellow prophets Zechariah and Malachi, stands at a significant moment in the history of Israel, and with them, in his own way, is part of a shift in focus and accommodation to a vastly different world from that which the exiles to Babylon had left some seventy years earlier. He may not scale the literary heights of Isaiah or plumb the personal depths of Jeremiah, but the manner in which he brings the word of the Lord has a rugged economy that bears its own beauty. And his unremitting focus on the temple rebuilding project is not so much a dilution of the message of his great predecessors as a sharp focus on the needs of a particular moment in the history of a people.⁶ Far from being distracted by a purely secular vision, a crime of which he is sometimes accused, Haggai and the book that bears his name bring a

---

2. P. Ackroyd, 'Studies in the Book of Haggai', *JJS* 3 (1952), pp. 1-13 (9).

3. Ackroyd, 'Studies', p. 9.

4. H.G. May, '"This People" and "This Nation" in Haggai', *VT* 18 (1968), pp. 190-97 (197).

5. H.W. Wolff, *Haggai: A Commentary* (trans. M. Kohl; Minneapolis: Augsburg, 1988), p. 11.

6. I appreciate the challenge of J.E. Goldingay, *Old Testament Theology. I. Israel's Gospel* (Downers Grove, IL: InterVarsity Press, 2003), p. 38, to the suggestion that 'the postexilic period was...a low point' in the Old Testament story. With him, 'I seek to avoid such assumptions. All these periods and all these stages in the story make it possible to see some things but also to miss others.'

surprisingly subtle exploration of the uncomfortable tension between the institutional focus of faith and the charismatic imperative to look beyond the institution to the God who ordains it. In a day when the institutional Church faces something of an identity crisis, when Western Christianity seems certain of what it is 'post-' but as yet unable to define itself in positive terms, the message of Haggai has something to say that is as particular to us today as it was to his hearers and to those who made the decision to preserve his words. For his own day and for ours, Haggai is a worthy member of the prophetic corpus, albeit as a supporting member of a larger team.[7]

Reading

It is the aim of this commentary to convey something of the particular significance of the book of Haggai. Several attitudes will characterize the attempt.[8] The first is intrinsic to the title borne by the series in which this volume appears, namely, that it is a 'reading'. Linguists, philosophers, literary critics and social scientists, to name but a few, wrestle with the nature and location of meaning; and they are joined by biblical scholars. Friedrich Schleiermacher's formulation of the problem by means of the metaphor of the hermeneutical circle has been influential. His circle was in the first instance an attempt to hold together a particular paradox which he described in a couple of key ways. First, Schleiermacher noted that it is not possible to understand the whole of a text without a detailed appreciation of the parts that go to make up that whole, and it is equally not possible fully to appreciate the parts of a text without understanding the whole of which it is a part, or its

---

7. Martin Luther, 'Lectures on Haggai', in *Luther's Works*. XVIII. *Lectures on the Minor Prophets* (ed. H.C. Oswald; trans. R.J. Dinda; St Louis: Concordia, 1975), pp. 365-87 (367), cautions the reader that 'one ought not to judge a work according to its greatness or smallness. Rather, we must judge a work according to the will of Him who commands such a work.'

8. The remainder of this Prolegomena is largely methodological. Those readers who prefer to move straight into commentary on the text should go to the Introduction at this point. Although this material, as Prolegomena, belongs at the start, it may also profitably be read at the end.

context, as it might be described today.⁹ He specified this further with his distinction between grammatical and psychological interpretation. Grammatical interpretation is that careful technical attention to the detail of a text, how each of the parts work and what they are able to say and what they are not able to say. Psychological interpretation is the attempt to appreciate not so much how the text works as the effect on the text of the person reading it and the experience and context that that reader brings with him or her to the reading of the text. The very format of this commentary illustrates the point. It would be an incomplete work without the introductory material that specifies the context in which to read the more detailed analysis of the text in its structure and details, and it would equally be incomplete without that detailed analysis to lend substance to the broader more contextual claims of the Introduction. The concept of the hermeneutical circle is intended to describe the perpetual conversation between those two aspects of interpretation.¹⁰

The hermeneutical circle has proved to be a useful tool for exploring a number of other paradoxes in the interpretive task. There is also a tension between the intention of the text or its author and the response that is given to the text,¹¹ between objective and subjective interpretation,¹² between the

9. See F.D. Schleiermacher, *Hermeneutics: The Handwritten Manuscripts* (ed. H. Himmerli; trans. J. Duke and J. Forstman; Missoula, MT: Scholars Press, 1977), p. 113. See also J. Verheyden, 'The Basic Features of Schleiermacher's Hermeneutics', in D.E. Klemm and T.N. Tice (eds.), *Papers of the Schleiermacher Group and Schleiermacher Society* (San Francisco: AAR, 1997).

10. I am using the term 'hermeneutics' in the sense of theorizing about interpretation, roughly as a synonym for 'theory of interpretation'. It may also be used to describe the task of interpretation. For example, a 'hermeneutic of suspicion' denotes a particular interpretive approach to the text.

11. See T.J. Meadowcroft, 'Relevance as a Mediating Category in the Reading of Biblical Texts: Venturing Beyond the Hermeneutical Circle', *JETS* 45 (2002), pp. 611-27.

12. This particular distinction is arguably more epistemological than hermeneutical. On their interaction, see M. Polanyi, *Personal Knowledge: Towards a Post-Critical Philosophy* (Chicago: University of Chicago Press, 1962), p. 267, who seeks a 'liberation from objectivism'. From within the field of biblical interpretation, see J.E. Goldingay, *Models for Interpretation of Scripture* (Grand Rapids: Eerdmans, 1995), p. 261.

interpretation and use of texts,[13] between interpretation and critique of texts,[14] and between what Anthony Thiselton calls the 'traditionalist' and the 'pluralist' interpreter.[15] There are other polarities that could be identified, or different ways of describing the same polarities. To extend the metaphor of the hermeneutical circle, each of these polarities may be thought to form a diameter to the circle, and the proper maintenance of each has the effect, like spokes in a wheel, of preventing the circle from collapse.

These polarities are all different ways of expressing that whenever a text is read a conversation develops between two parties, the author and the reader of that text. There are times when the author is quite inaccessible to the reader, and the intention to communicate can only be deduced from the text. For all practical purposes the text itself then becomes a partner in the conversation, but even in such an instance, I will argue below, readers assume as they approach the text that they are encountering an intention on the part of another party to communicate, even when that person may be known only within the text.[16] Anyone who encounters a text makes the decision, whether consciously or not, to privilege one or other of the conversation partners, the reader or the author/text.

To put it another way, one of two vantage points is chosen from which to view the text that is being interpreted. One extreme of each of the polarities mentioned above emerges when the text is viewed from the vantage point of the author.

13. See, for example, the distinction between interpretation and use tentatively made by U. Eco, *The Limits of Interpretation* (Bloomington: Indiana University Press, 1990), p. 62.

14. See D.J.A. Clines, 'Varieties of Indeterminacy', *Semeia* 71 (1995), pp. 17-27 (24).

15. A.C. Thiselton, 'On Models and Methods: A Conversation with Robert Morgan', in D.J.A. Clines, S.E. Fowl and S.E. Porter (eds.), *The Bible in Three Dimensions: Essays in Celebration of Forty Years of Biblical Studies in the University of Sheffield* (JSOTSup, 87; Sheffield: JSOT Press, 1990), pp. 337-56 (340-41).

16. R.W. Gibbs, *Intention in the Experience of Meaning* (Cambridge: Cambridge University Press, 1999), p. 206, notes 'that the multi-faceted nature of authorship complicates any simple view of intentionalism. Yet these complications don't eliminate the cognitive unconscious drive toward inferring something about both real and hypothetical authors'/ artists' communicative intentions'.

Meaning is sought in the search for the author's original intention in writing or compiling the text; intention is a privileged category in the interpretive process; the proper attitude of the reader is thought to be as one who seeks to understand what the author originally meant rather than to critique what the text is saying or to allow for ambiguities that the author may not have intended; and there are supposed limits to the uses to which a text may be put. The other vantage point from which the text may be viewed is the vantage point of the reader. From that perspective the meaning of a text is that which the reader perceives it to be; the response of the reader is privileged in the creation of meaning as against those who privilege authorial intent; texts may be critiqued and not merely interpreted; and the legitimacy or otherwise of the use to which a text may be put is for the reader to determine.

The adoption of the metaphor of the hermeneutical circle ensures that neither vantage point is able to operate to the exclusion of the other. Both are necessary, but a circle has to be entered somewhere, or, to continue with the mixed metaphor, a reader cannot begin to read without looking at the text from one particular vantage point. This is a 'readings' commentary, and so the opening contribution in the conversation with the text of Haggai is the reader and the questions which the reader brings to the text. In that respect it is a 'reading' rather than an interpretation.

To develop the point a little further, Robert Fowler has helpfully distinguished between the critic, who seeks to 'objectify' and master the text, and the reader, who is a subject serviced by the text. Of course the critic/reader distinction is a continuum, as there is no such thing as a pure critic or pure reader.[17] As will be explicated further, this particular reading strives to bridge the epistemological gap between subject and object, and accordingly works within the nexus of, in Fowler's terms, critic and reader. A commentary on the biblical text is *ipso facto* an intentional interpretation, so the commentator cannot avoid an element of criticism in the reading. Such a reader accepts some responsibility for the perception of meaning. However, I also seek to 'read' as well as possible, in

---

17. R.M. Fowler, 'Who is "The Reader" in Reader Response Criticism?', *Semeia* 31 (1985), pp. 5-23 (8).

the sense of hearing the text in its own terms rather than attempting to 'master' it.[18]

Context

Personal Context
A self-conscious 'reading', such as I have just been describing, is in the nature of things concerned with context, both of the text itself and of the reader of the text. A reader-oriented approach is not compatible with the view that meaning is an abstract generality to be distilled out of the text; it is something that is ultimately particular. What Haggai means cannot be determined apart from the circumstances in which the story is read. A 'reading' of Haggai is compelled therefore to convey an awareness of the reader's own context. My own personal context impacts on my reading of Haggai, as expressed in this commentary, in two ways in particular. First, it alerts me to features in the text itself and predisposes me to highlight some of those more than others. This will be evident, sometimes more to my readers than to me, throughout my reading of the text. Secondly, it also requires that a final section be compiled where there is more intentional discussion of the relevance of the words of Haggai to the world in which I find myself, and in which I detail what I see as key features of my personal context in my reading of Haggai.

Literary Context
But a reading's concern with context does not stop with that of the reader. In terms already discussed above in connection with the hermeneutical circle, there is also an interest in the whole of which the text in question is a part. So this reading must concern itself with the textual, linguistic and socio-historical context of the prophet Haggai. If the particularity of the reader is an integral part of a reader's encounter with the text, so equally the particularity of the text itself is an indispensable component of its meaning. An engagement of the

---

18. Or with 'competence', on which concept see J. Culler, 'Literary Competence', in J.P. Tompkins (ed.), *Reader-Response Criticism: From Formalism to Post-Structuralism* (Baltimore: The Johns Hopkins University Press, 1980), pp. 101-44.

one cannot occur without an engagement of the other. The Introduction that follows will elucidate Haggai's context further while the concluding reflection on contemporary relevance will address further the context of the reader.

An interest in narrative, discussed below, drives the critic to take literary context seriously. Any text is part of a longer story which needs to be acknowledged, and awareness of the wider literary context of Haggai will be a feature of my detailed comment. Some portions of the biblical narrative are relatively self-contained, but, I venture, cannot be fully understood entirely in their own terms. Joshua, for instance, needs a consideration of the possibility of a Hexateuch. Amos rewards reading against the background of the deuteronomistic enterprise. The rape of Tamar is an integral part of the succession narrative within which it is set. None of the Gospels can be read without reference to the others, and Paul's epistles need the Gospel context. If each of these examples also reward a reading in isolation, there are some narratives which are incomprehensible when read apart from their surrounding material. Jonah, for example, is reduced to a fantastic fable when read outside its setting within the Book of the Twelve, but becomes a thought-provoking reflection on the prophetic task when set in context. Haggai also, as we will see below, is best read nested within several contexts: as a unit with Zechariah 1–8; as one of the so-called prophets of the restoration along with Zechariah and Malachi; and as a member of the Book of the Twelve.

Narrative and Imagination

As we have begun to see, the category of narrative expresses well the focus on particularity of context which will be one of the distinctive features of my reading. I use the term 'narrative' in two senses. First, I use it roughly as a synonym of 'story'. Secondly, I use it to denote in broad terms an approach to the text which seeks to appreciate the aesthetics of a story and accepts the legitimate role of imagination in interpretation. This second sense of the term is roughly parallel to 'literary criticism'. There are other implications in the word 'narrative' which I do not intend. In particular, 'narrative' is not intended as a focus on one particular aspect of the story maker's craft as opposed to others, namely, the role of narrator and narrative technique as opposed to plot and characterization and so forth. Equally, my broad use of the term embraces some aspects of what others would describe as 'rhetorical criticism' and what at other points might include the methodology of discourse analysis.[19] I see both of these as sub-disciplines of the broader attempt to understand the art of the story implied by the term 'narrative'.

There is some debate over the use of imagination in interpretation. As John Goldingay points out, 'imagination is an ambiguous faculty'. To say that something is a product of the imagination can be to say that it is 'illusory or fanciful'.[20] Such a response implies that the search for truth within the text and the attribution of authority to the text is compromised by the employment of imagination in interpretation. One example of this hesitation is that expressed by Kevin Vanhoozer when he describes the process of Western culture and theology, beginning with an epigram invented by John Updike and used by Robert Funk: 'Priest, teacher, artist—the classic degeneration'.[21] To the priest reality is revealed, to the teacher it is rational, and to the artist, in the words of Vanhoozer, reality is 'marked by ambiguity, mystery, and irrationality'. The acceptance of textual indeterminacy, in the mind of Vanhoozer, is linked to the 'irrationality' of a speculative approach. Similarly, in his employment of Ricoeur Vanhoozer drives a wedge between history and the imagination thus: 'Ricoeur's is a faith founded not on history, but on the possibilities first grasped by the imagination'.[22]

In contrast, Goldingay, with whom I began this brief discussion, does not stop with his hesitations about imagination. He reminds us that imagination is no more ambiguous a

19. On 'rhetorical criticism', see J.I.H. McDonald, 'Rhetorical Criticism', in R.J. Coggins and J.L. Houlden (eds.), *The SCM Dictionary of Biblical Interpretation* (London: SCM, 1990), pp. 599-600. For 'discourse analysis' exemplified, see D.J. Clark, 'Discourse Structure in Haggai', *JOTT* 5 (1992), pp. 13-24.

20. J.E. Goldingay, *Models for Scripture* (Grand Rapids: Eerdmans; Carlisle: Paternoster, 1994), pp. 314-15.

21. K.J. Vanhoozer, 'A Lamp in the Labyrinth: The Hermeneutics of "Aesthetic" Theology', *TriJ* 8 (1987), pp. 25-56.

22. Vanhoozer, 'A Lamp in the Labyrinth', p. 49.

human faculty than reason when it comes to interpretation. For him, imagination is equally 'the far-seeing and realistic ability to see what actually is there or actually is possible'. Far from being characterized chiefly by irrationality and a nature antithetical to a historical perspective, 'imagination is the point of contact between divine revelation and human experience'.[23]

The present interest in narrative and narrative theology arises from this awareness that logic and proposition and the deductive method of reasoning from the general to the particular are not the only ways of making sense of what is encountered. It is possible that story can tell as much about truth as can a set of propositions. An appreciation of story or narrative form brings with it an interest in aesthetics and the imagination as well as an openness to the inductive method of reasoning from the particular to the general. Indeed, the greater part of Scripture is couched as narrative, and, it can be argued, other forms such as song and propositional argument are embedded in the story that we know as the Bible.[24] There is therefore something fundamentally appropriate about a narrative approach to interpreting the Bible. That in itself is reason enough for adopting a narrative-critical approach to the text. It is especially the case for Haggai, whose message is packaged in the most consciously crafted narrative of any of the so-called writing prophets, except possibly that of Jonah.

A narrative approach to the text does not absolutely require the critic to adopt a reader-centred approach, as a narrative can equally be considered in the light of the author's intent and context. Alternatively, a narrative approach can treat the text simply as artefact, with little regard for whence it came and what effect it may be having on the reader. An appreciation of the narrative itself, however, enables the commentator, by focusing on the story of the prophecy of

23. Goldingay, *Models for Scripture*, p. 315. In a similar vein, see S. Barton, 'New Testament Interpretation as Performance', *SJT* 52 (1999), pp. 179-208, on the concept of interpretation as 'performance'.

24. W. Brueggemann, *Theology of the Old Testament: Testimony, Dispute, Advocacy* (Minneapolis: Fortress Press, 1997), p. 66, argues that 'in other genres such as commandment, song, and oracle, I suggest that the same claims of narrative reality are generative, albeit one step removed from narrative rendering'.

Haggai and its impact on certain of his hearers, to retain a sense that the truth conveyed is discovered in the particularity of that story. And so the insights of narrative criticism are a key resource for this reading.

Received Form

In the nature of things a narrative approach cannot treat a text in an atomistic fashion. An appreciation of the workings of a story is impossible without a sense of the story as a whole. One expression of that is a concern to read what I will call the received form of the text, and that too is a feature of this commentary.[25] To read the received form does not imply necessarily that the critic is blind to the textual history of the unit under consideration. Indeed, an appreciation of that history can alert readers to features of the text that are themselves communicative in intent. This is one of the outcomes of the canonical-critical approach, which encourages readers to wonder why certain texts have been allied to other texts.[26] Think, for example, of the book of Daniel with its radical shift in genre at the start of ch. 7. A received-form reading acknowledges the history of composition that lies behind the distinction, but also wants to know what message lies in the incorporation of wisdom court tales (chs. 1–6) and apocalyptic visions (chs. 7–12) into the same story.[27] At other interpretive moments, composition history is more contentious. A case in point may be the Fourth Gospel, concerning which critics

---

25. I avoid the term 'final form' so as not to imply that there are other intermediate forms of the text that can be the subject of interpretation. I am grateful to Edgar Conrad, who clarified this point to me in a private conversation. The received form being read by this commentary is the MT as represented in translation by the NRSV, except on occasion where my own translation is supplied.

26. P.R. House, 'The Character of God in the Book of the Twelve', in *SBL Seminar Papers, 1998. Part Two* (Atlanta: Scholars Press, 1998), pp. 831-49 (833), defines a 'canonical' reading thus: 'By "Canonical" I mean analysis that is god-centred, intertextually oriented, authority-conscious, historically-sensitive, and devoted to the pursuit of the wholeness of the Old Testament message'.

27. See my comments in T.J. Meadowcroft, 'Narrative, Metaphor, Interpretation and Reader in Daniel 2–5', *Narrative* 8 (2000), pp. 257-78.

12 *Prolegomena*

debate the presence or otherwise of distinctive signs and discourse sources.[28] The very debate heightens the sensitivities of received-form readers to genre issues, but does not require them to reach form- or source-critical conclusions when none are readily available. In such instances the unanswered historical questions may be laid aside as a distraction from the task of appreciating the narrative in the form that we now have it, or a received-form reading may be offered as an antidote to historical-critical confusion about a text or portion of a text.

'Composite Artistry'
Various theoretical positions might undergird such an approach, but for this particular reader a key justification of received-form reading is to be found in Robert Alter's concept of 'composite artistry'.[29] By this he means the phenomenon whereby a text may grow over years and generations, but retain a conscious artistry and intent in the way this is done. The concept may be applied for example to the rich tradition that has been preserved in the Isaiah scroll with its deliberate exploration of key themes in the life of Israel across several distinct historical contexts, from Isaiah of Jerusalem in the eighth century down to the postexilic period.[30] Similarly, without denying the presence of redactive seams in the text, a synoptic reading of the narratives in 1 Samuel 15–18 concerning David's accession provides a subtle reflection on the tension between the sovereignty of God and the contingency of human action that are now woven together in the composite account.

The book of Haggai itself is an interesting case in point. There is a broad measure of agreement that the book consists

---

28. See, for instance, the approach articulated by F.J. Moloney, *The Gospel of John* (SPS, 4; Collegeville: Liturgical Press, 1998), pp. 11-24, in the Introduction to his commentary.
29. R. Alter, *The Art of Biblical Narrative* (London: George Allen & Unwin, 1981), p. 138. See also the critique and development of this concept by D. Damrosch *The Narrative Covenant* (Ithaca, NY: Cornell University Press, 1991).
30. H.G.M. Williamson, *Variations on a Theme: King, Messiah and Servant in the Book of Isaiah* (Carlisle: Paternoster, 1998), is one appreciation of this composite artistry in Isaiah. See especially pp. 203-208 on the growth of the tradition.

of the words of the prophet as well as editorial or narrative material about Haggai. There is, however, considerable debate over the source of the third person material. The main speculations are that they are the product of a Chronicler's redaction; they reflect a compilation by disciples of Haggai; or possibly they are the product of Haggai himself. A received-form reading appreciates the distinction between types of material, whether or not they are explicable on form-critical grounds, but is able to set aside for the moment the source of the apparently editorial material within the book. But a close reading also suggests that the tidy form-critical distinction between the prophetic words and the third person material is not nearly as easy to make in narrative terms, and that the two types of material act on each other to set up a particular dynamic. Sifting them out ultimately may prove no easier or more productive than separating out the colours that make up an oil painting, and then identifying the manufacturing source of each.[31] Accordingly, my reading of the received form also assumes that the sequence of narrative and oracle represented by MT is authentic.[32] This in itself, as well as constituting a rebellion against the form-critical method, may also contribute to the debate over the provenance of the narrative framework of the book of Haggai. The literary coherence of the material in its received form may provide an argument for a single author of the book, or at least a compiler who shares the provenance and sympathies of Haggai himself.

Discourse Analysis
My reading of the received form of the book of Haggai thus begins with a discourse analysis of the narrative around the speech formula. In that respect I am in conscious disagreement

---

31. Polanyi, *Personal Knowledge*, p. 382, expresses this epistemologically in the principle that 'lower levels do not lack a bearing on higher levels; *they define the conditions of their success and account for their failures, but they cannot account for their success, for they cannot define it*' (emphasis original). With respect to narrative theory, the sum of the parts cannot on its own account for the effect of a well-crafted narrative. It is in the nature of 'competent' reading to take account of this.

32. *Contra* P.W. Thomas and W.L. Sperry, 'The Book of Haggai', in G.A. Buttrick (ed.), *The Interpreter's Bible* (12 vols.; New York: Abingdon Press, 1956), VI, pp. 1036-49, and others.

with other analyses, including the form-critical. Out of this analysis, I form certain structural assumptions about the narrative on which the rest of the commentary is based. The levels of discourse identified there are assumed in the body of the commentary. The analysis is represented in diagrammatic form in Appendix A, and is explicated in the opening comments on Hag. 1.1-2 under the heading 'Structure'.

An Ethical Issue

So far I have indicated that the organizing perspective of this commentary is that of the reader with an interest in the context of the reader, while the methodology will include a received-form reading drawing on the insights of narrative criticism. But I have also alluded to the potential incompleteness of such an approach with my comments on the hermeneutical circle. In terms of that metaphor, I must be conscious of the dangers in concentrating too much on one end of the continua that form the supporting diameters of that circle.

In doing so I am confronted by the ethical issue that any reader-centred approach raises, for there is a certain irony about any written 'reading' of what somebody else has written. I am writing a commentary with the intention of communicating certain things about the prophecies of and narrative about Haggai and the potential effect of those on their readers. I expect that those who read the commentary will take an interest in my context and what I have to say. It is difficult to escape the challenge to treat the text of which I write in the manner in which I would like to be treated. I am therefore obliged to acknowledge that the book of Haggai has been formed out of a particular context and with an intention to communicate, and that I do the text less than justice if I do not take those facts seriously. So, a received-form reading cannot be at the expense of attention to socio-historical context and authorial intent.[33] To that extent, this piece of work resists the

33. See the reflection of M. Sternberg, *The Poetics of Biblical Narrative: Ideological Literature and the Drama of Reading* (Bloomington: Indiana University Press, 1987), pp. 41-57, on the drama of reading, and especially his comment (p. 50) that 'the Bible is difficult to read, easy to underread and overread and even misread, but virtually impossible to...counterread'.

trends of ideological criticism in that it does not seek to critique the text in the light of or use the text in the service of a pre-determined position. Nor do I accept that the text that I am presently examining is fundamentally indeterminate and that the only determinate factor in the exercise is my own context. Even when it is not explicitly stated, such a view of the text is implicit in many ideological approaches. In taking the approach that I do, I am heeding the warning of Anthony Thiselton against a

> socio-pragmatic hermeneutic which, on the basis only of narrative experience within a given context, excludes all interpretative options in advance which would give any other signals than positive ones for the journey already undertaken.[34]

I am also distinguishing between what I have called a reader-centred or reader-oriented approach, and the practice of Reader-Response criticism. As with most questions of literary and interpretive theory, the term 'Reader-Response' can mean different things to different people. But one of its classical formulations, and what I intend by spelling it with capital letters, is that contained in the work of Stanley Fish and in particular his book *Is There a Text in this Class?*[35] In that book, Fish argues that there is no such thing as a text in any objective sense. Texts only come into being through an interpretive act. In adopting this position, he effectively excludes the author and the concept of intention as any part of the equation for the discernment of meaning. In adopting a reader-centred approach to the creation of a 'reading' of Haggai, I am explicitly eschewing such an approach.

Speech-Act Theory

But I need a tool to enable me to hold together in my work a respect for the author and the intention to communicate along with my commitment to bring the interests of the reader into conversation with the text. So far my main help has been the metaphor of the hermeneutical circle, and that has proved to

---

34. A.C. Thiselton, *New Horizons in Hermeneutics* (Grand Rapids: Zondervan, 1992), pp. 439-40.

35. S. Fish, *Is There a Text in this Class? The Authority of Interpretive Communities* (Cambridge, MA: Harvard University Press, 1980).

be a useful diagnostic instrument. It provides a way of describing the problem and the challenge of interpretation. However, a diagnosis ought to lead to a prescription, and when it comes to prescribing a way ahead the hermeneutical circle becomes too blunt an instrument, capable only of describing a conversation between partners often at odds with each other. It ought not to be surprising that the metaphor of a circle results in a rather circular series of 'yes, but...' items in a conversation that struggles to hold together the varying poles in the hermeneutical diameters that I have described. I need something that enables me to venture beyond that circle.

Theories of communication provide a helpful boost in that direction. Whether it consciously espouses it or not, the hermeneutical circle assumes an analogy with the code model of communication 'whereby a sender encodes a thought in a linguistic message which is transmitted by some medium to a receiver, who in turn decodes the message to produce some replication of the original thought'.[36] Even when there is only a short distance between encoding and decoding, distortions may result as a result of what is sometimes metaphorically called 'noise'.[37] However, there are no categories provided by the model with which to describe what happens between the processes of encoding and decoding. So the hermeneutical enterprise, to the extent that it resembles the code model of communication, divides between those who focus on the action of encoding as crucial to the formation of meaning and those who focus on the action of decoding as crucial to the formation of meaning. For those who want to posit a conversation between the two poles, in the very conduct of which meaning is found, satisfactory categories are not available in the metaphor of the hermeneutical circle.

This is where the field of pragmatic linguistics can help. Anthony Thiselton's encyclopaedic *New Horizons in Hermeneutics* is wrestling with just the questions that I am now raising. It is intriguing to note the number of different contexts in

---

36. S. Pattemore, *The People of God in the Apocalypse: Discourse, Structure and Exegesis* (SNTSMS, 128; Cambridge: Cambridge University Press, 2004), p. 11.

37. See, for instance, the diagram in D. Sperber and D. Wilson, *Relevance, Communication and Cognition* (Oxford: Basil Blackwell, 2nd edn, 1995), p. 5.

which he finds Speech-Act Theory to be helpful.³⁸ This too is a linguistic model of communication, but its primary category is locution rather than code. Speech-act analysis distinguishes the locutionary act, the illocutionary intent and the perlocutionary effect of an utterance. With respect to its applicability to texts, the locution is the fact of a text; the illocutionary intent refers to the communicative intention of the text; and the perlocutionary effect indicates the effect of the text on those who encounter it. Locution is a category that acknowledges both intent and effect, or by analogy author and reader, as integral to the text itself. The achievement of speech-act is that it has made both intention and response, author and reader, indispensable to the understanding of a text. At the same time, the concept of locution allows the reader to be aware of intent within the text rather than understanding it as an external agent. It is no accident that Gibbs' work mentioned above on intention and meaning employs the language of speech-act at various points.³⁹

The danger with that position, though, is that a speech-act approach can become simply another manifestation of New Criticism's focus on the text as artefact. That is acknowledged by Gibbs, and provides part of the motivation for his quest for further methodological tools. But a speech-act based search for meaning in interpretation exhibits a yet more serious deficiency. Despite the care with which the practitioners of speech-act have differentiated categories of illocution and perlocution, they do not provide a convincing explanation of how the progression from illocution to perlocution works. How is it that a text's perlocutionary effect may end up at least for some readers at odds with the illocutionary intent? Or, what has happened to a text when it functions in, or is able to be used in, a way never intended?

A couple of examples illustrate some different angles on the problem, and why the problem matters to the interpreter. The debate over how to interpret the first eleven chapters of

---

38. Note, for instance, the index entry in Thiselton, *New Horizons*, p. 690. See also the work of G. Genette, *Narrative Discourse* (trans. J.E. Lewin; Oxford: Basil Blackwell, 1980), and S. Lanser, *The Narrative Act* (Princeton, NJ: Princeton University Press, 1981), on the application of Speech-Act Theory to the analysis of narrative.

39. Gibbs, *Intention in the Experience of Meaning*.

Genesis is fought on a number of fronts, around the basic problem of defining the genre of those chapters. At an illocutionary level, the intent of the text is contested. Is it history? Is it poetry? Is it a polemic in dialogue with a particular identifiable context? How those questions are answered is foundational to how those chapters are interpreted. There will be a perlocutionary outcome that is dependent on the illocutionary perceptions. A reading of the text as literal history determines how the reader interacts with a number of scientific disciplines, for example. A literary appreciation of those chapters, on the other hand, leads to an interest in the polemical context of the creation account and a different set of historiographical assumptions when it comes to the interpretation of Scripture.

In this example the perlocutionary effect has been expected to follow from the illocutionary intent, however problematic the identification of that intent might be. But a different problem concerns sections in the Old Testament that have subsequently been interpreted as messianic. The figure of 'one like a son of man' (NIV) in Dan. 7.13 is generally agreed to be a human figure who is imbued with divine authority in much the same way that 'the holy ones of the Most High' are imbued with the same authority later in the vision (Dan. 7.27).[40] Yet that text has become a key to understanding not 'one like a son of man' but 'the Son of Man'. Its perlocutionary effect on the New Testament writers is at odds with the likely illocutionary intent of Daniel 7. Similarly, the so-called fourth Servant Song in Isa. 52.13–53.12 has always been a challenge to interpreters, both Jewish and Christian. All attempts at historical interpretation of the figure in these verses stumble at some point, while the New Testament writers presume the fulfilment of the servant of Isaiah 53 in the person of Jesus.[41] Much as we would love to identify and find the prophet and ask him what he meant at that point, we cannot; but he probably would not have had in mind a portrait of Jesus so much as, in a way

40. On this interpretation, see T.J. Meadowcroft and N.D. Irwin, *The Book of Daniel* (ABCS; Singapore: Asia Theological Association, 2004), pp. 146-49.

41. See P. Stuhlmacher, 'Isaiah 53 in the Gospels and Acts', in B. Janowski and P. Stuhlmacher (eds.), *The Suffering Servant: Isaiah 53 in Jewish and Christian Sources* (trans. D.P. Bailey; Grand Rapids: Eerdmans, 2004), pp. 147-62.

only dimly understood by the speaker and preservers of the oracle, a personalized concept of the people as servant of God suffering vicariously in the cause of God's mission.[42] In the light of subsequent developments, that prophetic oracle has exercised a perlocutionary effect that cannot have had its roots in the intent of the prophet. Speech-act is not particularly helpful in describing this gap between illocution and perlocution in subsequent understandings of Daniel 7 and Isaiah 53.

I am grateful for the locutionary categories supplied by Speech-Act Theory, and will make use of them in this reading, but with caution and in a way that recognizes their inability fully to describe the impact of the text under examination on the reader.

Inference and Relevance

So, even with the deployment of Speech-Act Theory, my interpretive toolbox is not yet adequately equipped. Gibbs senses that also and points towards a further development in the field of pragmatic linguistics known as Relevance Theory.[43] This is a theoretical branch of pragmatic linguistics that is little known in the discipline of biblical studies, so what follows is a more extended (but necessarily simplified) account of the theory than the commentary context would normally demand, in the light of which it becomes possible to indicate the applicability of the theory to the process of developing a 'reading' of Haggai. I do not attempt a complete description of all the main categories and principles developed by Relevance Theory.

---

42. H. Spieckermann, 'The Conception and Prehistory of the Idea of Vicarious Suffering in the Old Testament', in Janowski and Stuhlmacher (eds.), *The Suffering Servant*, pp. 1-15, explores the dynamics of this possibility.

43. Gibbs, *Intention in the Experience of Meaning*, p. 121, comments that Relevance Theory 'holds much promise and should clearly be the focus of additional empirical research'. This is echoed by Pattemore, *The People of God*, p. 20, with the comment that Relevance Theory 'has proved to be a robust and seminal theory, as evidenced by the amount and diversity of continuing work based on it'. For much of my thinking on Relevance Theory I am indebted to Pattemore's work, in which he explores the applicability of Relevance Theory to biblical interpretation, and in particular interpretation of the Apocalypse.

Rather, I am highlighting the key points at which the concept of relevance and the task of literary, particularly biblical, interpretation intersect.

Relevance Theory

The chief architects are Dan Sperber and Deirdre Wilson in *Relevance, Communication and Cognition*.[44] Relevance Theory builds on the insights of Speech-Act Theory while also questioning its adequacy as a description of the communicative process. Sperber and Wilson take issue with the assertion that 'Perhaps the single most uncontroversial assumption of modern pragmatics is that any adequate account of utterance comprehension must include some version of speech-act theory'.[45] On grounds not too dissimilar from the psychological ones advanced by Gibbs, they move beyond the locutionary categories defined by Speech-Act Theory, and suggest instead that 'the principle of relevance makes it possible to derive rich and precise non-demonstrative inferences about the communicator's informative intent'.[46] Their enterprise is essentially to build 'an improved inferential model' which may be 'combined with a code model to provide an explanatory account of verbal communication'.[47] The result is known as Relevance Theory.

Despite the claim of Sperber and Wilson that the code and inference models complement each other in the production of relevance, the key to understanding their exposition of relevance is the notion of inference. This is a complex linguistic concept, but its essence for my purposes is that a hearer of an

---

44. Sperber and Wilson, *Relevance,* noted above. This is an expansion of the first edition of their work, which appeared in 1986.

45. Sperber and Wilson, *Relevance*, p. 243. It is important to distinguish what is meant by 'pragmatics'. Space does not permit a full exposition of the term, but as far as I can tell pragmatism can describe a particular philosophy of language, associated with such as Richard Rorty, while linguistic pragmatism is the study of utterance interpretation arising from the concept of inference, a model pioneered by H.P. Grice. Relevance Theory builds on the implications of inference. A linguistic pragmatism may undergird Relevance Theory, but it is not necessarily the case that a philosophical pragmatism does, and so it need not be the case that the use of linguistic pragmatics in the hermeneutical task requires agreement with a pragmatic philosophy of interpretation.

46. Sperber and Wilson, *Relevance*, p. 254.

47. Sperber and Wilson, *Relevance*, p. 3.

utterance uses aspects of his or her context to infer or deduce that certain things are meant by the utterance in question. Inference is necessary because the linguistic form of a statement is often inadequate on its own to convey what is meant. One statement can potentially mean different, even contradictory things, but despite that the hearer usually is able to infer what the speaker intends. I take inference to be the term that describes what happens when a hearer takes account of his or her own context, understands the speaker's context, assumes that the speaker is taking account of the hearer's context, and in the light of all that is aware of what a speaker means by a particular statement. To put it in somewhat more technical language, Adrian Pilkington expresses the 'inferential phase' of communication thus:

> An inferential phase brings non-linguistic contextual information to bear upon the output of decoding to arrive at the fullyfledged thoughts that are communicated. This inferential phase involves fleshing out the semantic representation by resolving ambiguities, assigning reference and enriching the content of concepts that contribute to the imposition expressed.[48]

By building on both the code and inference models of communication, the proponents of Relevance Theory work with both the intention of an act of communication and the contextualized response to that communication, or the inference that is drawn from it. According to Relevance Theory, one of the pre-conditions of relevance is that the speakers expect that their utterance is relevant, that there is sufficient in common with the hearers of the utterance that they will discern it to be something worth making the effort to listen to. Another important principle is expressed by Neil Smith and Deirdre Wilson thus: 'the greater the contextual effects the greater the relevance'. In other words, the more the hearer can discern that the utterance has something to do with his or her own context, the more likely is communication to be successful. At the same time, 'the smaller the processing effort, the greater the relevance'.[49] Or, the easier it is for a hearer to see where a

---

48. A. Pilkington, 'Introduction: Relevance Theory and Literary Style', *Language and Literature* 5 (1996), pp. 157-62 (157).

49. N. Smith and D. Wilson, 'Introduction', *Lingua* 87 (1992), pp. 4-6. Their introduction provides a useful summary of Relevance Theory, but

speaker's utterance impacts on the hearer's own context, the more likely is communication to be successful. The point of optimum balance between processing effort and contextual effect is the point of relevance.[50] To express this optimal point in crude terms, an utterance will be perceived by a hearer as relevant to the extent that it takes enough account of the hearer's own context while also drawing the hearer on to something new. If a statement is too foreign to the hearer, the absence of a contextual effect means it cannot be processed. If it is too familiar, no processing effort is required and it is likely to be discarded as unnecessary by the hearer. This type of exploration of the inferential interaction between hearer and speaker is just the gap left by Speech-Act Theory.

Inference in Texts

My description so far has been in terms of speakers and hearers and raises the obvious question: How may this be applied to texts, particularly to literary texts such as the book of Haggai, and readers? Let me turn first to 'contextual effect' and 'processing effort'. Although not all literary creations set out to demand as much processing effort as does a work like James Joyce's *Ulysses,* all in some way tend to reward processing effort beyond the normal call of conversational duty. And there are some biblical texts, the first readings of which exhibit little or no contextual effect for a contemporary reader. What are we to make of the repulsive narrative in Judges 19 of the abuse of the Levite's concubine and the subsequent butchering and parcelling out of her body? And do we care that the Israelites could not eat winged creatures with four legs unless the legs have joints above the foot (Lev. 11.20-21)? Any achievement of relevance is the result of a determined

---

for a full description of the possibilities of Relevance Theory, Sperber and Wilson, *Relevance*, is unavoidable.

50. Nam Sun Song, 'Metaphor and Metonymy', in R. Carston and S. Uchida (eds.), *Relevance Theory: Applications and Implications* (P&B, NS 37; Amsterdam: John Benjamins, 1998), pp. 87-104 (91), puts it like this: '(a) Other things being equal, the greater the contextual effect achieved by the processing of a given piece of information, the greater its relevance for the individual who processes it. (b) Other things being equal, the greater the effort involved in the processing of a given piece of information, the smaller its relevance for the individual who processes it.'

processing effort, where it is attempted at all. And how will the concept of relevance as developed by Sperber and Wilson cope with the notion of indeterminacy?

Some work has been done in answer to these questions, with promising results.[51] At a basic level, Relevance Theory's emphasis on inference is tailor-made for anybody attempting to describe what happens when a reader encounters a literary text. For, as David Trotter has expressed it, 'literature tests to the limit not our powers of encoding and decoding, but our powers of inference'.[52] Beyond the notion of inference, though, is the important relevance theoretic distinction between implication and implicature.[53] An implication is something drawn from the text when particular contextual assumptions are brought to bear on a text. An implication is entirely the manufacture of the reader, and as a result there is potentially no limit to the implications that can be drawn from a text. To draw a link with the classical reader-response commitment to indeterminacy, the development of ideological readings determined by the context of the reader may be described in relevance terms as implications. However, the quest for relevance is concerned not with implication but with implication that

---

51. The journal volumes *Lingua* 87 (1992) and *Language and Literature* 5 (1996) are devoted to Relevance Theory and literary style. In the *Language and Literature* volume see especially W. Clark, 'Stylistics and Relevance Theory' (pp. 163-78), and B. MacMahon, 'Indirectness, Rhetoric and Interpretative Use: Communicative Strategies in Browning's *My Last Duchess*' (pp. 209-23), who explores the relevance theoretic concept of 'echoic utterance' and its use in the analysis of irony. Pilkington, 'Introduction: Relevance Theory and Literary Style' (pp. 157-62) gives a useful overview but slightly overstates the case with his comment that 'Relevance theory rejects both code models of verbal communication and purely inferential accounts'. See also as a further example of Relevance Theory and literary text S. Uchida, 'Text and Relevance', in Carston and Uchida (eds.), *Relevance Theory*, pp. 161-78. See also Sperber and Wilson, *Relevance*, pp. 231-43, whose discussion of metaphor and irony provides some clues but is not explicitly directed at the question of relevance and reading texts.

52. D. Trotter, 'Analysing Literary Prose: The Relevance of Relevance Theory', *Lingua* 87 (1992), pp. 11-27 (12).

53. See the exposition by W. Clark, 'Stylistics and Relevance Theory', pp. 172-76, of the distinctions between implication and implicature, and between strong and weak implicature.

is intended or at least permitted by the author or speaker or text. Such implication is denoted using the neologism 'implicature'.

Further, utterances or texts are capable of generating a range of both strong and weak implicatures, which incidentally are best thought of as poles of a continuum rather than as discrete categories.[54] For the relevance theoretician, a strong implicature is that achieved by a minimum of processing effort with a maximum contextual effect. For some texts there may only be the one strong implicature available. For others, however, the presence of a strong implicature does not obviate the existence of further weaker implicatures that are intended to be picked up by the reader. They are achieved as a result of further processing effort on the part of the reader during which contextual effects are encountered. One of the features of poetic texts, a category of which narrative is a member, is the intentional creation of a range of weak implicatures which then become the responsibility of the reader to process. In that respect the concepts described by Relevance Theory prove useful also in developing a conscious methodology when reading texts. The dynamic nature of this process has been nicely captured in the phrase, 'on-line interpretation'.[55]

It is at just the point of accessing weak implicatures that Relevance Theory proves most beneficial to the interpretive quest undertaken by this commentary, concerned as it is to express a coherence between the intention of the text, the response to the text and the interaction of the two. This can be illustrated in two ways. The first is implicit in the question that Pilkington asks, 'Is poetic communication to be explained in terms of text-internal literary properties, or socio-cultural phenomena?'[56] The answer is that neither is adequate on its own, but each is critical to an understanding of the poetic communication. Relevance Theory acknowledges that the text itself guides the reader towards particular inferences by

---

54. Sperber and Wilson, *Relevance*, pp. 199-200, express it thus: 'the fiction that there is a clear-cut distinction between wholly determinate, specifically intended inferences and indeterminate, wholly unintended inferences cannot be maintained'.

55. Used for example in the context of a discussion on the nature of metaphor by Nam Sun Song, 'Metaphor and Metonymy', p. 91.

56. A. Pilkington, 'Poetic Effects', *Lingua* 87 (1992), pp. 29-51 (29).

means of properties that are 'text-internal' and, I might add, that can appropriately be described as intentional. It also acknowledges that this is not sufficient on its own, for the readers must respond to those text-internal properties. And that response is in terms of 'social-cultural phenomena', both within the text and in what readers brings to their reading of the text. At the intersection of the two, contextual effect is achieved.

Secondly, and to return to the idea of weak implicatures, if a strong implicature is explicitly the outcome of intention in the creation of a text, such weak implicatures as there may be are discovered as the text is responded to. This provides another snapshot of the interaction of text and reader, intention and response. Drawing again on the concept of a continuum of implicatures, Stephen Pattemore reminds us 'that there is no sharp dividing line between strong implicatures of an utterance which are clearly intended by the speaker and weak implicatures for which the hearer "takes the entire responsibility"'.[57]

Application to Biblical Interpretation

The application of these possibilities to biblical interpretation is yet in its infancy, although there has been some work done particularly among those concerned with Bible translation.[58] It is worth noting two provisos to the classic relevance theoretic formulations, which have arisen out of the attention of Ernst-August Gutt and Ernst Wendland to the theory. The first relates to the contextual effect—processing effort analysis. Gutt has modified the processing effort side of the equation to

---

57. Pattemore, *The People of God*, p. 19.

58. See the work referenced above of Pattemore, a United Bible Societies translation consultant. His work is an example of the theory in action. See also the endorsement of the theory and application of it to translation by E.-A. Gutt, *Translation and Relevance: Cognition and Context* (Oxford: Basil Blackwell, 1991), and his more popular *Relevance Theory: A Guide to Successful Communication in Translation* (New York and Dallas: UBS and SIL, 1992). *Contra* Gutt, E.R. Wendland, 'On the Relevance of "Relevance Theory" for Bible Translation', *BT* 47 (1996), pp. 126-37, only cautiously acknowledges Relevance Theory's occasional usefulness.

speak first of 'minimal processing cost' and then later of 'unnecessary processing effort'.[59] This will prove a helpful proviso in considering the question of the relevance of a text which is as 'foreign' to our own contexts as is the biblical text.

Although Wendland acknowledges Gutt's modification, his more substantial complaint concerns the almost exclusive focus of Relevance Theory, at least as presented by Sperber and Wilson, on the cognitive domain. He asks, 'What about the crucial "connotative" (emotive, affective, relational) overlay that accompanies all communication and which is paramount in certain types of discourse, from conversational pleasantries to classical poetry?'[60] This is a particularly apposite question for the interpretation of biblical texts, concerning which the expectation of the religious communities that read them is that the outcome of processing effort will be belief as well as knowledge.

Yet there seems no reason why the process of achieving relevance cannot work on the affective as well as the cognitive level. The notion of context itself is not inherently cognitive, and the processing of utterance and text normally takes place at a subjective level. One of the ironies of Wendland's complaint is that he allies it with the observation that the key categories in Relevance Theory are themselves 'highly subjective' in character and therefore an accurate measure of them is not possible. Of course he is right, but one wonders how he expects to measure the communication that occurs in the 'connotative' domain that he wishes to be recognized. The pairing of these two objections in itself is a concession by Wendland that communication is subjective in its essence, in the light of which his complaint about there being unmeasurable elements in a system that is attempting to describe the essence of communication remains problematic. To give him the benefit of the doubt, Wendland may be engaged in *ad hominem* argument at this point, in which case I accept with him that the operation of inference is only measurable in approximate terms. The fact that it functions at the relational and affective level as well as

---

59. Gutt, *Translation and Relevance*, p. 30, and *A Guide*, p. 25, cited by Wendland, 'On the Relevance', p. 127.

60. Wendland, 'On the Relevance', pp. 128-29.

Prolegomena 27

the cognitive renders this the case, although that is not explicitly acknowledged by Sperber and Wilson.[61]

Contextual Effect
In the light of Sperber and Wilson's commitment to the cognitive domain, I suggest a further amendment to Relevance Theory, namely, that it need not be an exclusively cognitive function. This can be tested by considering in the light of Relevance Theory the manner in which metaphor is processed by a reader. Sperber and Wilson avoid the issue of the connotative or affective functions by describing the processing of metaphor in terms of weak implicatures and 'a wide array of contextual implications'.[62] An essay by Ted Cohen proves helpful at this point. Like Sperber and Wilson, Cohen does not attempt to describe what metaphor is but remains focussed on the operation of metaphor within its narrative context.[63] His thesis is that the primary purpose of a narrative's employment of a metaphor is the achievement of what he calls a 'community of feeling' between reader/hearer and writer/speaker where the same connection may not have been possible on a cognitive level. His key illustration is the biblical one of the prophet Nathan's encounter with David after his affair with Bathsheba and murder of her husband Uriah (2 Sam. 12.1-15). The metaphor of the sheep stealer achieves a community of feeling, indignation, between prophet and king and between reader and narrative. In terms of Relevance Theory, Cohen might have been talking about the achievement of 'contextual effect' and it is noteworthy that he does so in affective or relational terms. There is no doubt much that remains unsaid in Cohen's approach to metaphor, and some opinions from which one might want to demur, but he has illustrated the operation of relevance beyond the cognitive domain. That

61. In their discussion of the relationship of relevance to truth, Sperber and Wilson, *Relevance*, p. 263, reiterate their commitment to the cognitive domain, commenting that the 'notion of relevance has to do with considerations of cognitive efficiency, and the notion of cognitive efficiency cannot be divorced from that of truth. The function of a cognitive system is to deliver knowledge, not false belief'.
62. Sperber and Wilson, *Relevance*, p. 236.
63. T. Cohen, 'Metaphor, Feeling, and Narrative', *Philosophy and Literature* 21 (1997), pp. 223-44.

possibility is particularly apposite for the employment of Relevance Theory in the task of reading the Bible.

Relevance Theory categories cohere to a considerable extent with other priorities outlined above for this reading of Haggai, and because of that play a role in developing the reading. Its emphasis on contextual effect induces a sensitivity to context, both of the contemporary reader and of the prophet and editor of the book itself. The concept of implicature is useful in exploring the move from contextual effect in the late fifth century BCE to the early twenty-first century CE. Its emphasis on the responsibility of the reader and the importance of contextual effect is in tune with the emphasis on the particularity of story outlined above. It also helps to ensure that the responsibility of the reader in interpretation does not become untrammelled privilege. Limits of interpretation are encountered in Relevance Theory's concept of communicative intent. At the same time a relevance approach reminds the commentator of the ethics of interpretation, and in particular the requirement to give the same attention to intention within the text as is assumed by the act of commentary itself. In this way Relevance Theory is a tool that helps to hold together in a creative way both intention and response as partners in the hermeneutical endeavour rather than as rivals coexisting restlessly together.[64]

Incidentally, as befits readers who take the received form of the text seriously, who are alert to inference within the text and who value context, from time to time relevant intertextual effects will be encountered in the book of Haggai. The identification of intertextuality is more of a reading craft than an exact science, and will always be the result of subjective judgment, but when I propose intertextual echoes I will do so mindful of the seven rules of thumb developed by Richard Hays: availability, volume, recurrence, thematic coherence, historical plausibility, history of interpretation and satisfaction.[65]

---

64. For more on this point, see Meadowcroft, 'Relevance as a Mediating Category'.

65. Hays himself refers to them as 'tests'. See R.B. Hays, *Echoes of Scripture in the Letters of Paul* (New Haven: Yale University Press, 1989), pp. 29-32.

Reading the Text as Scripture

So far the status of Haggai as a book within the canon of Jewish and Christian Scripture has remained implicit in the discussion. By virtue of the socio-cultural context in which most Western commentators read the Bible, they have little choice but to adopt one of two positions with respect to the sacred or otherwise status of the Bible. Whether the reader likes it or not, the text is surrounded by a deeply embedded assumption of special status arising from its membership of a special context, the canon of sacred Scripture, whether Christian or Jewish. A reading can assume that or it can consciously adopt an approach that treats the material like any other example of ancient literature.

This latter position is the harder of the two to sustain. Walter Moberly highlights why:

> There is a nice irony in the fact that the recurrent rhetoric on the part of biblical scholars about freeing the Bible from ecclesiastical and dogmatic presuppositions, so that it can speak for itself, tends to coexist largely uncomplainingly with the preservation of that ecclesiastical and dogmatic construct, the Bible itself.[66]

Any treatment of, say Haggai, that is determined to read it simply as an ancient classical text must be indefatigable in its determination to unpick Haggai from its literary and communal context, for that very context bespeaks an attribution of the sacred to Haggai itself. The failure to do this unpicking thoroughly results in the kind of dissonance that dogs many post-Enlightenment treatments of biblical texts. The fact that they are being read at all remains strangely at odds with the manner in which they are being read. But that dissonance is not my problem, because, as has already been implied on a number of occasions in this Prolegomena, I am reading Haggai on the premise that it is part of the text of sacred Scripture through which I expect to hear God speak. Although that is in one sense an easier position to adopt than the alternative, it

---

66. R.W.L. Moberly, *The Bible, Theology, and Faith: A Study of Abraham and Jesus* (CSCD, 5; Cambridge: Cambridge University Press, 2000), pp. 13-14.

still raises a couple of related questions: the nature of the relevance of the biblical text and the manner in which that relevance may be discerned. It is to those questions that I now turn.

Scripture and Contextual Effect

In my comments above about the applicability of Relevance Theory to a reading of the book of Haggai, I did not directly deal with the relevance concept of 'contextual effect'. But it is an important concept because it helps us to understand a little better the nature of the relevance (using the term in its technical sense) of the biblical text. I have already alluded to what I have called the 'foreignness' of the text. In using that word I am attempting to express the sense that there is so little in common between the world of the biblical authors and their first hearers and the contemporary reader that any achievement of contextual effect is hazardous.[67] Yet I have also put the descriptor 'foreign' when applied to the Bible in quotation marks, to express the empirical fact that this same text is assumed by many who read it to be relevant because it is familiar.[68] Why, then, is the biblical text perceived to be relevant despite its 'foreignness'.

A primary reason is that in one sense it is not really a foreign text; rather it is a text that is at the heart of the context of many who read it. This can come about by at least two factors. On the one hand, as Moberly has pointed out, the relevance of any particular segment of the Bible in the twenty-first century owes much to the consensus concerning the wider collection of which Haggai, for example, is a part. Haggai is relevant because of the expectation that the Bible is relevant. There could be any number of reasons or combination of reasons for this being the case. For one who is interested to see how the Bible has formed cultural and religious traditions, the relevance may simply be phenomenological. Or it may be relevant in the sense that a contextual effect is achieved when a reader meets archetypal themes relating to the encounter

67. This achievement of contextual effect is sometimes described metaphorically as the meeting of 'horizons' of the reader and the text.
68. This sense of foreignness is properly preserved, I think, for it prevents the reader too easily assuming that the intent of a text may be known.

between the human and divine, or a particular literary tradition whose enduring appeal lies in the nature of the narrative or poetics or rhetorical effect. Or the reader may be a member of a society in which the biblical stories and metaphors are deeply rooted in the culture. In any one of these ways the relevance of the Bible may be consciously or unconsciously perceived as parts of it are encountered.

To that extent the Bible functions like any other classical text, the relevance of which is to be found more in its cultural significance than in its accessibility. But there is another sense, beyond the general significance of a classical corpus, in which the text of the Bible is not foreign. This can be exemplified negatively. It is a fact that most people do not put any processing effort into the sacred literature of other religions than their own, and so perceive no relevance in those other texts. To most Muslims the *Rig Veda* is not relevant, to most Hindus the *Book of Mormon* has no contextual effect, and most Christians do not attempt to interpret the *Qur'an*.[69] The corollary to all this is that those who have a faith commitment to one or other of those traditions are committed to the relevance of their sacred texts, although the role played by the sacred texts may differ sharply between traditions. For the Christian or the Jew, the Bible is relevant because of the role that it is believed to play as sacred text in the encounter of God with humanity.[70] And because of that, to such a person the book of Haggai is also relevant. An intention to communicate is presumed on the part of an author, however difficult it sometimes is to perceive that author. There is a preparedness to

---

69. In making this comment I am not denying the desirability of mutual appreciation of one another's faith traditions. Rather, I am making an empirical observation. Nor do I wish to imply that the examples of texts given necessarily play an equivalent role within their religions to that of the Bible in Christianity. In fact, the understanding of other faith traditions is probably more necessary now than it has ever been in the modern era.

70. I am content to understand a text as 'sacred' in the senses already implied, that it mediates an encounter with the divine and that it has been set apart with this in mind by a particular faith community. For a fuller exploration of the topic, see the conversation between R. Detweiler, 'What is a Sacred Text?', *Semeia* 31 (1985), pp. 213-30, and D. Rutledge, 'Faithful Reading: Poststructuralism and the Sacred', *BI* 4 (1996), pp. 270-87.

work away at even obscure texts until, in relevance theoretic terms, a range of weak implicatures gradually emerge into focus. Exactly which implicatures emerge will vary according to the points at which the context of the text and the context of the reader intersect with one another. At each point also 'limits of interpretation' are respected as response and intention meet one another.

Implicature and the Biblical Text
But more needs to be said. A trenchant criticism of Relevance Theory has been that it is unable to deal in truth claims. This is obviously a criticism that I must take seriously, given my interest in the application of this theory in the interpretation of a sacred text. It is a question that Sperber and Wilson address in some detail in their revised edition of *Relevance*. They concede the point and attempt some revisions in the light of it, but it remains inescapable that Relevance Theory is not finally about what is true, but about how communication occurs. Yet interpretation must be concerned both with truth claims and with how they are communicated. Where Relevance Theory is helpful is in its recognition of both intention and context in the process of communication. It therefore challenges any hermeneutical approach that either denies the possibility of communicative intent or denies the importance of non-literal implication. I would argue therefore that this gives rise to a hermeneutic that is relational and is likely to allow for truth claims in its process. The question of what is true and false, however, will remain subject to debates about authority and the nature of sacred texts.[71]

I have acknowledged the 'limits to interpretation' of intention that come into play when a reader responds to a text with a search for relevance. It would make sense, then, to consider the issue of truth claims by asking the question: What 'limits of interpretation' are imposed by the nature of the biblical text? If it is agreed that the claim that 'God speaks' is fundamental to the Scriptures, then that assumption forecloses the

71. Indeed, at several points this Prolegomena begs a fuller treatment of the question of authority with respect to the tasks of reading and interpretation. This is a task for another occasion, but in the interim note the discussion of Goldingay, *Models for Scripture*, especially Part II.

possibility of a tension between relevance and truth, in that any contextual effect achieved in the reading of something with the intent of divine discourse must be true.[72] In such a context, to achieve relevance is to achieve an acquaintance with truth. The range of implicatures, as opposed to implications, that may be achieved are consistent with the fact of what Nicholas Wolterstorff calls *Divine Discourse* in his book of that title. It cannot be denied that this position entails huge commitments on the part of the reader as to the nature of God. Such a position accepts that God is inherently truthful. Hard as that may be to adopt, an even harder implication—harder because it engages with the rough edges of human experience —is that God communicates in a manner that may be at times puzzling or inscrutable but is not ultimately malicious or capricious or deceptive.[73] These are both positions underpinning this reading of Haggai, and intrinsic to the assumption that relevance is achievable.[74]

'Divine Discourse'

The assumption of divine discourse as the intent of the Bible is inescapably a faith commitment. It is best to face that fact and admit it. But that does not mean it is either irrational or beyond the sphere of critical examination. There are some further points that can be made in support of that position. Wolterstorff defends, in the words of the subtitle of *Divine Discourse* noted above, 'the claim that God speaks'. By drawing on what he calls the 'illocutionary stance of biblical narrative', he is able to differentiate between divine authorship and

---

72. Note the subtitle in N. Wolterstorff, *Divine Discourse: Philosophical Reflections on the Claim that God Speaks* (Cambridge: Cambridge University Press, 1995).

73. This is a view not shared by all. P.R. Davies, *Whose Bible is it Anyway?* (JSOTSup, 204; Sheffield: Sheffield Academic Press, 1995), p. 113, concludes from the story of the near sacrifice of Isaac that, 'The story says to them: do not trust a deity. He or she or it almost certainly does not trust you, and has no reason to tell the truth.' Moberly, *The Bible, Theology, and Faith*, pp. 170-83, responds to Davies' highly suspicious reading of the story.

74. Although I would want to nuance his claim, note the comment by Sternberg, *Poetics of Biblical Narrative*, p. 179, that 'the Bible must have an omnicompetent God and a privileged narrator to serve his cause'.

34 *Prolegomena*

divine discourse.⁷⁵ Wolterstorff arrives at the view concerning the significance of Scripture that 'the discourse of biblical writers is an instrument of divine discourse'.⁷⁶ He argues that God may appropriately be described as the author of Scripture by thinking of the nature of inspiration. For him, 'inspiration does not determine the agent of the discourse generated'.⁷⁷ Rather, human discourse has become the vehicle of divine discourse as the human authors have discerned what God is saying. The discernment can take as many forms as are represented in Scripture and could be described in any number of ways.⁷⁸ This has something in common with the view of Meir Sternberg that biblical narrative's ability to portray the inner states of God points to an omniscient author and beyond that to the divine authorship of the Bible.⁷⁹ But, while appreciating the gains of Sternberg's approach, Wolterstorff is clear that his concept of divine discourse is different again.⁸⁰ As Sternberg's author is ultimately not obtainable, he is forced to depend on the category of 'implied author' and is in danger once again of taking New Criticism's path of too great a focus on the text for text's sake, with a corresponding loss of sensitivity to the context both of the text and of the text's reader.

Wolterstorff's focus on divine discourse keeps the human authors in view, and buttresses his perspective with the concept of entitlement. Rather than say that an author who can know such things about God as are portrayed in biblical narrative must be divine, Wolterstorff argues that the human authors are entitled to know these things about God.⁸¹ In a

---

75. Wolterstorff, *Divine Discourse*, Chapter 14, 'The Illocutionary Stance of Biblical Narrative' (pp. 240-60).

76. Wolterstorff, *Divine Discourse*, p. 284.

77. Wolterstorff, *Divine Discourse*, p. 284.

78. Wolterstorff himself does not engage with Goldingay, *Models for Scripture*, but note Goldingay's four-fold analysis of Scripture—witnessing tradition, authoritative canon, inspired word and experienced revelation—as one model for describing the various ways in which human authors have discerned what God is saying.

79. See Sternberg, *Poetics of Biblical Narrative*, Chapter 2, 'Narrative Models' (pp. 58-83).

80. Wolterstorff, *Divine Discourse*, pp. 248-52.

81. See Wolterstorff, *Divine Discourse*, Chapter 15, 'Are We Entitled?' (pp. 261-80), on the question, are we entitled to believe that God speaks?

carefully argued chapter he accepts that such knowledge on the part of the biblical authors is the outcome of belief. However, he takes belief as a given entitlement which must then be tested by what he calls 'doxastic practice'. By this he means effectively the process of taking all steps that are reasonably available to the believer to examine the belief in the light of experience. It is in the entitlement of the human authors to convey a narrative in which God is character, and in a similar entitlement of readers to see in the discourse so created a divine discourse, that the claim that God speaks is realized. This opens a way to respect the divine intentionality of the biblical texts, while also appreciating the importance of the reader and acknowledging the potential for indeterminacy in the communicative act.

Obviously such an approach is inimical to a rationalist epistemology. It describes a particular type of knowing that is inescapably attached to belief. This calls forth two responses. The first and most basic is the ethical one noted above, the obligation of a relevance theoretic approach to read a text as fully as possible in the terms in which it presents itself. As Scripture itself expects to facilitate an encounter with God, then there is an ethical imperative to approach it in those terms.[82] Secondly, as discussed above, post-critical epistemologies open up possibilities in that they seek to break down the disjunction between the objective and the subjective and challenge Cartesian categories by means of a re-appreciation of the role of belief in knowing.[83]

Scripture and Belief

Such an epistemology confronts head-on the question posed by Philip Davies in the provocatively titled *Whose Bible is it Anyway?*[84] The view of this commentary is that, while the Bible is properly the subject of critical academic study in the sense that it must be a factor in the human search for understanding

---

82. Note again Goldingay, *Models for Scripture*, which is a comprehensive attempt to grasp the self-understanding of Scripture.

83. See for instance the influential project already referred to of Polanyi, *Personal Knowledge*.

84. P.R. Davies, *Whose Bible is it Anyway?*, especially Chapter 2, 'Church, Theology, Academy', pp. 17-55.

and truth, the Bible is also the Scriptures of the Church and has been formed by the Church. Therefore it is appropriate to acknowledge the particular stewardship that has been vested in the Church to read and interpret the Scriptures.[85] As a corollary to that, it is to be expected that the role of the Scriptures in the formation of belief and relationship with God in Christ can inform the reading of the text. That expectation is a feature of this particular reading of the book of Haggai. According to one's view of the Church with respect to the rest of human society, this need not exclude a study of the Bible that disregards the ecclesiastical context. That I expect to encounter divine discourse as I read the book of Haggai requires me the more to engage with all readers of that same text regardless of their presuppositions or faith positions. Indeed the empirical facts are that the two contexts, the Church and the academy with their varying presuppositional commitments, engage fruitfully if not always amicably with each other.

So far the justification for this type of reading has been in terms of communication theory, along with some epistemological comment. I have also just noted that there is an implicit ecclesiology that is part of such a position. There is also a theological observation to make, which Phyllis Bird hints at but does not develop in her comment that, 'The Bible shares the incarnational character of the One to whom it bears witness'.[86] Goldingay speaks of the link as an analogical one, the divine–human nature of Scripture being somewhat like the divine–human nature of the Word incarnate. He writes,

> The analogy with the incarnation helps us to see that the words of God in scripture can be expressed in a context and be culture-relative and could yet have absolute significance; their contextuality need not imply that they are limited to their context.[87]

---

85. S.M. Schneiders, *The Revelatory Text: Interpreting the New Testament as Sacred Scripture* (New York: Harper Collins, 1991), p. 92, comments that 'living within the Christian tradition of faith is not only not a threat to scholarly objectivity in interpretation of the biblical text but provides a privileged thematic and intuitive access to its meaning'.

86. P.A. Bird, *Missing Persons and Mistaken Identities: Women and Gender in Ancient Israel* (OBT; Minneapolis: Fortress, 1997), p. 264.

87. Goldingay, *Models for Scripture*, p. 239.

He develops this further with the suggestion that just as the divine Christ may be met in relating to the human Christ and *vice versa*, so

> it is possible to understand scripture by starting from the fact that it is God's word and from that base investigating its humanness, or by starting with its humanness and letting the human word speak as a divine word.[88]

In terms of the discussion so far, an encounter with 'divine discourse' can begin either with a focus on the intention of the discourse or with the contextualized response of the reader. Either approach is in keeping with the nature of the text, yet each needs to take account of the other. Relevance Theory and also a speech-act approach both provide a reading methodology that helps to ensure that that remains the case.

Writing much earlier in the last century, Wilhelm Vischer, on the subject of Christ in both the Old and New Testaments, also perceived the link between the incarnation and the nature of the Bible, but took the point further than Goldingay appears willing to. His comments bear quoting at some length:

> If the words of the Bible were not really words of men they would not be the true swaddling clothes of the Son of Man. The *scandalon* of the human contingency of the Bible, which historical and literary criticism has brought to our attention, corresponds precisely to the *scandalon* of the incarnation of the eternal Word in the historical appearance of Jesus of Nazareth at a certain point of time.[89]

There is an element of the analogy observed by Goldingay in his remarks, but Vischer's comments take us beyond that to a christological point. He also asks us to see that the written testimony to Christ that the Church has received and formed could be of no other nature if it is to be a true expression of the incarnation, of the fact of Christ Jesus incarnate in the flesh. Accordingly, 'In their fleshliness, in their temporal contingency and historical fortuitousness, the writings of the Old and New

---

88. Goldingay, *Models for Scripture*, p. 239.
89. W. Vischer, *The Witness of the Old Testament to Christ. I. The Pentateuch* (trans. A.B. Crabtree; London: Lutterworth, 1949), p. 15. See also the discussion of Vischer's position by Moberly, *The Bible, Theology, and Faith*, pp. 134-38.

Testament bear witness to the incarnation'.[90] Correspondingly, not only do we perceive the nature of the Scriptures in the incarnate one to which they bear witness, but we are helped to understand the nature of the incarnation by means of the nature of the Scriptures which bear it witness.[91] Accordingly, any hermeneutical process that hopes to enter into the divine discourse must itself be able to reflect the incarnational nature of God's self-revelation.[92] This makes it all the more crucial that any methodology for reading Scripture be able to discern both the divine intent of and the contingent response to the text, and be able to distinguish the two. To return to an earlier section of this Prolegomena, it also provides a theological basis for a focus on context and particularity. The very particularity of the incarnation and God's engagement with human history invites such an approach.

There is no escaping that this is a risky position to adopt, but it is the nature of the case that there is no safe or foolproof way through for the reader. If there were, if it were possible to take shelter in either the absoluteness of Scripture or the absolute privilege of a reader reading an indeterminate text, we would no longer be participating in the mystery of knowing God. I have already commented that there are few who are using relevance theoretic categories to illuminate the reading of the Bible. However, as a final comment in this section on reading the text as Scripture, a number of scholars are presently interested in a believing reading, although none of them would categorize what they are doing with that exact phrase. I have already noted something of Goldingay's work. Reference has also been made to Moberly whose recent study, *The Bible, Theology, and Faith*, addresses what he calls 'the question of God in and through scripture', and who incidentally concludes with a profound trinitarian reflection on the interaction of the

---

90. Vischer, *The Witness*, p. 14.
91. Goldingay, *Models for Scripture*, p. 241, warns that 'there are limits to the analogy between inspiration and incarnation. There is not such an intrinsic link between the nature of Christ and the nature of scripture that one can argue directly from the one to the other.' This remains, however, an assertion rather than a demonstrated position.
92. See a defence of this position in T.J. Meadowcroft, 'Between Authorial Intent and Indeterminacy: The Incarnation as an Invitation to Human–Divine Discourse', *SJT* 58 (2005), pp. 199-218.

incarnation, the particularities of the divine discourse found in the biblical text and what he calls the 'paradigms of human life in relationship with God'.[93]

Conclusion: Interpretation as Performance

Following on from the foregoing point, and as a way of concluding these methodological notes, I note the study by Stephen Barton on what he has chosen to call 'New Testament Interpretation as Performance'.[94] In his focus on that particular metaphor to describe the interpretive task, Barton urges on his readers the necessity to 'locate our work as exegetes in a wider context of divine and human action'.[95] His work is characterized by the desire to develop a new paradigm for biblical interpretation cast in a trinitarian framework with a lively sense of the relational and the ecclesial context in which interpretation may take place. The metaphor that Barton is elucidating is attractive to one in search of a hermeneutic that seeks to hold together both the intention of the divine discourse and the reader response to that discourse as it is encountered in a reading of the text. The emphasis on 'performance' is a telling one as it speaks in a creative way of the processing effort that is called for in order to achieve relevance in the encounter with a text whose accessibility often lies as much in its status as in its form, a text whose very nature seems to call forth an engagement on the part of the reader. The spreading circle of witness in the Gospel of John leads to a focus on those who will read the text and themselves become witnesses; the book of Jonah ends with a question; sections of Second Isaiah are so indeterminate that the reader must seek to re-appropriate the material into ever-changing contexts; the apocalyptic material points onwards to something yet just out of reach. Each calls forth a response from and implies a responsibility for the reader. In a similar metaphor to Barton's 'performance', Tom Wright suggests the authority of Scripture

---

93. Moberly, *The Bible, Theology, and Faith*, pp. 45, 232-37. Note also his comments on the 'enduring significance of the story' (pp. 64-69).

94. S.C. Barton, 'New Testament Interpretation as Performance', noted above.

95. Barton, 'Interpretation as Performance', p. 179.

is in the nature of an incomplete five-act play that calls forth the creation of a fifth act by its respondents.[96]

By now, we have moved some way beyond the technicalities of a cognitive model of communication which has dominated parts of this discussion. We stand at the edge of an encounter with a text that bears witness to the mysterious meeting of heaven and earth in the realm of human history. But more than that, it embodies and, as both church and synagogue bear witness, somehow enables that meeting to happen.[97] The understandings of the nature of the texts and ways of reading are pressed into the service of that conviction. As readers bring to a reading of Haggai a lively interest in context, a concentration on the narrative form of the received text, a sensitivity to the ethics of reading, and a conviction that a responsible hermeneutic must take account of both reader response and authorial intent, the truths of Scripture will gradually emerge.

---

96. N.T. Wright, 'How Can the Bible be Authoritative?', *Vox Evangelica* 21 (1991), pp. 7-32.

97. While I am reading Haggai as a Christian, I am aware that Christianity is not the only faith community that reads Haggai as sacred Scripture and from time to time some commonality with a Jewish perspective will emerge in my reading. However, it is not part of my purpose to distinguish in any systematic way between readings that are common to both faiths and those that are not. There are some aspects of my reading that are obviously Christian. Where that is the case, my comments do not implicitly question the validity of the Jewish perspective on the same text and context.

INTRODUCTION:
HAGGAI AND HAGGAI'S READERS

In the Prolegomena I noted the importance of context to any self-aware 'reading' of the text. Part of the aim of a commentary is to achieve a meeting of the two context 'horizons' of contemporary reader and ancient text or author. The conclusion to this commentary, an exploration of contemporary relevance, examines the scenery at the point at which those horizons meet, a point at which 'transformation' might occur.[1] The contemporary context of this particular 'reading' is addressed there.

The focus of this introduction is the setting in which Haggai uttered his words and in which they were first heard and subsequently preserved. The historical background and the literary setting of the book are both traditional concerns of the commentary, and are to be expected. More particular to this type of reading of Haggai is the additional concern to uncover the thought world that lies behind the emphasis on the temple as well as an interest in the personalities of Joshua and Zerubbabel and the people whom they lead. I also consider the way in which prophecy is conceived by Haggai and his hearers, for the conclusions we reach on that affect our perception of the significance of his words. As part of the bridge between the two horizons mentioned above, I also look at the history of reception of the book of Haggai by the faith communities that have accorded it authoritative status in the centuries since the Haggai narrative was formed.

---

1. Another scholar engaging in what I termed a 'believing reading' towards the end of the Prolegomena is Schneiders, *The Revelatory Text*, pp. 169-78, who speaks of 'transformative understanding'.

Historical Context

Date

The words of Haggai the prophet can be as precisely located as any of the oracles of the so-called classical prophets. Within the book of Haggai everything takes place within a time frame of about three and a half months in the second year of Darius, and is dated by most scholars between August and December 520 BCE.[2] All of the oracles are placed by the narrative in the second year of the reign of Darius (see Appendix C). The first is on the first day of the sixth month (1.1); the second is undated but presumably on the same date (1.3); the third is on the twenty-fourth day of the sixth month (1.15); the fourth on the twenty-first day of the seventh month (2.1); the fifth on the twenty-fourth day of the ninth month (2.10 and repeated in 2.18); and the final oracle again is on the same day as the previous one, the twenty-fourth day of the ninth month (2.20).[3] This succession of dates continues into the first chapter of Zechariah (Zech. 1.1, 7).[4] In a detailed reading it will be seen that these dates also play a key role in the literary appreciation of the words of Haggai.

Despite a widespread consensus, there remain a couple of points of debate about the dating. One concerns the way in which to understand the regnal years of Darius, and the second lies in the fact that Darius's attainment of the Persian throne was not straightforward and the start of his reign could be pinpointed at various moments. To take the second point first, remember that Cyrus, the Persian conqueror of the Babylonians, ruled until his death in 529 BCE. He was succeeded by his son Cambyses, who took considerable interest in his mastery of Palestine as a base for a planned invasion of Egypt. His death in 522 BCE led to a period of uncertainty and rebellion

---

2. J. Finegan, *Handbook of Biblical Chronology: Principles of Time Reckoning in the Ancient World and Problems of Chronology in the Bible* (Princeton, NJ: Princeton University Press, 1964), especially pp. 210-11.

3. Most interpreters of Haggai identify five oracles rather than six. For a defence of the six-oracles schema on which this commentary is based, see Appendix A and the comment on Hag. 1.1-2.

4. See the time chart in C.L. Meyers and E.M. Meyers, *Haggai, Zechariah 1–8: A New Translation with Introduction and Commentary* (AB, 25B; Garden City, NY: Doubleday, 1987), p. xlvi.

within the empire for about a year, until Darius finally established himself in power.⁵ Principally, Darius faced rebellion in Babylon where Nidintu-Bel, also known as Nebuchadrezzar III, reigned for about three months until his defeat.⁶ About a year later, Araka, styled as Nebuchadrezzar IV, ruled for a similar period of time until his defeat by the Persians. From that point, November 521 BCE, Darius appears to have been accepted as the ruler of the entire empire. The question concerns whether he dates his accession from his defeat of Nidintu-Bel in December 522 BCE, or from his final defusion of the Babylonian threat about a year later.

The other problem with dating lies in how to understand the regnal years. Assuming that Darius dates his reign from his defeat of Araka, Babylonian reckoning of the second year of Darius's reign puts the events of Haggai in 520 BCE, a time when peace has been established in the empire. If the accession year is counted as year one, then Haggai is set a year earlier, in the latter part of 521 BCE. So, although the general view is that events in Haggai occurred in 520, there are two reasons why they may not have been. This would not ordinarily be critical, but in this case the difference sets the book of Haggai either during a period of instability and some privation within the empire, or it sets it in a time of emerging calm and consolidation. There have been attempts to read the prophecies of Haggai and Zechariah against a background of provincial rebellion throughout the empire.⁷ In fact, the argument for a background of a secure emperor Darius is the more compelling, has won the day with most commentators, and is the assumption of this commentary. Certainly that would have been the case by the time the oracles of Haggai were compiled into their narrative shape, on which see further below.

Conditions within Judah

Conditions within Judah were far from easy, as is clear from the words of Haggai, but they were not as fraught politically

---

5. R.J. Coggins, *Haggai, Zechariah, Malachi* (OTG; Sheffield; JSOT Press, 1987), p. 11.
6. P.R. Ackroyd, 'Two Old Testament Historical Problems of the Early Persian Period', *JNES* 17 (1958), pp. 13-27 (14-15).
7. See Ackroyd, 'Two Old Testament Historical Problems', for an exposition of such.

as they would have been a year or two earlier. Indeed, Yehud appears to have been the beneficiary of Darius's increasing security as he gradually reasserted policies of tolerance for and promotion of local governance originally instituted by Cyrus. As well as that, Darius was able to indulge a particular interest of his own, the reorganization of the satrapies.[8] With regard to the particular issue of the temple in Jerusalem, the liability of the inhabitants of Yehud to taxation was moderated and some redistribution of tax for the benefit of the temple was also in evidence. These matters lie behind events depicted in the first six chapters of Ezra. There we see the reiteration of the original decree of Cyrus in 538 BCE which initiated the first wave of returnees to Judah under the appointed leadership of Sheshbazzar. For some reason the initial impetus flagged and somewhere along the line another figure, Zerubbabel, was appointed as governor to work alongside Joshua, the earliest individual on record to bear the title 'high priest' (see below for further on the origins of that title).[9] These two, spurred on by Haggai in 520 BCE, revive the temple-building effort nearly a generation after the initial wave of return to Palestine. As governor, Zerubbabel must have been an appointee of Darius, and the close working relationship with Joshua depicted in the biblical account suggests the same of the high priest also. Despite a number of historical problems in the book of Ezra, it is generally agreed that chs. 5 and 6 in Aramaic provide a fairly accurate picture of the period leading up to the work of Haggai.[10] Ironically, Haggai and Zechariah demonstrate no interest in reporting the completion of the temple, something which we know from Ezra 6.14 and 15 was achieved by 516 or 515 BCE, when the dedication of the house

---

8. See the summary of Meyers and Meyers, *Haggai, Zechariah 1–8*, pp. xxxviii-xl.

9. This commentary accepts the premise argued by A. Laato, *A Star is Rising: The Historical Development of the Old Testament Royal Ideology and the Rise of Jewish Messianic Expectations* (Atlanta: Scholars, 1997), p. 190, that Sheshbazzar was the predecessor of Zerubbabel, contra H.M. Barstad, *The Myth of the Empty Land: A Study in the History and Archaeology of Judah during the 'Exilic' Period* (SOFS, 28; Oslo: Scandinavian University Press, 1996), p. 63, who claims that Zerubbabel is the Akkadian name for Sheshbazzar.

10. Coggins, *Haggai, Zechariah, Malachi*, p. 12.

of the Lord was celebrated. This in itself is suggestive for the argument of this commentary that the Temple itself is not as important as what its building represents of the relationship between Yahweh and the people of God.

Context of Those who Preserved the Narrative

A further aspect of the historical context, one that I consider more fully in the commentary on 2.18-19, is the context of those who preserved the narrative and its oracles as against the putative hearers in 520 BCE. Zerubbabel, who was part of the prophet's narrative audience, disappears into a historical lacuna subsequent to the book of Haggai. It is reasonable, therefore, to suppose that the endowment of a special status on him remained in the future at the time in which the narrative was set, otherwise the book of Haggai could not have spoken of him in the terms in which it does. Therefore, these oracles would probably have been compiled at a time not too distant from the dating preserved in the narrative, when the hopes invested in Zerubbabel were still alive.[11] They are likely to have begun as a continuing encouragement to people who were experiencing similar conditions to those of the first hearers and needing ongoing encouragement to maintain the temple restoration with the hope of a better day to come.

Temple Context

Haggai brings his special interest in the temple into this historical context. I am using the 'temple context' as a catch-all phrase to cover a number of overlapping concerns, all of which surface in the book of Haggai. There is an interest in the priesthood, specifically the high priesthood, and correspondingly in matters of purity and impurity. Linked to this is the

---

11. See the argument of J. Kessler, *The Book of Haggai: Prophecy and Society in Early Persian Yehud* (VTSup, 91; Leiden: Brill, 2002), p. 41, for a late sixth-century redaction. J.E. Tollington, 'Readings in Haggai: From the Prophet to the Completed Book: A Changing Message in Changing Times', in B. Becking and M.C.A. Korpel (eds.), *The Crisis of Israelite Religion: Transformation of Religious Tradition in Exilic and Post-Exilic Times* (Leiden: E.J. Brill, 1991), pp. 194-208 (208), identifies 'an initial oral proclamation' and then 'a literary compilation after a relatively short space of time'.

concept of holiness. A question also lurks in the background concerning the role of the king and more specifically the Davidic tradition. This relates to the part played by the first two recipients of Haggai's words, Joshua the 'high priest' and Zerubbabel the 'governor' of Judah. The message to Joshua and Zerubbabel is also received by 'the people', always a term charged with covenant possibilities. Indeed, these overlapping concerns cumulatively reflect an interest in the covenant, which comes into focus around the rebuilding of the temple and the possibilities that reside therein.[12] Elizabeth Achtemeier goes so far as to say, 'That is what the book of Haggai is about—God's yearning to enter into covenant fellowship with his Chosen People once more'.[13] A backdrop of covenant is assumed by both the commentary and my subsequent assessment of Haggai's contemporary relevance.

An understanding of the significance of the temple to Haggai and his hearers may be derived from the considerable amount of Second Temple material that is available to us. My approach to this particular section is to consider first the temple at Qumran, and then to demonstrate the link between that and some of the biblical precursors to the book of Haggai.

The Idea of the Temple at Qumran
Regarding the Qumran material, a relevant question to ask is how early the ideas on the temple reflected therein may be. It could be that they echo a tradition reaching back into the third or even fourth centuries BCE, although the dates of the texts themselves are somewhat later.[14] If that is the case, then the

12. G. Larsson, *Bound for Freedom: The Book of Exodus in Jewish and Christian Traditions* (Peabody, MA: Hendrickson, 1999), pp. 208-10, explores the sense in which the Mosaic sanctuary established in Exod. 25 is not merely a holy place but reflects a dwelling of God with the people.

13. E. Achtemeier, *Nahum–Malachi* (Interpretation; Atlanta: John Knox Press, 1986), p. 97.

14. L.H. Schiffman, *Reclaiming the Dead Sea Scrolls: The History of Judaism, the Background of Christianity, and the Lost Library of Qumran* (New York: Doubleday, 1994), p. 65, considers that the corpus of scrolls reflects the confrontation with Hellenism primarily after the conquest of Palestine by Alexander in 323 BCE, and that 'the information the scrolls provide us is the most relevant to the years between the Maccabean Revolt of 168–164 BCE and the turn of the era'. He cautiously admits the possibility that the Temple Scroll 'may have emerged from a

ideas represented therein are not far removed in time from the late sixth-century date of the book of Haggai, and indeed even possibly pre-date the production of the LXX of the Book of the Twelve. Although there is no interpretive tradition of Haggai explicitly available to us from Qumran, there is evidence for a climate of reception very soon after the compilation of the Book of the Twelve and particularly the prophets of the restoration, the shorthand that I have adopted to describe the Haggai–Zechariah–Malachi grouping.[15] In the heterodox context of the Second Temple period, generalizations cannot be made from one particular grouping. However, the hints of some consonance that we will see between Qumran and LXX, deriving as they do from quite different religious contexts, are suggestive, as are further hints of consonance between Qumran and a developing biblical tradition that almost certainly predates Haggai.

There is a huge interest within the Qumran material in the temple and its fate, all of which reaches its encyclopaedic

related group either contemporary with or earlier than the Qumran sect' (p. 258).

15. The term 'restoration' assumes a particular stance on 'the myth of the empty land' debate. Barstad, *The Myth of the Empty Land*, pp. 30-39, sees plenty of evidence of a functioning community in Judah during the exile, *contra* J. Kessler, 'Reconstructing Haggai's Jerusalem: Demographic and Sociological Considerations and the Search for an Adequate Methodological Point of Departure', in L.L. Grabbe and R.D. Haak (eds.), *'Every City Shall Be Forsaken': Urbanism and Prophecy in Ancient Israel and the Near East* (JSOTSup, 330; Sheffield: Sheffield Academic Press, 2001), pp. 137-58 (144-51), who proposes a demographic decline and a weak Jerusalem during the same period. I take a lead from L.S. Fried, 'The Land Lay Desolate: Conquest and Restoration in the Ancient Near East', in O. Lipschits and J. Blenkinsopp (eds.), *Judah and the Judeans in the Neo-Babylonian Period* (Winona Lake, IN: Eisenbrauns, 2003), pp. 21-54, who argues that, regardless of the extent to which the land was depopulated, 'the impetus to build could not come from the local Judean population, who did not control the tangible visible proof of YHWH's presence' (p. 51). This proof was to be found in the return of the temple vessels under Cyrus. There would have been an accompanying destruction of infrastructure, such that the re-establishment of Judah as a functional province in the Persian empire and the rebuilding of the temple can properly be described as a 'restoration'. Goldingay, *Old Testament Theology*, p. 701, terms the experience of exile a 'mammoth rupture'. See further below in the comments on 1.5-6.

culmination in the Temple Scroll (variously 11QT or 11Q19 and 11Q20). In all this material there seem to be three trajectories of thought interacting with one another. These may be characterized as the communal, the physical and the eschatological. The physical temple is never reduced to a notional concept useful only as symbol. There was great interest in the particularity of the physical temple and the rites to be observed within it, especially in 11QT as just indicated. Yet despite the sheer volume of detail concerning the temple and its rites, little is said about the 'meaning and significance' of all this.[16]

There is much more concerning meaning and significance where the sanctuary is apparently perceived communally. One point at which this is explicit is in 1QS (Rule of the Community) around Columns 8 and 9. There we read of the community as 'the tested rampart, the precious cornerstone' and 'a most holy dwelling' (8.7 and 8).[17] In this context of community as temple, the reference to 'foundation of the community' (8.10) is strongly reminiscent of the physical temple building in Hag. 2.18. There is also the problematic construct phrase *mqdsh 'dm* in 4QFlorilegium (4Q174), the ambiguous construct phrase 'temple of man' (4QFlor 1.6).[18] This may be a reference to the physical construction but it may also apply to the construction of a community that fulfils the function of the temple in the midst of the people.[19] The ambiguity in itself reflects the interweaving of the two themes. Reflection on the temple as community extends to attribution of a role *vis-à-vis* the people and the land. In 1QS, this community will be 'a house of perfection and truth in Israel'; it will offer up sacrifices on behalf of Israel ('a pleasant aroma'); and it will 'atone for the

16. C.T.R. Hayward, *The Jewish Temple: A Non-Biblical Sourcebook* (London: Routledge, 1996), p. 4.

17. All quotes from the Dead Sea Scrolls follow *The Dead Sea Scrolls Study Edition* (eds F. García Martínez and E.J.C. Tigchelaar; 2 vols; Leiden: Brill, 1997–98).

18. Hayward, *The Jewish Temple*, p. 123, reads it as 'sanctuary of men'.

19. See the survey of views and exposition by D. Dimant, '*4QFlorilegium* and the Idea of the Community as Temple', in A. Caquot, M. Hadas-Lebel and J. Riaud (eds.), *Hellenica et Judaica, Hommage à Valentin Nikiprowetzky* (Leuven: Peeters, 1986), pp. 165-89.

land' (8.9-10).²⁰ Moreover, this house of perfection and truth is called to 'establish a covenant in compliance with the everlasting decrees'. The same link between temple building and covenant is present in Haggai, although less explicitly than in the Rule of the Community. Rather, it is implicit in such phrases as 'their God' (1.14) and the bringing forth from Egypt (2.5).

George Brooke draws attention to the 'community as sanctuary' thesis while warning against pursuing this line to the exclusion of any aspirations for a physical temple.²¹ It is important to read it in the context of the communal and eschatological aspirations that are interwoven with the physical. As we have seen, the possibility is not excluded that one day an ideal physical temple may be built. At the same time, the temple is lent a wider significance than either the physical or the communal are able to express on their own. In the midst of the Temple Scroll comes 11QT 29.7-10:

> They shall be for me a people and I will be for them for ever; and I shall dwell with them for ever and always. I shall sanctify my temple with my glory, for I shall make my glory reside over it until the day of creation, when I shall create my temple, establishing it for myself for all days...

The phrase 'the day of creation' is slightly problematical both textually and in terms of meaning, but despite that the scope of the temple as *'olam*, 'for ever', is a clear theme. The usual English translation of *'olam* is inadequate as the English tends to suggest a chronological understanding. It is, however, as much a spatial term as a temporal one. Its application to the

---

20. According to B. Gärtner, *The Temple and the Community in Qumran and the New Testament: A Comparative Study in the Temple Symbolism of the Qumran Texts and the New Testament* (SNTS, 1; Cambridge: University Press, 1965), p. 30, 'the point is that the holiness of Israel has become concentrated in the community, which thereby becomes a substitute for the Jewish temple' in 1QS 5 and 8.

21. G.J. Brooke, *Exegesis at Qumran: 4QFlorilegium in its Jewish Context* (JSOTSup, 29; Sheffield: JSOT Press, 1985), p. 193. Dimant, '4QFlorilegium', p. 177, is similarly cautious with her argument that '...the Temple of Men represents an interim stage between the Temple of Israel of the past (and present?) and the eschatological Temple of the future'.

temple indicates a role for the temple as the repository of the glory of God far beyond that which is temporally and geographically located.²² The entire fragment 1 of 4QFlor develops this theme more fully with a midrash on an assortment of passages liable to messianic interpretation. The writer's expectation for the temple is that 'He (Yahweh) will appear over it for ever; foreigners shall not again lay it waste as they laid waste, in the past...' (4QFlor 1.5-6).

What is interesting about 4QFlor is the way it combines a perception of the temple as eternal in scope with the hopes invested in both the kingdom and the Zadokite heritage for the preservation of the covenant. This may be noted in 4Q252 column 5, in which the throne of David is not cut off. The Hebrew is a little uncertain at this point, but it is clear that one aspect of this Davidic kingdom is that it is 'the covenant of royalty'. Here again the hopes of an eternal kingdom linked to covenant hopes may be seen. The implication of the Zadokite priesthood in this eschatological hegemony, again tied into the covenant, occurs at numerous points at Qumran, two of which I instance. At CD 4.3-4, 'the sons of Zadok are the chosen of Israel, the men of renown, who stand...at the end of days'. 1QS^b 3.6 refers to a covenant of an '[eternal] priesthood' for the faithful sons of Zadok. In many of the references to Zadok, the priesthood is charged with responsibility to separate out the good and the evil. This is true both for the temporal community of the sanctuary and for the eschatological temple (see, e.g., 1QS 5 and 9).²³ Related to this is another relevant example from 1QS 9, where the formation of a 'holy community' is

22. It is difficult to settle on the best term with which to express this sense of *'olam* in English. 'Eschatological' does not quite do justice to the cosmic or spatial scope of the vision, while 'cosmic' does not quite do justice to the eschatological or temporal scope of the vision. I have chosen to express this with the term 'eschatology' as it takes us closer to the sense than 'cosmic' quite does. Nevertheless, I acknowledge that it is not a perfect expression of the Semitic concept of *'olam*.

23. Schiffman, *Reclaiming the Dead Sea Scrolls*, pp. 319-21, distinguishes between 'restorative' and 'utopian' views of Israel's future. He links the figures of Zerubbabel and the high priest in Haggai/Zechariah with the restorative strand that he sees in the Dead Sea sect. I will see it in terms of a rootedness in history and contemporary events with a future aspect also at work.

envisaged. The community consisting of 'men of holiness who walk in perfection' contrasts with 'men of deceit' and the 'goods' of each are to have nothing to do with each other. The eternal temple is not explicitly in view, as it has been in the examples highlighted above, but the discourse at this point indicates the interaction on each other of the themes of holiness/unholiness, temple and community.

In his exposition of liturgical anthropology in the Dead Sea Scrolls, Crispin Fletcher-Louis draws out in some detail an important corollary to all of this, namely, the concept of temple-as-microcosm that is also prevalent in the Qumran material. This is especially the case in his exposition of the Songs of the Sabbath Sacrifice and the War Scroll (1QM).[24] The concept is that the temple is a 'microcosm of the universe, its rituals and drama effect the power of the creator within the cosmos'.[25] As a result of this,

> There is a parallelism between Israel's actions in the cult and God's actions in creation as a whole. And this means there are two more specific analogies at work. One looks upwards from the sanctuary: Israel, her priesthood and liturgy act in imitation of the life of heaven and God's wonders therein. One looks outwards and downwards from the sanctuary. Israel, her priesthood and liturgy are somehow parallel to the events within the earthly realm and history and, in particular, in [the War Scroll] the eschatological battle with God's enemies.[26]

This concept is of course not created out of nothing by the Qumran community. Psalm 150.1 contains a suggestive parallel between 'sanctuary' and 'firmament'. Somewhat later, Ben Sira links the firmament to the Jerusalem temple (Sir. 24 and 50).

The question before us is the extent to which this material enhances an understanding of Haggai's own context, and hence of the oracles that he uttered and the narrative in which they are reported. Certainly there are some immediate connections, and at points they have much in common with the biblical

---

24. C.H.T. Fletcher-Louis, *All the Glory of Adam: Liturgical Anthropology in the Dead Sea Scrolls* (STDJ, 42; Leiden: Brill, 2002), Chapter 8–12.
    25. Fletcher-Louis, *All the Glory of Adam*, p. 183.
    26. Fletcher-Louis, *All the Glory of Adam*, p. 474.

tradition. The concern for the fate of the physical temple and the temple vessels is a feature of the period leading up to and during the exile. The final insult perpetrated by Nebuchadnezzar appears to have been his appropriation of the temple vessels (Jer. 52.17-23). This concern surfaces regularly through the early chapters of the book of Daniel, culminating in the story of Belshazzar (Dan. 5).[27] Haggai is part of a cluster of material that sees the rebuilding of the temple and the repossession of the temple vessels (Ezra 1.7) as the realization of a restored Israel, however that may be understood. This is the focus of Ezra–Nehemiah. The notion of a restored Israel includes also an interest in the purity of the people who are associated with the temple (see, for example, the campaign against marriage with foreigners in Ezra 10). The eschatological and communal significance of the temple is perhaps not so obvious in the biblical tradition of the exile, but it is arguably not entirely absent. Ezekiel's vision of the temple (Ezek. 40–48) appears to imbue the building with a transcendent significance. At the same time, Haggai's own command to the people in 2.18 to 'set their heart' (my translation) on the day of the foundation of the temple is suggestive of a significance beyond the building itself, and perhaps prefigures the 'community as temple' concept noted above as evident in 1QS and 4QFlor.

The Zadokite Priesthood
A further connection is through the Zadokite priesthood. It is difficult to argue against the conclusion that Joshua is considered by Haggai and Zechariah to be in the Zadokite line, although the origins of the Zadokite line are subject to speculation. A few freeze frames on the biblical tradition illustrate the grounds on which Joshua is linked to that tradition. Zadok is probably the first Jerusalemite priest, and as such is intimately linked with the development of a centralized temple-based form of religion, although, unlike Joshua, he is not entitled 'high priest' (see, e.g., 2 Sam. 8.17; 1 Kgs 1.32; 1 Chron.

---

27. I assume a Persian provenance for the court tales in Dan. 2–6, although the final form of the book may date from mid-second century BCE. See T.J. Meadowcroft, *Aramaic Daniel and Greek Daniel, A Literary Comparison* (JSOTSup, 198; Sheffield: JSOT Press, 1995), pp. 272-77.

29.22).²⁸ Indeed, the office of high priest does not emerge until the return from exile. 1 Chronicles 6.1-15 places Zadok in the line of the Aaronite priesthood as a direct descendent of Aaron. Part of Ezekiel's vision for the new temple is that 'the levitical priests' of the 'family/descendents of Zadok' (Ezek. 43.19; 44.15) should play a pivotal role in it. Whether or not Zadok was physically a member of the Aaronite family, the work of the Chronicler illustrates that the tradition gradually has come to invest the hopes for a renewed temple and priesthood in the person of Zadok as the true continuation of the levitical tradition. The same genealogy of 1 Chronicles names a descendent of Zadok, Jehozadak, as the priest taken into exile by Nebuchadnezzar. The chief priest who emerges for the rebuilding of the temple is persistently named as the son of this Jehozadak.²⁹ In that respect the lineage of Joshua, described by both Ezra (Ezra 3.8) and Haggai as 'son of Jehozadak' (or 'Jozadak in Ezra 3.8), is significant in that it provides a bridge between the temples and builds on the hopes that came to be invested in the Zadokite priesthood during the exile experience.

Zerubbabel's Davidic Significance

As Zadok is a significant figure in the hopes of Qumran, so is a Davidic figure, whether or not an explicit restoration of royalty is envisaged. Just as Joshua's Zadokite heritage is derived from other biblical evidence, so we must look elsewhere to discover Zerubbabel's Davidic significance. The key link is once again provided by the Chronicler, this time in a genealogy at 1 Chron. 3.17-19.³⁰ In Haggai, Zerubbabel bears the patronymic Shealtial; in the 1 Chronicles reference he is the son of

28. D.W. Rooke, *Zadok's Heirs: The Role and Development of the High Priesthood in Ancient Israel* (Oxford: Oxford University Press, 2000), p. 72.

29. For further on the figure of Zadok in the growth of the biblical tradition, see G. Boccaccini, *The Roots of Rabbinic Judaism: An Intellectual History, from Ezekiel to Daniel* (Grand Rapids: Eerdmans, 2002), pp. 56-63.

30. D.L. Petersen, 'Zerubbabel and Jerusalem Temple Reconstruction', *CBQ* 36 (1974), pp. 366-72 (369), attributes the links between Chronicles and Haggai to a 'Chronistic redactor' of Haggai. However, the links may be as readily explicable in terms of a shared literary and historical provenance.

Pedaiah, a brother of Shealtiel. Whatever the explanation of this discrepancy might be, in either case he would be the grandson of Jehoiachin, and therein lies his significance, for Zerubbabel's grandfather was the unfortunate royal who found himself, after three months as a vassal king, deposed and deported to Babylon by Nebuchadnezzar (see 2 Kgs 24).[31] There are several variations on his name, and in the Chronicler's genealogy referred to above he appears as Jeconiah. Zerubbabel is therefore a direct descendent of the last king to sit on the throne of David. As I will consider in more detail in the body of the commentary, this historical understanding is crucial to an appreciation of the apparently royal status given to Zerubbabel in the final verses of Haggai. It builds upon the hopes in a branch of David expressed in Jer. 23.5, 6; 33.15, 16, a theme that is developed further in the post-exilic period by Zechariah (Zech. 6.12-13). The observation of Zerubbabel's patronymic also helps to provide a bridge over which Haggai can reach back to pre-exilic times as the basis for a restoration hope in what has gone before. It has also been speculated that the figure named in 1 Chron. 3.18 as Shenazzar, an uncle of Zerubbabel, may have been the shadowy figure Sheshbazzar, about whom little definite can be determined but who was Zerubbabel's predecessor as governor. Sheshbazzar is mentioned as Cyrus' appointee as first governor of Judah and the one who caused the temple vessels to return to Jerusalem with the returning exiles, but apart from that he does not figure in the account of the return at all (see Ezra 1.11; 5.14-16). Although his place in the tradition cannot finally be determined, it may be that the link between Zerubbabel and Shenazzar is also another link back to the pre-exilic period.

Qumran and the Biblical Tradition
A number of the Qumranic themes concerning the temple, as I have outlined, are incipient in the biblical tradition, and may be detected in the book of Haggai itself. Haggai in one sense stands between the embryonic hopes for the temple expressed in such places as Ezra and Ezekiel 40–48, and their more fully developed form in the writings from Qumran. Care must be

---

31. For a detailed discussion of this issue, see Meyers and Meyers, *Haggai, Zechariah 1–8*, pp. 68-69.

taken not to apply the Qumran material anachronistically, but where we find potential developments of the earlier post-exilic and exilic traditions, it can enhance our appreciation of the thought world in which Haggai was doing his work.[32] With respect to the temple and the life of the people focused on the temple, there are a number of such points. The trajectories of understanding of the temple as eschatological, physical and communal inform the context into which Haggai spoke. Within the book the physical temple is in view but it is linked constantly with the life of the people. The inclusion of the final oracle with its apocalyptic imagery, while not explicitly linked to the building of the temple, by association has the effect of linking the hopes of the temple with eschatological concerns. The importance of the Zadokite priesthood alongside the hopes in a Davidic figure also figures prominently in the minds of those to whom Haggai spoke. Likewise the link between creation and the sanctuary so evident at Qumran is suggested by the 'desolation' of both the temple and the land in Haggai. Each of these aspects of the temple in Haggai are productive in the search for contemporary relevance.

Zerubbabel and Joshua in Haggai/Zechariah 1–8

The comments, however, about the Zadokite priesthood and the Davidide Zerubbabel must be qualified because they mask an important question about the roles of Zerubbabel and Joshua with respect to one another. At this point the distinction between the temple context and the history of reception becomes blurred, and some of what is said more properly belongs to the history of reception, but I treat it at this point as a kind of bridge between two aspects of the wider discussion. The problem that has long exercised interpreters concerns the apparent difference in the way that Joshua and Zerubbabel are treated respectively by Haggai and Zechariah. This is intensified by the fact that Haggai and Zechariah 1–8 function so obviously as a pair, to the point that some have read them as a single literary unit.[33] The present discussion assumes that

---

32. On the understanding the unity of Second Temple Judaism, the diversity of the 'Judaisms' of the same period, and the relationship between the two, see Boccaccini, *Roots of Rabbinic Judaism*, pp. 8-14.

33. For example, Meyers and Meyers, *Haggai, Zechariah 1–8*, p. xliv, consider them a composite work.

the two are closely linked (see below for a literary and historical discussion of those links).

Until the final oracle, Zerubbabel and Joshua are always addressed together in the book of Haggai, and most of the time their patronymic and title is included in the address. The only exception to that is in 1.12, where Zerubbabel is not named as 'governor'. What has exercised interpreters is the exclusive focus of the final oracle on Zerubbabel alone, who therein acquires the additional accolade 'my servant' (2.23). At the same time, whenever the two figures are named together Zerubbabel appears first—thus, so it is claimed, indicating a priority in the mind of the writer or compiler. This raises the possibility that the figure of greater interest to Haggai, or at least to those responsible for his narrative, is Zerubbabel.

The governor and high priest relate somewhat differently to each other in Zechariah 1–8. Joshua is given a special role in Zechariah's fourth vision (Zech. 3) in the purification of the land. In the next vision (Zech. 4), Zerubbabel occupies the front of the stage, as his role both in laying the foundation of the new temple and in completing it is highlighted. So far the treatment is even-handed, although the same explicit roles are apparently ascribed to each figure as is the case in Haggai. Complexities arise in the coronation scene of Zech. 6.9-15. Verse 11 is clear that the high priest Joshua, known already from Haggai, is to be crowned. In v. 12, the high priest is addressed and a figure known as Branch is pointed out to him. This figure will be responsible for building the temple, and furthermore (v. 13) he is imbued with an implicit royal spleendour as he sits on a throne. In the context of Zechariah 1–8 and Haggai, explicitly the references to the signet ring in Hag. 2.23 and the role assigned to Zerubbabel in Zechariah 4, it is difficult to avoid the identification of the 'Branch' as Zerubbabel. There is some intertextual effect with other passages of hope which backs up this identification (see especially Jer. 22.24 and 23.5).[34] The MT of Zech. 6.11-13a makes more explicit than does the NRSV translation that there are two distinct figures in

---

34. Although there is no lexical coincidence, the branch from the stump of Jesse in Isa. 11.1 is working with the same idea. Incidentally, this is one of a number of links between Haggai and the oracles attributed to Isaiah of Jerusalem that will emerge.

view here, the crowned high priest Joshua and 'a man whose name is Branch'.

These two figures appear to fulfil some kind of joint function in v. 13b, and as they do so there is *shalom* between them. The problem lies in the position each one occupies with respect to the other. The NRSV conveys a picture of 'Branch...on his throne' with the priest 'by him'. This is a rendition of the LXX variation, which literally reads 'on his right side'. In contrast, the MT has both Branch and Joshua the high priest on a throne, in the kind of joint stewardship that is implied by the phrase, 'with peaceful understanding between the two of them'. It is difficult to see any transmission reason for the LXX variation. There is nothing resembling 'right side' in the surrounding text of the Hebrew version, nor any similar phrasing elsewhere in the corpus that may have been imported. Moreover, there is no possibility of the difference coming about by a misreading of the consonantal text. It seems most likely that this variation indicates a variation in the tradition, whether the LXX represents a variant *Vorlage* or an interpretive translation of the tradition represented in the MT.

The two possibilities form the basis of the debate over the significance of this verse. Commentators tend to adopt one of three positions. Branch may be Zerubbabel, thus continuing the pairing of Joshua and Zerubbabel as the twin authorities in the restored Israel.[35] A second view is that Joshua himself is referred to as Branch. Notwithstanding my comments above, the Hebrew of Zechariah 6 is sufficiently ambiguous to allow for that interpretation. This argument is used to support the view that the prophecies of Zechariah shift the focus away from the Davidide Zerubbabel to the Zadokite high priest Joshua as the source of both civil and religious authority in the reconstituted Israel, at least in the interim.[36] An intermediate position is adopted by Joyce Baldwin, who sees both priestly and kingly authority coalescing around the figure called Branch, representing a corporate identity exercised by Joshua and Zerubbabel together.[37]

---

35. This is the view of Rooke, *Zadok's Heirs*, pp. 146-49.
36. So Meyers and Meyers, *Haggai, Zechariah 1–8*, p. 371.
37. So J.G. Baldwin, *Haggai, Zechariah, Malachi* (TOTC; London: Tyndale Press, 1972), pp. 135-37.

58 *Introduction*

The differing views of the commentators may well represent a tension that was present in the earliest sources. Even within the Jeremiah material already referred to, a couple of traditions are apparently in tension with each other. In Jer. 22.30, we read with respect to Jehoiachin (there denoted Coniah) that neither he nor his descendants will ever sit on David's throne or rule in Judah again.[38] This seems at odds with the hymn to the righteous branch in Jer. 23.5-6, a branch which will come from David's line. The tension lends some support to the notion that there was a tussle for significance between the position of high priest and that of the Davidic ruler, particularly as expressed in the person of Zerubbabel.[39] The MT of Zech. 6.12-13 is ambivalent over the question of whether the high priest participates in the rule from the throne, until it comes to the phrase that places the priest also upon 'his throne'. At that point Rooke's view loses some credibility, and the placement of the priest supports the case that he is being moved into the role apparently envisaged for Zerubbabel by Haggai. In contrast to all that, the LXX appears at odds with the general thrust of Zechariah in favour of Joshua, and has more in common with the primacy of Zerubbabel implied by the narrative of Haggai and his oracles.

The debate is far from settled. The final oracle in Haggai is a surprising and definite focus on Zerubbabel at the expense of Joshua, while the detail of the signet ring does seem to pick up explicitly on the hopes hinted at in the book of Jeremiah for a branch. While that may be evidence of a kind of primacy for Zerubbabel in the high priest–governor relationship, a point which remains debatable, the detail that Zerubbabel is always listed first in Haggai can bear little weight. Zechariah in contrast surprises by the accretion of traditionally understood royal accoutrements to the high priest Joshua. The version variation in Zech. 6.13 may well reflect a debate over how far royal expectations can be permitted to settle on the priest, but there is not enough evidence to arrive at an assured conclusion.

38. W. McKane, *Critical and Exegetical Commentary on Jeremiah* (ICC; 2 vols.; Edinburgh: T. & T. Clark, 1986), I, p. 546, reads: 'none of his children will gain custody of the throne of David'.

39. *Contra* C.L. Feinberg, *Jeremiah: A Commentary* (Grand Rapids: Regency, 1982), p. 160, who reads Jer. 23 as the prophetic response of hope for a new king in light of the extinction of Jehoiachin's line.

The MT form in which we have received Zechariah suggests a joint stewardship between the two figures, while there is elsewhere in Zechariah 1–8 a slightly greater emphasis on Joshua than on Zerubbabel. Such difference as there is in emphasis remains slight. Consequently, there is some wisdom in Baldwin's approach, which is to read the *shalom* among Branch and priest to be evidence of a coalescing of priestly and gubernatorial responsibility although still represented in two figures.[40] The jury remains out as to which of the two is the more important. Haggai may think one and Zechariah may think another, reinforced by the LXX tradition of Zech. 6.13. Readers do well to allow the two emphases to exist side by side in the text as it has been received, and to read synoptically—in other words, to allow the two traditions, if in fact they are distinguishable, to inform each other, to allow the hopes invested in the line of David and the hopes for the re-establishment of a Zadokite priesthood to work together in a single restoration and eventually in an eschatological hope.

There is some irony that follows from such an approach, which gives pause to the temptation to make simplistic assumptions. The fifth oracle of Haggai (2.10-19) concerns the concept of ritual purity, and entails a conversation with the priests. The place of this oracle in the context of the wider narrative is addressed in the body of the commentary, and is not without its problems, but whatever literary or form-critical solution is proposed, it occupies a striking place in the narrative. In contrast, there is little apparent interest in this topic in the prophecies of Zechariah. On another theme the contrast is even more marked. The fate of the nations is observed largely negatively in the book of Haggai. In the final oracle (Hag. 2.20-23), part of the eschatological hope is that the kingdoms and nations will be overthrown and destroyed and put to the sword. The fourth oracle (Hag. 2.1-9) is less negative, but still sees a day when the role of the nations *vis-à-vis* Israel will be primarily as suppliants. In comparison, although Zechariah hopes for vengeance on 'daughter Babylon'

---

40. Baldwin, *Haggai, Zechariah, Malachi*, p. 135, writes that Zechariah's 'hearers had been prepared for the Branch to fulfil priestly and kingly functions and therefore would realize that both Joshua and Zerubbabel contributed to the work of the coming Branch, while neither alone adequately represented him'.

(Zech. 2.7-9), he is able to accommodate in his eschatology a more generally inclusive vision (Zech. 8.20-23) for the nations. If Haggai is primarily concerned to promote Zerubbabel and Zechariah primarily concerned to promote the high priesthood to a distinctive role in the restored nation of Israel, as some have claimed, these variations in focus are surprising. I would have expected the opposite. This warns us further against a dependence on easy categorizations, and is an argument in favour of allowing the priestly and the royal to act on one another through these two books. In that way Haggai and Zechariah 1–8 are understood as a staging post on the way to the realization of a 'priestly kingdom and a holy nation' (Exod. 19.6). Just as that phrase defies conventional categorizations—priest with kingdom and holiness with *goy*—so does the eschatological vision of Haggai and Zechariah 1–8 when read together.

Recipient Context

If that is how the book of Haggai functioned in those early days of the restoration, it has been interpreted in other ways since. A commentary that is interested in drawing together the contexts of the book of Haggai itself with that of present day readers of the book is perforce interested in the history of reception that bridges those two contexts.[41] The earliest evidence we have on the reception of the book of Haggai is via the LXX, the early translation into Greek, and also the material that has been preserved by the Qumran community. As noted above, the Qumran material provides little if any evidence of a particular attitude to the book of Haggai itself, but a considerable amount of material relevant to the possible provenance in which Haggai was working. There is a little more direct evidence in the LXX.

41. E. Ben Zvi, 'Twelve Prophetic Books or "The Twelve": A Few Preliminary Considerations', in J.W. Watts and P.R. House (eds.), *Forming the Prophetic Literature: Essays on Isaiah and the Twelve in Honor of John D.W. Watts* (JSOTSup, 235; Sheffield: Sheffield Academic Press, 1996), pp. 125-56 (149-50), reflects on 'meanings evolving out of the interaction between the ancient readers for which the book was written and the text being read'. The premise of such an interaction undergirds the interest of this commentary in reception context.

The LXX

A perennial question concerns the extent to which variations between the LXX and the MT are interpretational or theological as opposed to merely technical. To the extent that variations demonstrate a *tendenz*, they can tell us something about the earliest reception of the book by subsequent generations of readers. Where the reasons for variation are explicable in text-historical terms, or seem in concert with the overall sense of the MT, I will not pursue them. A commentary such as that by Wolff provides ample technical notes on the MT/LXX variations in the text.[42] The assumption I am adopting is that variations are likely to be technical or insignificant unless there is a compelling reason to think otherwise.

But there are several instances where a *tendenz* is arguable at least, partly in that there appears to be some concordance between the LXX emphasis and developments in the thought world indicated by some of the Qumran material. The first is in 1.11 where the land is said in the MT to be suffering from 'drought' (*choreiv*), the same consonants used of the word to describe the temple in v. 9 and translated by NRSV as 'in ruins'. Whether 'drought' and 'in ruins' derive from the same root or from different ones that are spelt the same (so BDB), in either case a translation in both v. 9 and v. 11 could be 'desolate' or 'desolation', and the rhetorical effect of the Hebrew pun is to identify the fate of the land in v. 11 with that of the temple in v. 9. The LXX does not represent that. It employs the expected translation of 'in ruins' in v. 9 with *ereimos*, 'desert', but translates the same Hebrew consonants in v. 11 with *rhomphaia*, 'sword'. Again, that is a possible translation of that group of Hebrew consonants, in fact the expected one in a different context. But the effect of the choice made here is to deflect the rhetorical effect of MT while at the same time opening up the possibility that the LXX reads the fate of the temple a little more portentously than does the MT. Mention of the sword introduces apocalyptic and possibly eschatological echoes. This may be completely unintended by the translator and therefore insignificant. That the LXX opts in 2.6 for a synonym for 'desert' where 'the dry land' (NRSV, MT *charabah*) could

---

42. Wolff, *Haggai*, pp. 27-31, 57-79, 87-88, 97-98.

legitimately be translated as 'desolation' cautions us against reading too much into the appearance of a sword in LXX.

However, another variation is found in 2.9, where the LXX includes a long explanatory phrase not in the MT, which can be translated thus: 'and peace of soul for protecting (or strengthening) those who are bringing about the rebuilding of this temple'. There are two interesting aspects of this extra phrase. First, it includes the verb *anhisteimi*, a verb which incidentally later became charged with theological significance, but here has the sense of building or setting in place and is the commonplace translation for a commonplace Hebrew word, *qum*. It is, however, not the usual term used by LXX in Haggai for building the temple, which is *oikodomeo*, a term without the same sense of rebuilding. The word *anhisteimi* introduces the concept of 'rebuilding' and thus of more than one temple, which is not present in the Hebrew. The MT simply draws a comparison between later splendour and earlier splendour of the temple (2.9). The second point of interest is the focus on those who are doing the building as especially chosen. This too is not a theme in the MT, but may point towards a reception tradition beginning to grow up around the temple, that there is particular blessing and cursing associated with the attitude that is adopted towards the temple. This too is tinged with an eschatological interest.

A further long addition in 2.14 adds to the effect. The addition comes at the end of the verse and says, 'because of the receipts of their daybreaks, they suffer from their wickedness. And you hate those who are speaking in the gate.'[43] The phrase 'their daybreaks' is more or less inscrutable, but is not crucial to the main point being made, which is that there is here also a stronger emphasis on the culpability of the people for the fate of the temple than is the case in MT.

The two LXX pluses that I have just looked at seem to work out chronologically from the date of the oracles of Haggai in opposite directions. The first one seems to echo the eschatological significance of the temple that is so much a feature of the Qumran texts. The second points back to an earlier

---

43. Wolff, *Haggai*, p. 88, speculates 'their morning profits' as an explanation of 'receipts of their daybreaks'.

tradition of prophecy with its reference to those speaking in the gate (see Amos 5.10). However, both focus more strongly on the attitude of the people than does the MT of Haggai itself. In the MT of Haggai 'the people' is a more or less monochrome category. They are either working for the building of the temple or they are not. At Qumran, the temple project is invested with a wider eschatological significance, and there is a steady dualism between good and evil and those who ally themselves with good or evil. When the two pluses and the variation in the LXX text are taken cumulatively, the *tendenz* of the LXX of Haggai, such as it may be, leads in a similar direction as do the ideas reflected in the Dead Sea Scrolls. I am not claiming for the LXX exactly the same type of agenda evident in the Temple Scroll, namely, a massive focus on the ideal physical temple precisely as part of an understanding of an ideal society. And of course the contexts are quite different: one is Palestinian and one is of the diaspora; one is probably more sectarian and the other more at peace with religious establishment. Yet despite these differences, and the more noteworthy because of them, from a time not too distant from the original formation of the material, the temple that Haggai was writing about and the life surrounding that temple was invested with a significance beyond the building itself, but still a significance to which the building remained an indispensable pointer.

Philo

A further point of interest in LXX Zech 6.12 is its employment of the word *anatolei* to render the MT *tsemach*, 'branch'. The Greek has the sense of 'rising one'. This does not necessarily imply a move to a messianic understanding of 'Branch', by whom I have suggested Zerubbabel is probably intended. Indeed, the same translation move is made in Jer. 23.5 and Ezek. 16.7; 17.10, and in each case the LXX translator seems to be working with an agricultural metaphor in mind. That which rises is that which sprouts like a shoot or a branch. However, Philo of Alexandria, working just a generation or so before the destruction of the Second Temple in 70 CE, does considerably more than the LXX with Zech. 6.12. He draws on the term *anatolei* and writes of it that it is the strangest of titles, surely, if you suppose that a being composed of soul and body is here described. But if you suppose that it is that Incorporeal one, who differs not a whit from the divine image, you will agree that the name of 'rising' assigned to him quite truly describes him. (*Confusion of Tongues* 62)[44]

Philo does not develop the idea further with respect to the figure denoted in Zechariah, instead moving into a kind of midrash on 'rising ones', but he provides a clue as to how the material in Zechariah and Haggai could be read at the end of the Second Temple era. If the reading demonstrated by Philo is not explicitly eschatological, it at least indicates a desire to interpret in transcendent terms.

Sirach

The work of Ben Sira is also relevant. It is generally agreed that this wisdom book dates from early in the second century BCE, most likely before the Maccabean crisis of the 160s.[45] Although apparently from a school of thought different from that of Qumran, Ben Sira's work is preserved and respected by the Qumran community. He is also referred to with approval by the rabbis, to the extent that his book is quoted some eighty-two times in the Talmud and other rabbinic writings. This was despite the rabbinic inability to agree on whether or not the Wisdom of Ben Sira 'defiled the hands' (i.e. deserved canonical status).[46] He seems to have been widely read among Jews of varying shades of opinion. Of particular interest are his treatment of the high priest Simon II (ch. 50) and his hopes for the Zadokite priesthood in chs. 45 and 50. These chapters indicate the hope invested in the Zadokite dynasty of priests and the importance of their descent from Phinehas. Although it may have been appropriated to an eschatological cause, the primary function of the work of Ben Sira among his later readers was to continue to remind Jews of how things had been before the

---

44. *Philo IV* (trans. F.H.C. Colson and G.H. Whitaker; Loeb Classical Library; London: Heinemann, 1932), p. 45.
45. A.A. DiLella, *The Hebrew Text of Sirach: A Text-Critical Study* (London: Mouton, 1966), pp. 150-51, comments in detail on the age and history of the Hebrew text of Ben Sira.
46. P.W. Skehan and A.A. DiLella, *The Wisdom of Ben Sira* (AB, 39; New York: Doubleday, 1987), p. 20.

despoliation of the temple by Antiochus IV in 167 BCE.[47] In that respect he reflects an ongoing hope in the Zadokite dynasty such as that reflected in Haggai. Even more importantly he links the Davidic covenant to the figure of Phinehas, an ancestor of Zadok (Sir. 45.24-25). In doing so, Hayward argues, he 'has in some measure transferred to Simon and the Zadokite dynasty royal attributes which were once characteristic of the House of David'.[48] Here too Ben Sira follows a line of thought whose beginnings may be detected in the synoptic reading of Zechariah 1–8 and Haggai suggested above.

Targum Prophets

If there is some debate over the extent to which the LXX may be regarded as intentional interpretation, there is none over the Aramaic paraphrases of the Hebrew text known as the Targums. As befits their status as paraphrases, these texts are interpretive in intent in a way that the LXX is not. Robert Gordon and K.J. Cathcart place Targum Prophets after 70 CE, although they see some pre-70 CE elements represented therein.[49] Of particular interest in the Targum of the Twelve Prophets is the concept of the *shekinah* or glory of the Lord resident in the temple. On balance, Gordon considers that this element should be dated post-destruction of the Second Temple.[50] At 1.8 the Targum reads concerning the rebuilt temple, 'and I shall be pleased to make my *Shekinah* dwell in it in honour, says the Lord'.[51] The MT reads as translated by NRSV, '...so that I may take pleasure in it and be honoured, says the Lord'. Assuming that this is a post-destruction tradition, the targumic terminology 'shall be pleased' perhaps locates the

---

47. Hayward, *The Jewish Temple*, p. 40: 'The dissemination of ben Sira's work suggests that his stance towards the Zadokite priesthood embodied in the text may have commanded respect long after the Zadokites had ceased to rule as high priests'.

48. Hayward, *The Jewish Temple*, p. 51.

49. R.P. Gordon and K.J. Cathcart, *The Targum of the Minor Prophets: Translated, with a Critical Introduction, Apparatus, and Notes* (Aramaic Bible, 14; Edinburgh: T. & T. Clark, 1989), p. 17.

50. R.P. Gordon, *Studies in the Targum to the Twelve Prophets: From Nahum to Malachi* (VTSup, 51; Leiden: Brill, 1994), pp. 132-37.

51. I am using the translation of Gordon and Cathcart, *The Targum of the Minor Prophets*.

hope in an indeterminate future.[52] In line with this the Targum at 2.15 renders the infinitive construct 'placed' with an imperfect form of the verb. The infinitive construct is indeterminate as to time, but the imperfect is more likely to be expressing a future aspect, a time of building that has not yet begun to happen. There is just the hint that for the Targumist the temple represents a future hope rather than a realized physical, communal or symbolic reality.

At the same time, the Targum goes some way beyond the MT in its location of the *shekinah* in the physical temple that is to be built. The MT is content to see the honour from the rebuilt temple bringing about an indwelling of God throughout the created order. This is expressed by the MT through the link between the absence of the temple and the poverty of the land in ch. 1 and the location of hope in the latter part of ch. 2 in both the created order and events in the world of the nations. The Targum introduces in *shekinah* an entirely new term to the text, and in so doing indicates a move to invest greater eschatological expectation concerning the Temple.

It is also notable that in the Targum on Haggai the term 'house' in the phrase 'house of the Lord' is almost always rendered as 'sanctuary' (*mqdsh*; 1.2, 4, 9, 14; 2.3, but not 1.8; 2.7). As a result, the Targum seems deaf to the rhetorical effect in MT of the house of the Lord in contrast to the houses of the people. This has a two-fold effect. First, it shifts the focus onto the function of the house of the Lord as the place of the sanctuary in which the rite is conducted. Haggai himself is relatively uninterested in this aspect of the life of the temple. At the same time, the use of the root *qdsh* emphasizes the holiness of the place. This is intriguing given the probability that the Targum reflects a time after the destruction of the temple in 70 CE, when the rebuilding of the temple is primarily thought of as an eschatological event. It indicates the concern for holiness and the need to root the religious life of the people into some sort of physical expression. This is not unlike the developments in the Qumran approach to the temple, where there is tremendous physical detail for what is primarily a transcendent concept.

52. Gordon, *Studies in the Targum*, pp. 134-63, eventually opts for a post-destruction date, but warns against a 'definite conclusion about the historical standpoint' of the Targum.

This possibility is reinforced by two other variations, neither of which can bear great significance on their own, but which cumulatively add to the effect. The first is the Targum's employment of the phrase 'My *Memra* is your support' for MT 'I am with you' (1.13; 2.4). This is a 'standard translation' on the part of the Targum.[53] It is also a rich evocation of the theological content of the divine name Yahweh, centred on the temple of Jerusalem.[54] In that respect, if *Memra* is a standard translation, it does not merely represent a rabbinic shift of focus onto the Torah after the destruction of the temple; it is also a theology located in the transcendent significance of the temple. This is a recognizable end point to the trajectory on which Haggai's own understanding of the significance of the temple is situated. At the same time, the Targumic interest in Haggai's temple is primarily an introverted one at 2.14 where MT 'nation' becomes Targum 'congregation'. This avoids describing the people of the covenant with the word *goy* while also '[redirecting] the oracle against the Judaean community' much more explicitly than does the MT.[55]

Josephus
This is not to say that all Jews of the Second Temple period saw things the way the Targumists or even Philo or the Qumran community saw them. In his retelling of the temple rebuilding and the conduct of Joshua and Zerubbabel, Josephus makes no comment at all about the eschatological hopes invested in these two figures by Haggai and Zechariah.[56] Given Josephus' Roman sympathies and that the same Romans

---

53. Gordon and Cathcart, *The Targum of the Minor Prophets*, p. 178.

54. C.T.R. Hayward, 'The Holy Name of the God of Moses and the Prologue to John's Gospel', *NTS* 25 (1979), pp. 16-32 (24), sums up: '*Memra* is God's Name 'HYH, which by midrashic exposition refers to his presence in past and future creation, history and redemption'. D.J. Harrington, 'Review of Robert Hayward, *Divine Name and Presence: The Memra*', *CBQ* 45 (1983), pp. 133-34 (133), notes that the centre of this theology was the Jerusalem temple. I am grateful to Abilash Vergheese for drawing my attention to this understanding.

55. Gordon and Cathcart, *The Targum of the Minor Prophets*, p. 180.

56. *Jewish Antiquities* 11.52-120, in *Josephus. VI. Jewish Antiquities, Books IX–XI* (trans. R. Marcus; Loeb Classical Library; London: Heinemann, 1937), pp. 336-73.

68 *Introduction*

are the target audience for his *Jewish Antiquities*, it is hardly surprising that he makes no mention of the hopes invested in Zerubbabel for an ongoing Davidic dynasty. If anything he highlights the benevolent role of the Persians and in particular Darius (*Jewish Antiquities* 11.96, 106). In any case, hope in the ancestral Davidic dynasty would have run extremely low in the light of events by the time Josephus did his writing.

Rabbinic Materials

The need that emerges in the Targum to read Haggai in quite a different way would have become acute in the rabbinic era, after the destruction of the temple and after hopes for an imminent rebuilding of a physical third temple faded in the wake of the failure of the Jewish Revolt (132–35 CE). In the Talmud itself, such references as there are to the book of Haggai tend to employ the oracle on purity (2.10-13) in debates over purity issues. The line on silver and gold (2.8) is also occasionally referred to but with no particular reference to the historical context of Haggai. There are two direct references to the temple in the context of Haggai, and both indicate an interpretive tradition concerning the 'former' and 'latter' in 2.9. The MT's Hebrew is sufficiently ambiguous to allow that the former and latter could refer to distinct temples, but that is the more unlikely reading. The more likely is that the splendour is being compared in terms of different times rather than different buildings. Certainly this is the understanding of the LXX. In *b. Yoma* 21b we read:

> ...in five things the first Sanctuary differed from the second: in the ark, the ark-cover, the Cherubim, the fire, the *Shechinah*, the Holy Spirit, and the *Urim-we-Thummim*... They were present, but they were not as helpful as [before].[57]

And *b. Baba Batra* 3a-3b records that 'greater shall be the glory of the latter house than the former...one referring it to size and the other to the duration; and both are correct'. The principal point of interest in the latter quote is the comparison between different temples in terms of glory rather than a comparison of the glory itself as implied by MT and LXX. This

---

57. All Talmud quotations are from I. Epstein's English edition: *Babylonian Talmud* (ed. I. Epstein; London: Soncino, 1938).

is reflected also in the *b. Yoma* quote, although with the added element there of the inclusion of *Shechinah* as a key item in the temple, a feature also of the Targumic interpretation.

The *Midrash Song of Songs Rabbah* reflects the same interpretive tradition as the Talmud on 2.9 with the comment that 'the glory of this latter house shall be greater than that of the former' (2.13.3).[58] But there are two more interesting interpretive developments evident in the Midrashim that do not feature in the Babylonian Talmud. The first of these deals with the contradiction surrounding the person of Zerubbabel as a scion of David (Jer. 22 and 23). I have noted the problem that Jeremiah with one hand appears to eliminate the dynasty of David entirely and with the other appears to reinstate it. *Song of Songs Rabbah* concludes that repentance has brought about the nullification of the earlier decree (8.6.23). *Numbers Rabbah* does not refer explicitly to repentance, but writes concerning the events of 2.22 that by them 'Thus was annulled that which he had said to his forefather' (20.20).

Of more enduring interest to a contemporary interpretation of Haggai, though, is the view of Zerubbabel that is found in *Genesis Rabbah*. Writing in a period when the hopes invested in a Second Temple have no further cash value, the midrash opines,

> Thus from the tribe of Judah were descended Solomon, who built the first Temple, and Zerubbabel who built the Second Temple; and [from him will be descended] the royal Messiah, who will rebuild the Temple. (XCVII.NV)

Two interpretive moves are indicated by this statement. First, the restoration of the temple is now linked with the messianic hopes. These remain in the future and the understanding of the temple indicated thereby is now an idealist or eschatological one. Hopes of a physical rebuilding have been left far behind. Secondly, the midrash represents an attempted solution to the puzzle of Zerubbabel in the biblical tradition. Haggai/Zechariah invest him with extraordinary significance,

---

58. All *Midrash Rabbah* quotations are from H. Freedman and M. Simon's English edition: *Midrash Rabbah* (ed. H. Freedman and M. Simon; London: Soncino, 1939), in which volume *Genesis Rabbah* is translated by H. Freedman; *Song of Songs Rabbah* by M. Simon; and *Numbers Rabbah* by J.J. Slotki.

yet that significance remains apparently unrealized. *Genesis Rabbah*'s move distances Zerubbabel from any kind of messianic status that may have been implied by 2.23. At the same time, it confirms his Davidic importance by naming him as one in the succession from which will eventually emerge the Messiah who will rebuild the temple.

By way of illustrative contrast, E.B. Pusey reads in Rabbi Akiba's endorsement of the Jewish leader Bar-Kokhba in the Jewish revolt a final impulse on the part of the Jewish people that the messianic fulfilment of the desire of nations must take place before the destruction of the temple.[59] Indeed, Pusey also quotes a Jewish controversialist, R. Isaac Chiz. Em., as maintaining a messianic hope based on the seed of Zerubbabel.[60]

Early Christian Interpretations

Early Christian interpretations of the book of Haggai, and their interests, would clearly have been different from those of Judaism. Presumably the New Testament book of Hebrews guided the early Christians towards a typological approach to the temple and the religious life focused on it. At the same time the Johannine tradition of identification of Jesus with the temple must have been active, as must have been the final vision of the Apocalypse which sees the end of a necessity for a temple and the culmination of its functions in the people of God themselves.[61] In the New Testament, the temple is thought of either as fulfilled and surpassed in the person of Jesus or in some way resident in the people of God. The two themes act on one another, in a way that reflects the identification in both Daniel 7 and the Apocalypse of the son of man and the people of God. At the same time, the early Church Fathers made a clear identification of Zerubbabel as wearer of the signet ring with the Christ.[62]

---

59. E.B. Pusey, *The Minor Prophets with a Commentary Explanatory and Practical, and Introductions to the Several Books. VII. Zephaniah and Haggai* (London: James Nisbet, 1907), pp. 250-51.

60. Pusey, *The Minor Prophets*, p. 275.

61. For a fuller appreciation of these possibilities, see the work of G.K. Beale, *The Temple and the Church's Mission: A Biblical Theology of the Dwelling Place of God* (Downers Grove, IL: Apollos, 2004).

62. Pusey, *The Minor Prophets*, pp. 274-75.

The Reformation

This approach is well in place by the time of the great exegetes of the Reformation, Martin Luther and John Calvin. Of the two, Luther goes into less detail than Calvin but is the more historically measured in his approach. He reads the book of Haggai as primarily about the question of building the Second Temple of the Jewish people. But he then faces the problem of what to do with a prophecy that is entirely about something, the rebuilding of the Temple, that from his vantage point is no longer relevant. His solution is to read the prophecy as pointing forward to the coming kingdom of Christ. With respect to 'Once again, in a little while' in 2.6 he writes,

> Because of Christ the external people were being preserved, and God was calling them His people, separate and select from all the nations of the earth. But now the Jews are not a people of this kind, for they have neither a kingdom nor a priesthood.[63]

Sadly, Luther's Christian messianism is fuelled here, as elsewhere in his writings, by a commitment to the elimination of the physical Jewish race. In line with that logic, he interprets Zerubbabel as the forerunner of Christ who has to move out of the way for the new king, Christ.[64] The signet ring therefore applies not to Zerubbabel but to Christ.

Calvin's approach is even more dominated by messianic expectation than Luther's. He takes up the theme as early as the second verse of Haggai with the comment that the Lord's house is significant in 'that thence might come forth the Redeemer of the world'.[65] The oracle in 2.6-9 is interpreted entirely in terms of the Christ event. For Calvin, everything still in the future is Christ. He is the 'treasure of all nations' (2.7), of which the gold and silver is illustrative, and his is the

---

63. M. Luther, 'Lectures on Haggai', p. 381.

64. Luther, 'Lectures on Haggai', p. 387: 'Christ, who came from the Jews, changed everything with His coming, namely, through the preaching of the Gospel. You see, as long as Zerubbabel lived that change did not occur. It came after his death when the new King, Christ, was born.'

65. J. Calvin, *Commentaries on the Twelve Minor Prophets. IV. Habakkuk, Zephaniah, Haggai* (trans. J. Owen; Edinburgh: Calvin Translation Society, 1848), pp. 321-22.

glory yet to come.⁶⁶ On a slightly different tack from Luther, Calvin writes of Haggai that 'There is no doubt but he points out Christ in the person of Zerubbabel'.⁶⁷

At the same time, because he lacked Luther's agenda concerning the Jews, Calvin was not so concerned with the fact that the temple has been utterly surpassed. He is more able to see contemporary lessons arising from the challenge of building the Second Temple that Haggai was addressing himself to. Principally, he discusses the importance of spiritual matters that are indicated by the external and visible building. For the hearers of Haggai's words, '...it was not enough to Satisfy God, though they spared neither expense nor labour in building the Temple; but that something greater was required, even to worship God in it in a pure and holy manner'.⁶⁸ By means of his christological interpretation, Calvin also considers the interest in the temple to be indicative of more heavenly concerns. He writes,

> Though then the Temple itself was of no great importance before God, yet the end was to be regarded; for the people were preserved by the visible Temple in the hope of the future Christ; and then it behoved them always to bear in mind the heavenly pattern that they might worship God spiritually under the external symbols.⁶⁹

The words of Haggai could also be put to the cause of reformation in a more secular fashion. William Jenkyn preached a sermon before the English House of Peers in February 1645 on the text of Hag. 1.2.⁷⁰ In the context of the battle for

---

66. Calvin, *Twelve Minor Prophets*, pp. 358-63.
67. Calvin, *Twelve Minor Prophets*, p. 384.
68. Calvin, *Twelve Minor Prophets*, p. 366. His application of the principles to the papists against whom he was defining the church (p. 371) would be problematic in our own day.
69. Calvin, *Twelve Minor Prophets*, p. 332.
70. W. Jenkyn, 'Reformation's Remora; or, Temporizing the Stop of Building the Temple: A Sermon Preached before the Right Honourable the House of Peers, in the Abbey-Church at Westminster, upon the 25th of February, 1645, being the Day Appointed for the Solemne and Pulike Humiliation', in R. Jeffs (ed.), *The English Revolution. I. Fast Sermons to Parliament, Volume 22 Feb 1645/6–Mar 1646* (London: Cornmarket Press, 1971), pp. 10-50.

supremacy that was the English Civil War, Jenkyn equates the post-exilic return from Babylon with delivery of the English Church and state from 'Prelaticall thralldom'.[71] For him, the temple is no longer a physical temple nor even an eschatological event, but is rather an expression of the people of God during the age of the Church. Haggai's warning against 'sloth' is then applicable to whatever the contemporary institutional expression of the people of God may be, and such people are then deemed to be a communal expression of temple. Jenkyn's warning is against the Peers to maintain the work of the Reformation lest they be found among 'those, be they never so high, that are slothfull in the work of the spirituall temple'.[72] The sermons of John Rainolds in the later years of Elizabeth's rule take a similar line and are first printed in 1649 because of their applicability 'for these times', that is, the time of the Civil War in England.[73] An intriguing twist in them is the equation of Cyrus with Henry VIII as the Lord's anointed in the Reformation. As Darius stands in succession to Cyrus in the outworking of God's plan for Israel and the temple, so Elizabeth stands in succession to Henry in the formation of the people of God as spiritual temple.[74]

A Nineteenth-Century Treatment

A thorough nineteenth-century treatment of the minor prophets is that of E.B. Pusey, the tractarian apologist. Again, he evinces little apparent concern with the context of the Twelve, apart from an acknowledgment that the three final prophets on the scroll belong to the period of the restoration. Pusey's work is characterized, though, by an appreciation of the early and mediaeval Jewish and patristic comments on the books on which he comments. He also exhibits a close attention to the historical and political background of the work of Haggai,

---

71. Jenkyn, 'Temporizing the Stop', p. 23.
72. Jenkyn, 'Temporizing the Stop', p. 18.
73. J. Rainolds, *The Prophesie of Haggai, Interpreted and Applyed in Sundry Sermons* (London: William Lee, 1649), p. 86, writes on 1.12-13, 'The Church is said to be edefied by a Metaphor, when they that are believers are layd as living stones one upon another, being edefied, that is built as a spirituall house is by Gods ministers, who are therefore called Gods builders...'
74. Rainolds, *The Prophesie of Haggai*, p. 8.

closer than was exhibited in the Reformation context. For him, 'Prophetic descriptions of the future are but incidental to the mission of Haggai'.[75] His emphasis is rather on the contemporary necessity of the message of Haggai. For Pusey, any reading of Haggai is ultimately certain that 'we, by aid of the Holy Spirit, so enter upon what Haggai here speaketh, as not doubting that he altogether aimeth at Christ'.[76] At the same time, he retains a lively sense of the applicability of the struggle over the temple to the contemporary Church.

Recent Interpretations

Most recent treatments of the book of Haggai concern themselves primarily with historical and literary questions.[77] There is correspondingly much less certainty in the treatment of eschatological and temporal issues raised by the prophets of restoration than was a feature of earlier Christian and Jewish exegesis.[78] W. Emery Barnes typifies the hesitancy. His comments on the critical final oracle are astonishingly brief. Regarding Zerubbabel, he says merely of the title 'servant' in 2.23, 'Perhaps the title here is quasi-Messianic', and then concludes with the historical comment that 'The choice of Zerubbabel involves the choice of the Jews. Jehovah chooses Israel again.'[79]

In contrast to that brevity, much ink continues to be spilled on the question of when exactly in Darius's reign events took place. The problem of the roles of Zerubbabel and Joshua is also a feature of recent treatments, as is the related concern for the nature of the prophetic understanding that lies behind the work of Haggai and his companions. The tendency in such historical treatments is not so much to discern the messianic

---

75. Pusey, *The Minor Prophets*, p. 201.
76. Pusey, *The Minor Prophets*, p. 212, here quoting with approval Rupert of Deutz (1075–1129/30).
77. See the overview by Coggins, *Haggai, Zechariah, Malachi*.
78. An intriguing exception is J. Kodell, *Lamentations, Haggai, Zechariah, Malachi, Obadiah, Joel, Second Zechariah, Baruch* (Wilmington, DE: Michael Glazier, 1982), p. 52, who employs 'the times' in a reflection on Vatican II and the respective roles of Pope John XXIII and his detractors.
79. W.E. Barnes, *Haggai, Zechariah and Malachi: With Notes and Introduction* (Cambridge: Cambridge University Press, 1934), pp. 19-20.

significance of Zerubbabel the signet ring as to puzzle over the subsequent insignificance of Zerubbabel in the judgment of history. This also raises questions of which communities may have been behind the prophecy of Haggai. These matters are treated in more detail below.

Hinckley Mitchell, writing in the early part of the twentieth century, commented of Haggai that 'the book is so brief that it seems almost ridiculous to suspect its unity'.[80] Despite that, many modern commentators have concerned themselves with literary and redactional issues, particularly around the distinction between editorial and oracular material and related historical composition questions. The debate over these matters has been a feature of commentary on Haggai through the twentieth century. One example is the fine commentary by Wolff, whose work makes a clear distinction between what he calls the sketch-scenes and the Chronicler.[81] Others have made the same distinction by noting a narrator's organization of collected prophetic oracles, with each of the two hands distinctly evident.[82] It remains a matter for debate whether or not this distinction is defensible on form- or redaction-critical grounds. However such questions are answered, they feed into the contemporary interest in narrative and alert the reader further to the narrative shape of the book of Haggai. The result is a shift in concern from the message of Haggai to an appreciation of the form in which the message has been couched, without denying that a full appropriation of the text requires that form and message inform each other.

This interest in form is also linked to an interest in literary context. Apart from the wider question of the Book of the Twelve, of which Haggai is a part, the recognition of the last three prophets of the Twelve as a unit under the general rubric

---

80. H.G. Mitchell, 'A Critical and Exegetical Commentary on Haggai and Zechariah', in H.G. Mitchell, J.M.P. Smith and J.A. Bewer, *A Critical and Exegetical Commentary on Haggai, Zechariah, Malachi and Jonah* (ICC; Edinburgh: T. & T. Clark, 1912), pp. 1-362 (28).

81. Wolff, *Haggai*, pp. 18-19.

82. For example, the articles by P.R. Ackroyd, 'The Book of Haggai and Zechariah I–VIII', *JJS* 3 (1952), pp. 151-56, and 'Some Interpretive Glosses in the Book of Haggai', *JJS* 7 (1956), pp. 163-67. See Appendix B for a composite representation of various form and redaction-critical approaches.

76 *Introduction*

of 'prophets of the restoration' has become commonplace. In particular, the even closer link between Haggai and Zechariah 1–8 is a feature of recent commentary. This often goes hand in hand with a view of Zechariah that proposes a radical separation between chs. 1–8 and 9–14. This growing interest in the literary context of Haggai can be readily illustrated. The Calvin Translation Society's collection of Calvin's commentaries on the Twelve Minor Prophets treats Habakkuk, Zephaniah and Haggai in one volume while the final volume deals with Zechariah and Malachi. Although Calvin himself was not blind to the prophets of restoration as a significant grouping, his collectors in the nineteenth century are apparently interested in each book of the Twelve as independent entities. In contrast, the Anchor Bible two-volume project on Haggai and Zechariah by Meyers and Meyers treats Haggai and Zechariah 1–8 in one volume and Zechariah 9–14 in a second. Similarly, the Old Testament Library two-volume work by David Petersen on the three prophets of the restoration makes the volume division between Zechariah 8 and 9.[83] These matters of literary form and context are also treated in more detail elsewhere in this introduction.

The eschatological and messianic questions of an earlier age have not entirely been abandoned by the present, however. More conservative treatments have continued to read Haggai with such questions in mind. Eugene Merrill, for example, in his comments on 2.23, reads Zerubbabel as a 'prototype'.[84] Others bring a more nuanced historical sense to their work. Baldwin in her Tyndale Old Testament Commentary continues to take the historical context of the text seriously in her interpretation.[85] The significance of the rebuilt temple to the Jews recently returned from exile remains firmly in view. The eschatological hopes that took centre stage in the Reformers' treatments have not been pushed to one side, but they are viewed much more through the work of God among the people

---

83. Meyers and Meyers, *Haggai, Zechariah 1–8*, and D.L. Petersen, *Haggai and Zechariah 1–8: A Commentary* (OTL; London: SCM Press, 1984).

84. E.H. Merrill, *An Exegetical Commentary, Haggai, Zechariah, Malachi* (Chicago: Moody, 1994), p. 57.

85. Baldwin, *Haggai, Zechariah, Malachi*.

at a particular moment in their history. So, for Baldwin, 'God's universal kingdom, in which the warring nations find their peace in capitulating to Him...is the ultimate goal of history, but Haggai sees it beginning in his own time as personal and community affairs are submitted to God's rule'.[86] Accordingly, her treatment is less explicitly christological than those of earlier times. For example, at 2.7 Baldwin notes that the messianic expectations in the phrase 'desire of all nations' have 'rightly been abandoned' by recent translators, given that the Hebrew plural verb requires a plural subject.[87] And when it comes to the figure Zerubbabel, Baldwin does not draw a direct link with Christ as the ancient readers were wont to do. Her Christian eschatological reading of the book of Haggai is more focused on the temple itself, which she sees as having been fulfilled in the person of Jesus Christ. To the degree that he is more glorious than the temple, God's future purpose remains more glorious than anything achieved in the building of the temple in the fifth century BCE.

Literary Context

The Book of the Twelve in Canonical Context

There are three key aspects of the literary context in which the book of Haggai appears: its place within the Book of the Twelve; its membership among the writings of the prophets of the restoration; and its particularly strong links with Zechariah 1–8.

The Book of the Twelve is the name that has long been given by the Jewish Scriptures to the twelve writing prophets known in the Christian tradition as the 'minor prophets'. The Twelve have been grouped together virtually for as long as there has been manuscript evidence for their existence. This includes the evidence from the scrolls at Qumran, which reaches back to

---

86. Baldwin, *Haggai, Zechariah, Malachi*, p. 33. See also W.J. Dumbrell, 'Kingship and Temple in the Post-Exilic Period', *RTR* 37 (1978), pp. 33-42.

87. Baldwin, *Haggai, Zechariah, Malachi*, p. 48, *contra* R.T. Siebeneck, 'The Messianism of Aggeus and Proto-Zacharias', *CBQ* 19 (1957), pp. 312-28, who argues from 2.2-9 for the central role of the temple in the messianic era.

the Hasmonean period (150–30 BCE), and in the Greek tradition a scroll which suggests that the grouping of the Twelve in the LXX was as old as the first century BCE.[88] This fact has been taken seriously by interpreters only sporadically until recently. Before focusing on the Book of the Twelve itself, though, it is worth considering the place of its contents within the various canons of Scripture, as therein lies a history of reception of its own.

By the time of the destruction of Jerusalem in 70 CE, the tripartite division of the Hebrew Bible was in clear outline, whether or not it was actually codified.[89] In that division the pentateuchal books are privileged as Torah. Following them come the books of the Prophets, that is, Samuel and Kings and the writing prophets. That second division culminates in the scroll of the Twelve. The third part of the Hebrew Bible is the collection known as the Writings, within which there was some variation in ordering. In the tripartite division, the Book of the Twelve brings to a conclusion the story of the establishment of the covenant people, and the long prophetic task of determining what it means to live as a covenant people and where the covenant road might lead in the face of sin and political disaster. In terms of the way ahead for the covenant, the prophets of the restoration, Haggai, Zechariah and Malachi, have the last word. What follows them is the Writings, which can be characterized as a working out of patterns of worship and responses to the realities of daily life within the attempt to be faithful to the covenant that God has made. For much of the material gathered as Writings, the presence of the covenant as a background is only evident by means of the canonical context. In that context, the promised restoration is not fulfilled

---

88. On this evidence see R. Fuller, 'The Form and Formation of the Book of the Twelve: The Evidence from the Judean Desert', in Watts and House (eds.), *Forming the Prophetic Literature*, pp. 86-101 (87-91).

89. R.T. Beckwith, *The Old Testament Canon of the New Testament Church and Its Background in Early Judaism* (London: SPCK, 1985), pp. 110-65, argues for an Old Testament canon structured into its three parts and closed 'not less than 250 years earlier than the currently accepted date of AD 90' (p. 165), *contra* J. Barton, *Reading the Old Testament: Method in Biblical Study* (London: Darton, Longman & Todd, 1984), pp. 91-97, who probably represents a majority of scholars with his view that an early concept of canon is essentially anachronistic.

eschatologically, but we do see the effect of its promise on the daily life and worship of the people of God. Today, that tripartite tradition constitutes the Scriptures of the Jewish people and is known as the Hebrew Bible.

Alongside the development of the Jewish tripartite tradition in the period of the Second Temple was the development of a Greek tradition, based on a historical process of translating the Hebrew Bible into Greek and culminating in the version known to us as the LXX. Included in the LXX were a group of other Greek texts, which we know today as the apocryphal or deutero-canonical material, and which became attached to the translated biblical texts.[90] The ordering of the books of the Scriptures in the LXX was quite different from the tripartite division of the Hebrew Bible, and is roughly reflected in the order familiar to modern readers of the Christian Bible. Notwithstanding occasional variations in that order, the Twelve were always grouped together in a similar but not identical format to that of the Hebrew Bible. In any case, the three prophets of the restoration retained their place at the end of the collection. Sometimes the Twelve are followed in the Greek tradition by the big three of Isaiah, Jeremiah and Ezekiel as well as Daniel (with Susannah and Bel and the Dragon), who was considered by the Greek tradition to be one of the prophets. In this scenario the prophets play a culminating role in the canon of the Jewish scriptures. The last part of the collection focuses on the struggle towards hope in the face of covenant failure and exile. The more mundane focus of the Writings occupies a more central place in the collection. This reflects a reception tradition that provides a focus for people alienated by the demise of the Second Temple, now looking in the same direction as the prophets of the restoration towards a promised future yet awaited.

During the centuries immediately after the destruction of the temple in 70 CE, the Christian Church adopted the LXX as

---

90. In the case of each deutero-canonical book, it is a matter of debate whether or not the Greek text is a translation of a Semitic original, although my comments imply that they are original in the Greek. Only in the case of Ben Sira is there hard evidence for a Semitic *Vorlage*, although even then its status is debated. On the complex textual history of Ben Sira, see Skehan and DiLella, *The Wisdom of Ben Sira*, pp. 51-59.

its Old Testament scriptures while the synagogue reverted to the Hebrew tradition, effectively relinquishing the Greek tradition to the Christians. While the Church eventually turned to the Hebrew tradition as canonical, it retained traces of the Greek tradition, including the deutero-canonical books and the broad outline of the order of books. In the Christian canon, the Book of the Twelve came to occupy without rival the final place in the canonical Old Testament (as distinct from the collection that included the deutero-canonical books). Now, instead of representing a fulfilled hope pointing towards the Writings, or an eschatological hope, in the canonical arrangement of the Christian scriptures the Twelve function neither fully eschatologically nor completely temporally. Rather, they are the last signpost to the fulfilment of Jesus Christ encapsulated in the New Testament. This is part of the context in which Haggai is read today by Christians. I will argue that this is in tune with a text that forces us to take seriously both its eschatological possibilities and its contemporary significance, without allowing either to dominate.

The Book of the Twelve

There are two ways to approach the manner in which the Twelve itself may constitute a literary unity. One is that typified by Paul House in his *The Unity of the Twelve*, which may be called a formalist approach.[91] Such an approach is only marginally concerned with redaction-critical matters, preferring to read the text in its received form and noting the manner in which the parts relate to the whole in more classical literary terms. House's treatment, for instance, considers plot, characters, theme and point of view. Another approach, that typified by Paul Redditt, asks how the Book of the Twelve came to be compiled into its present form.[92] Neither approach is mutually exclusive, and I have noted above that redaction-critical observations can alert the reader to literary features, whatever the explanation of their origins may be. However, the more fruitful approach for a reading of this nature is to keep

---

91. P.R. House, *The Unity of the Twelve* (JSOTSup, 97; Sheffield: Almond Press, 1990).

92. P.L. Redditt, 'Zechariah 9–14, Malachi, and the Redaction of the Book of the Twelve', in Watts and House (eds.), *Forming the Prophetic Literature*, pp. 245-68.

focused on the received form of the text and to consider how it works rhetorically. The assumption in doing so is that the compilation of these diverse anthologies of prophetic ministries at some stage made sense, or created some sort of perceived unity. My purpose is to consider what the nature of that unity might be with special emphasis always on Haggai.

Assuming that the three prophets of the restoration may be so considered, it is helpful to adopt House's basic plot summary. The prophets Hosea–Micah focus on various types of sin, both in the context of life lived within the covenant and in cosmic terms. Nahum–Zephaniah then draw out the logical consequences of that sin. That both Israel and its neighbours are singled out highlights the ongoing focus on both covenant and cosmic significance. The task of the final three prophets, Haggai–Malachi, then, is to bring to a concluding focus the restoration both of Israel and of the wider cosmic context in which Israel lives out its calling.[93]

Of course, it is not as tidy as that. It is not all darkness until the point of restoration, nor is it all lightness of step once we get to the prophets of restoration. Malachi is as hard hitting as any of his predecessors. And in the earlier focus on sin and judgment there is an ebb and flow of hope. Hosea gives us the haunting love songs of chs. 11 and 14, Amos provides hints of both a remnant and of a hope in a restored Judah (9.8-15), Joel promises the coming spirit (2.28-32) and Habakkuk is unable to abandon hope in the face of agricultural desolation (3.17-19). It is best to think of the final prophets of the restoration taking these hints of hope and drawing them on to completion.

Think, for example, of the theme of the Day of the Lord, a theme that remains slightly out of focus in the early parts of the Book of the Twelve. In Joel, Amos and Obadiah, it is conveyed entirely in terms of the judgment of God. The prevalent mood is one of terror as the sins of the people rebound on their own head (Joel 1.15; 2.1, 11, 31; 3.14; Amos 5.18, 20; Obad. 15). This reaches a culmination in Zephaniah 1. Malachi's vision of the Day of the Lord, when read in that context, provides a significant contrast. The awful judgment of that day is not modified, yet now it is accompanied by the promise that 'the sun of righteousness shall rise, with healing

---

93. See the summary of House, *The Unity of the Twelve*, p. 109.

82 *Introduction*

in its wings' (Mal. 4.2). At the same time, the prophet anticipates Elijah and the work of reconciliation that he will bring (Mal. 4.5-6). In this way the restorative possibilities of the Day of the Lord are drawn out by one of the prophets of restoration, and, as House observes, the final scene in the middle section of the Book of the Twelve, Zephaniah, points towards the possibilities of restoration.[94]

Prophets of the Restoration
After this bridging material in Zephaniah, the final prophets in the Twelve move in with an extended treatment of the possibilities that Zephaniah has hinted at. A marked change in emphasis is evident, of the sort instanced above concerning the Day of the Lord. Indeed Haggai, in his focus on the building of a second temple, introduces a reversal of much that has gone before. The attitude of the earlier prophets to the religious establishment is ambivalent, instanced sharply by the inscrutable question at Amos 5.25: 'did you bring to me sacrifices and offerings the forty years in the wilderness, O house of Israel?'[95] The religious establishment is not rejected out of hand, but there is a marked lack of enthusiasm for it in places. In a collection whose concern is for the right appropriation of the cult rather than for the cult itself, the sudden focus on the physical temple that Haggai brings is notable, if not almost discordant.

In that very reversal, though, lies part of the genius of the book.[96] In a close reading of the text, the focus on the physical temple is more apparent than real. What is really at issue is the obedience of the people and the possibility of blessing that arises from that obedience. The reversal is in fact the shift in focus from judgment for disobedience, the primary focus of so much that has preceded Haggai in the Twelve, to the possibilities of blessing through obedience.[97] The final oracle of

94. House, *The Unity of the Twelve*, p. 89.
95. In the Hebrew it is simply impossible to determine whether the answer to this question concerning that idealized desert experience is expected to be yes or no.
96. See the summary in House, *The Unity of the Twelve*, pp. 152-60.
97. See House, *The Unity of the Twelve*, pp. 99-100. In this respect at least the Twelve represent a deuteronomistic understanding. R.L. Smith, *Micah–Malachi* (WBC, 32; Waco, TX: Word Books, 1984), is particularly alert to this in his commentary.

Haggai contains the tantalizing hint that simply building the temple is not the sum total of the divine plan.

The culmination of the book of Haggai with the promise to Zerubbabel does leave an implied question, however. A received-form reading has to take that question seriously, and the context of the three prophets of the restoration provides part of the answer. Zechariah maintains the momentum that Haggai has begun but shifts the focus on to Jerusalem as a whole rather than the temple in particular. In doing so, he clarifies for the reader something that Haggai has only been able to imply, that the re-formation of the temple is crucial primarily in that it points to the re-formation of the people of God. Key components of the people of God and the covenant that has brought the people into being are Jerusalem and an accompanying eschatological focus on Zion. These are themes to which Zechariah turns. At the same time, he hints at an enhanced role for the priestly Joshua in contrast to how he is presented in Haggai. But even that theme must point beyond itself to the people of God and their relationship with Yahweh. In that light, the final puzzling little book of the Twelve, Malachi, begins to make more sense, for Malachi treats the concerns of both Haggai and Zechariah. In bringing the priesthood into sharper focus, Malachi looks towards the health of Jerusalem that was a concern of Zechariah and towards the health of the temple and the sacrificial system therein which was the presenting concern of Haggai. The outcome is the re-formed people of God in Malachi 3 and 4.[98]

As a footnote to this, with their differing emphases, all three of the final prophets in the Twelve bring their message into sharp focus on an individual. In Haggai, there is Zerubbabel, of whom more will be said in the body of the commentary. Setting aside the debate that each mention causes, in both sections of Zechariah there is a figure of some sort; Branch

---

98. House, *The Unity of the Twelve*, p. 108, observes, 'Without Haggai–Malachi the *other* books become shadows of what they are when completed by these post-exilic writings' (emphasis original). And on an even broader canvas (p. 119): 'Despite the difficulty of the formulation of the denouement, Yahweh has accomplished the major goal in the Twelve. Israel and all creation have been reconciled to the divine plan for them.'

of Zechariah 6 and the king riding on a donkey in Zech. 9.9-10. And in Malachi there is the 'messenger of the covenant' (Mal. 3.1), the one whose role is to restore the covenant with Levi, a covenant of a pure priesthood (Mal. 2.4-9).[99] The use of the term *mal'ak* leaves an ambiguity as to whether the 'messenger' in Malachi is a prophetic figure, as in Haggai, or an angelic one, as in Zechariah 1–8. As the role implied is more akin to that of Haggai than that of the intermediary angel in Zechariah, a prophetic figure is probably in view. This would dovetail nicely with the final mention of the 'prophet Elijah' (Mal. 4.5) before the great and terrible day of the Lord. If that is the case, it is interesting to note across the three prophetic books that when the individual figures of hope are assembled, they form a collective of the royal, priestly and prophetic, all aspects of the eschatological hope that was subsequently to grow during the Second Temple period, and all of which reach a culmination in the temple community.

A particular irony about the reversal being argued for at this point is found in the situation and attitude of the people. In the pre-exilic and exilic prophecies, the prophets constantly have to confront an unwarranted optimism on the part of the people, commonly expressed as the complacency of misplaced trust. The prophet's task is to disabuse the people and their leadership of this complacency. After the return from exile, and the possibility of restoration becomes measurable in physical terms, ironically the people are found to be without hope and motivation. After years of misplaced trust they are apparently now incapable of trust at all. The prophet's task now is to show them a future that they have lost sight of, rather than to disabuse them of a future which will turn out to be a mirage.

Haggai/Zechariah 1–8

At a literary level, within the prophets of the restoration Haggai has the most in common with Zechariah 1–8. The temporal markers and setting, the themes and the interest in Joshua and Zerubbabel, lead naturally to a pairing of the two. This is so evident as only to require passing mention, and the question of whether this pairing should be thought of as an

---

99. House, *The Unity of the Twelve*, p. 159.

adversarial or a complementary one has been discussed above. The context of a pairing with Zechariah 1–8 will be assumed throughout the commentary. The place of Zechariah 9–14 is more problematic for the thesis that the three final prophets in the Twelve function in a unified direction. Many treatments simply read these chapters as interlopers in what would otherwise be a tidy schema, as witness the number of commentaries that treat Haggai and Zechariah 1–8 and then break off. As an exception to this approach, House argues that 'regardless of the prophecy's origin it *functions* as a unified literary construction'.[100] Indeed, with its continued emphasis on Jerusalem, it may be said to occupy the central place in the corpus of the prophets of restoration.[101]

Personal Context:
Haggai as Prophet and his Hearers

Haggai
A discussion of Haggai himself, from whom the book takes its name, and of those who first heard his message rounds off this treatment of the context of the book of Haggai. As with most of the prophets, there is little personal information available on Haggai. He may have been a priest, and there are some who think that he was old enough to have seen the first temple before its destruction. If that is the case, the concern of the book of Haggai to build bridges between the two temples, as already noted, can be seen to have its roots in the life of the prophet himself. It has also been suggested that the lack of any patronymic suggests that he was a well-known member of the by now rare breed known as prophets. But this is to ask a slender piece of evidence to carry far too much weight, while the matters of Haggai's age and priestly status are speculation.

---

100. House, *The Unity of the Twelve*, pp. 100-101 (emphasis original).
101. See also the rationale of E.W. Conrad, *Zechariah* (Readings; Sheffield: Sheffield Academic Press, 1999), pp. 20-22, for reading Zechariah as a unity within the Book of the Twelve, and the analysis of R.W. Pierce, 'Literary Connectors and a Haggai/Zechariah/Malachi Corpus', *JETS* 27 (1984), pp. 277-89, and 'A Thematic Development of the Haggai/Zechariah/Malachi Corpus', *JETS* 27 (1984), pp. 401-11.

The possible age of Haggai is an inference drawn from his question in 2.3, which has gathered the weight of a Jewish tradition that he had lived much of his life in Babylon.[102] Concerning a possible priestly lineage, the evidence is equally thin. Mitchell cites an early Christian tradition, a statement of one Dorotheus, that Haggai 'was buried with honour near the sepulchre of the priests, where the priests were customarily buried'. Hesychius adds the explanation that this was 'because he was of priestly stock'.[103] The LXX ascriptions of Psalms 146–49 add some weight to this suggestion. On the other hand, Haggai's reference to the priests as 'other' in 2.11 may point in the opposite direction. These things cannot be known of Haggai.

What can be determined is his status as a prophet in the minds of those who collected and created a narrative of his work. The name Haggai appears nine times in this brief book. Five times he is named 'the prophet Haggai'. These ascriptions cluster as the first mentions of Haggai (1.1, 3, 12; 2.1, 10) interrupted only by a mention of 'Haggai, the messenger of the Lord' (1.13). Several things are of interest here. First, the number of ascriptions of prophet to Haggai is as insistent as the number of times the phrase 'oracle of the Lord' or an equivalent appears. The editors are determined to name Haggai as such.[104] A second point of interest is the term 'messenger', an unusual one to apply to a prophet. The Hebrew is *mal'ak*, which in other contexts (including in Zechariah) has angelic connotations. Is it possible that this choice of vocabulary unwittingly reflects a time when the confidence expressed in the writing prophets was on the wane, to be replaced by the apocalyptic device of the angelic messenger of Yahweh whose task is to convey the message as revelation to an earthly recipient? Another intriguing form of expression appears in each of Haggai, Zechariah and Malachi. It is the habit of speaking of the prophetic oracle coming 'by the hand of' (a literal translation of the MT) the prophet (Hag. 1.1, 3; 2.1; Zech.

---

102. E. Cashdan, *The Twelve Prophets* (London: Soncino Press, 1948), p. 254, cited in Baldwin, *Haggai, Zechariah, Malachi*, p. 28.
103. Mitchell, *Haggai, Zechariah, Malachi and Jonah*, p. 26.
104. M. Boda, 'Haggai: Master Rhetorician', *TynBul* 51 (2000), pp. 295-304 (298), comments further on this phenomenon.

7.12; Mal. 1.1), which also signals an attribution of authority to the prophet in question.[105] Could this also represent an era when the identification of the prophetic persona with the word of Yahweh is no longer as complete, an era just beginning to conceive of the need for an intermediary in the experience of revelation? Certainty is not possible on these questions, but they do perhaps hint that we are reading in Haggai and his colleagues the last surge of the prophetic impulse that has coursed through the Book of the Twelve and brought the people to a hope represented by a restored temple and people (for further on this see comments on 1.1-2).

Haggai's Hearers
As for the context of those who first heard Haggai's words, a picture will gradually emerge in the course of the commentary. As I have indicated in remarks on date and historical context, the experience of inadequacy expressed in the second oracle is a key. As a second comment at this introductory stage, a *crux interpretum*, concerns two distinctions: one between 'these people' (e.g. 1.2), 'the remnant of the people' (1.12; 2.2) and 'the people of the land' (2.4), and a second between 'people' and 'nation' (2.14). The question of whether the text in using these terms reflects distinct groupings, or whether a conflict between the resident Samaritans and the returning exiles is in mind, will be addressed more fully at relevant points in the commentary. Suffice it for now to signal the conclusion that the terms are broadly synonymous and are not intended to reflect a conflict among the people.[106]

---

105. See the argument of J.E. Tollington, *Tradition and Innovation in Haggai and Zechariah 1–8* (JSOTSup, 150; Sheffield: JSOT Press, 1993), p. 65.

106. For further on 2.14, see R. Pfeil, 'When is a *Goy* a "Goy"? The Interpretation of Haggai 2.10-19', in W.C. Kaiser and R.F. Youngblood (eds.), *A Tribute to Gleeson Archer* (Chicago: Moody Press, 1986), pp. 261-78, *contra* Thomas and Sperry, 'The Book of Haggai', p. 1046. On the distinction between 'people' and 'remnant' see J.M. O'Brien, *Nahum, Habakkuk, Zephaniah, Haggai, Zechariah, Malachi* (AOTC; Nashville: Abingdon, 2004), p. 145.

HAGGAI 1.1-2
(SECTION A, THE FIRST ORACLE):
SETTING THE SCENE

The first two verses of the book of Haggai are crucial in establishing the credentials of the narrative, erecting the profiles of the plot structure and introducing the reader to the main characters. I am working from the premise that the first two verses form a distinct unit within the book of Haggai as a whole, on a par with each of the other five units in the book (see the discourse analysis in Appendix A). Hence the first two verses are given a section of commentary on their own. That is a premise that goes somewhat against the flow of opinion and needs to be justified. The justification will be presented in terms of a simple analysis of the discourse of the book as a whole.

The Structure

The usual approach of recent critical scholarship to the structure of Haggai has been to make a form-critical distinction between the narrative material and the words of Haggai that come as oracles from the Lord. Although conclusions vary a little depending on who is doing the analysis, generally the narrative material has been identified as follows: 1.1, 3, 12-13a, 14–2.1; 2.10, 20-21a. The intervening material consists of six oracles of the Lord addressed to one or more of Joshua, Zerubbabel and the people (see Appendix B). It is obvious that the narrative material is evidence of another hand at work collating the material from Haggai and shaping it into a narrative form. There have been some attempts to identify the particular interests of the redactor as distinct from the interests of the prophet himself as seen in the oracles, although a consensus has not emerged.

Some Structural Dissonances

The verses that contain dates in the reign of King Darius more or less coincide with the form- and redaction-critical identification of narrative material (1.1, 15; 2.1, 10, 20; see Appendix B). This does not include reference to the date in 2.18, which is part of the oracle introduced by 2.10 and functions as a reminder of the date of that oracle. There are a couple of dissonant notes struck when the narrative/oracle structure is set alongside a structure around dates in the reign of Darius. The first is that the brief oracle embedded in several verses of narrative material at 1.13b, 'I am with you', is dated retrospectively rather than in anticipation (see on 1.13 for the argument to this effect).

A second dissonant note is that, on the discourse analysis that I have adopted (see below), the introduction to the second oracle (1.3) contains no date. Linked with the fact that the first oracle (1.1-2) is the only one not to conclude with a *n'm yhwh (tṣb't)* ('says the Lord [of hosts]'), this has led commentators to treat 1.1-12 as a single oracle and to ignore the structural force of the prophetic formulae. This could be seen as a weak point in my argument that 1.1-2 should be regarded as a distinct oracle. Nevertheless, on balance I suggest that the coherence achieved through a discourse analysis based on the introductory prophetic formulae, as expounded below, outweighs the variations noted around the end of the first oracle in v. 2 and the start of the second in v. 3.

A more important and more jarring dissonance relates to the distinction between oracle and narrative which is often presented as if the two were watertight categories. In fact, when the narrative is read carefully, that is found not to be the case. In the first place, the entire book of Haggai is cast as narrative. Of all the books within the Twelve, with the possible exception of Jonah, none is so consciously crafted as a narrative as Haggai. It is a story about a person and his message and the manner in which that message is received. By contrast, the other books in the Twelve, and indeed the other major classical prophets, may best be described as coherent anthologies. Although there are narrative aspects in each, they set out more to convey a message than to tell a discrete story. The oracles within Haggai, as will be seen, function within the dynamics of the narrative. A less subjective point can also be made, that the genre of narrative also insinuates itself into what is traditionally identified as oracle material. This is most evident in the fifth oracle, the one beginning at 2.10. Within the oracle is an extended (for Haggai) dialogue between Haggai and the priests which in its turn leads into further oracular material (2.14-19). Whatever the form- or redaction-critical merits of the distinction between narrative and oracle, the distinction at the level of genre cannot be maintained.

A further problem should be noted in response to the argument that ascribes a concern with Zerubbabel and Joshua exclusively to the narrative material as opposed to the oracles themselves. For when the book is divided into sections by dating, it is found that the people stray into the narrative material and Joshua and Zerubbabel feature in the oracular material. The two blocks of narrative in 1.12–2.1 respectively describe the response of Joshua, Zerubbabel *and* the people or the remnant of the people (who 'the remnant' may be will be considered when they are encountered in the narrative), and is addressed to Joshua, Zerubbabel *and* the remnant of the people. At the same time, the fourth identified oracle, the one in 2.1-9, is not only to the people of the land but also mentions Joshua and Zerubbabel.

A Different Structural Proposal

The dissonance introduced by the usual ways of reading a structure in Haggai indicates the need for a different approach. One of the features that leaps out of the narrative is the prevalence of formulaic introductions to oracles of the Lord. When these are collated alongside the several other occurrences of dialogue-introducing verbs, some interesting patterns emerge (see Appendix A). For my purposes at this point, I note the formulae identified as level 1 in the discourse. With one exception, they draw together the 'word of the Lord' and 'Haggai' in a regular pattern of expression. The exceptional reference at 1.13, 'Haggai, the messenger of the Lord, spoke to the people with the Lord's message', has particular problems that will be treated in context. Translated literally, the first three of the other level 1 formulae read, 'the word of the Lord became by the hand of Haggai the prophet' (1.1, 3; 2.1). The final two read, 'the word of the Lord became to Haggai' (2.10, 20; in 2.10 the ascription 'the prophet' is included also). Despite the small variations, a clear picture emerges of a narrative structured around the reception of the word of the Lord by Haggai. What then follows in each instance is an account of Yahweh's command to Haggai to speak, an account of what Haggai actually says, and in some cases the response in turn of Joshua, Zerubbabel and the people. These episodes form the basis of the structure of the book, which is laid out diagrammatically in Appendix A, and this reading of Haggai will be informed by that structure.

Given the literary and text-historical difficulty in preserving a neat distinction between narrative and oracle, this paves the way for a more integrated appreciation of the plot as a whole. The question of the function of the dates may then be treated in narrative terms rather than redaction-critical terms, as we move through the story of Haggai and his message (in further justification of this approach, see also my comments on 1.12).

The first episode is that introduced by the first occurrence of 'the word of the Lord became by the hand of Haggai the prophet' (1.1, my translation), and it is to that that I now turn.

Dating

The opening words of the book of Haggai are 'in the second year of King Darius, in the sixth month, on the first day of the month'. The detail of this date has a number of immediate effects. First, it links the message of Haggai with the material of which it is a part. In the corpus of the prophetic writings, most of the prophets are given some sort of historical and geographical context within which their words are to be heard and read. Haggai is no exception, located as he is in the land where Joshua and Zerubbabel are doing their work during the reign of the Persian king Darius I. In that respect, the provenance of his task is similar to that of other prophets. We know roughly what to expect when we read or hear about the word of the Lord coming to a prophet during the reign of a certain king.

Distinctiveness of Dating in Haggai
On a closer look at the prophetic corpus, though, the nature of the dating is seen also to separate Haggai from many of his prophetic colleagues. The most obvious difference is that the date is in terms of a Gentile king. This is the first time that

92 *Haggai 1.1-2*

this has been the case, and consequently foreshadows two aspects of Haggai's message. It signals that he is beginning to talk about the return from exile without a monarch, about a time when the rules of the game are radically different from what they were when the earlier prophets were doing their work. It is a time when the life of Israel must be computed and recorded against a background of accommodation with the Gentile powers of the day. Ironically, a period which has been characterized by Ezra and Nehemiah as one of rigorous demarcation between Israel and the other nations is now compelled to acknowledge those nations in its dating. And this in fact will turn out not to be as antithetical to the message of Haggai as Ezra–Nehemiah might have led us to expect. The mention of Darius as the third Hebrew word in the book foreshadows a concern with the nations beyond Israel that will gradually emerge through the six oracles of Haggai.

And there is another variation. Most of the prophetic anthologies that begin with a general date do so in terms that indicate a period during which the prophet is active without explicitly dating the oracles. For instance, the prophet may be described as active 'in the days of' certain kings (Isa. 1.1) or around the time of certain events, such as the earthquake pinpointed by the compilers of the Amos material (Amos 1.1). The book of Jeremiah gives exact dates for the opening and closing of Jeremiah's ministry, but does not consistently date the particular oracles. Certain oracles within the collections may be dated precisely, 'in the year that King Uzziah died' (Isa. 6) being one example that springs readily to mind; but in no other prophetic collection does dating play so large a part in the structure of the narrative. Indeed, the introductory date in Haggai is the first of five dates in the space of only thirty-eight verses. This variation on most other introductions to prophetic collections is the opening gambit in a narrative framework that is unique within the corpus of writing prophets.

There are two possible exceptions to these observations. One is the prophet Ezekiel whose corpus does indeed open with a dated oracle, but this is not sustained through the anthology in quite the same way as in Haggai, and the date itself is thoroughly ambiguous (Ezek. 1.1). The second exception is the prophet Zechariah, who also opens with a prophetic oracle precisely dated also in the reign of Darius. There are dates also at Zech. 1.7 and 7.1, but they do not dominate the structure of the narrative in the way that the dating does in Haggai. Indeed, when the book of Zechariah is read as a whole, they become even more incidental in character. The tight narrative format of Haggai is not sustained into the book of Zechariah, but the initial link achieved by the dating formulae remains important. This can be described in terms that have already been noted. First, it continues the characteristic post-exilic necessity of dating events in terms of the king of another nation. Secondly, it is a reminder that the book of Haggai on its own is an incomplete story needing as a minimum the book of Zechariah and also that of Malachi, fellow prophets of the restoration.

This dependence on the wider context of the restoration prophetic material is also a reminder of the key exceptions to the observation that most of the written prophetic anthologies have some sort of temporal and spatial setting built into them. Those exceptions are Obadiah, Joel, Jonah, Nahum and Habakkuk, all of whom are members of the Book of the Twelve and all of whom begin with no dating formula at all. Paradoxically, the link between Haggai and Zechariah made most evident by the dating formulae and the absence of dates in those five members of the Twelve both point to the role of the wider corpus in determining the significance of one member of the corpus. The struggle to locate Obadiah, Joel, Jonah, Nahum and Habakkuk which has been a feature of their study is much less of a concern if part of their *Sitz im Leben* is their context within the scroll of the Twelve.

The Message of the Dates
Quite apart from the narrative and contextual significance of the date at the start of Haggai, the fact of the date is an important message in its own right. It indicates to the reader that 'the word of the Lord' is not a context-free concept. Rather, it is received and understood within the circumstances of the recipients. The word of the Lord that comes through Haggai is the word of the Lord because it is received in the 'second year of King Darius, in the sixth month, on the first day of the month'. The exactness of the date reinforces this notion, as does the repetition of that formula for each of the oracles of Haggai, bar one.

The mention of the second year of King Darius also recalls a particular background of international events, which I have detailed in the Introduction. I am assuming that 'the second year' refers to the year 520 BCE, rather than a year or more earlier. Even more exactly, the date of 29 August in that year for the first oracle has been widely accepted as accurate (see Appendix C). This is significant as it means that Darius has by this time consolidated his hold on the Persian imperial throne and has embarked on his programme of reorganizing the satrapies and attending to local concerns within the empire. Therefore the word of the Lord through Haggai is heard in the context of relative stability in the imperial province of Judah, after some difficult years both economically and politically. In fact, not only is it a time of stability; it is also a time when the Jewish people's re-establishment of their religious and ethnic identity is on the agenda of the Persian empire itself.

Darius

Apart from the backdrop function just described, another function of this first brief section in the narrative is the introduction of key participants in the drama that is about to unfold. With the exception of 'this people', all the main characters are encountered in section A at the top level of the discourse; that is, before the second layer introduced by 'thus says the Lord of hosts' (1.2). This amount of information in level 1 is unique to this particular section. The start of each of the other sections also begins usually with a date and always with some kind of note that the word of the Lord came to Haggai. But nowhere else are Zerubbabel and Joshua included at that level; when they are mentioned, they come in at a lower level of discourse (see 1.14; 2.2, 21). This highlights the importance of this first section of the narrative as introductory of the main characters. Accordingly, the remaining comment on level 1 of the discourse in this oracle is devoted to meeting each of them.

By reason of the dating formula, the first of these is Darius. The reader has already seen him from a distance, and in fact he never comes much closer. At one level, the story can be told entirely without him. Probably the only way available to the writer and editor to date the oracles was by reference to the imperial reign. Yet, on a literary level, the repetition of the dates is not necessary only to provide regular temporal markers. Their effect is also to keep the backdrop to events constantly in focus. They remind the reader and hearer of the commission of Cyrus in 538 BCE, in the terms of which the exiles were organized for a return to Judah and the rebuilding of the temple in Jerusalem (Ezra 1). They also call to mind the stop–start nature of the building projects, a history which has been recorded in the early chapters of Ezra, and the re-establishment of Cyrus' commission by explicit command of Darius (Ezra 6). This re-commissioning comes with some economic support in the form of tax relief for the temple project. Alongside a backdrop of imperial support sits the absence in the Haggai narratives of the local opposition that features in the Ezra–Nehemiah account. The Haggai narrative assumes that the imperial power is benevolent and supportive, and that the barriers to progress are found within the people themselves. Economically and spiritually, they have the wherewithal to build the temple if they want to do so.

Zerubbabel and Joshua

As Complementary Figures

This amalgam of imperial support and religious impulse continues as the text introduces two figures, both of whom feature in the narrative more explicitly than does Darius. They are, of course, 'Zerubbabel son of Shealtiel, governor of Judah' and 'Joshua son of Jehozadak, the high priest' (see Ezra 6), of whom critical questions concerning their identity and function relative to each other have been discussed in the Introduction. The Ezra material is curiously silent on events leading to the appointment of Zerubbabel. His function as 'governor' gives him an imperial role within the province of Judah, which itself was probably a sub-satrapy within the Persian empire. He must have been an imperial appointment, and his sphere of influence would have been, for want of a better term, the secular governance of the imperial province. We also know frustratingly little about Joshua, or about the genesis of the title he bears, 'high priest'. By the time of Haggai, was the term one of appointed office or simply indicative of a senior figure? If the former, we have no inkling of its evolution during the period of the exile. In a sense it is not essential to determine an answer. Whatever the title may have meant to Joshua's contemporaries, it is clear from the narratives both of Haggai–Zechariah and of Ezra–Nehemiah that Joshua is doing his work in a recognized appointed capacity of leadership. His sphere of influence would have been complementary to that of Zerubbabel, with a particular concern for the religious institutions of the people of Israel as reconstituted in the Persian province of Judah.

The type of sacred–secular distinction that I have implied is in a sense anachronistic, as it is clear that temple and palace function as a complex over which the king traditionally ruled as representative of Yahweh (see the so-called Royal Psalms, such as Pss. 2; 18; 110). The king fulfilled sacral functions within the cult (see, e.g., 2 Sam. 24.21; 1 Kgs 1.9; 12.32) and had an ongoing responsibility for the maintenance of the temple–palace complex. However, from the time of the Deuteronomic reforms, the sanctuary was the preserve of the priesthood at the apparent exclusion of the king (see Deut. 12.5-7, and the story of Uzziah's indiscretion in 2 Chron. 26.16-23). Against that background, it seems likely that, while Zerubbabel would have had special responsibility for re-establishing the temple and the cult, Joshua was a necessary complement to him. As the narrative unfolds, governor and high-priest are seen together in a corporate function. To extrapolate a little to the eschatological implications of Zerubbabel and Joshua in the Haggai–Zechariah corpus, I earlier observed of the coronation scene of Zech. 6.9-15 that royal and sacral authority coalesce around the figure called 'Branch', who represents a kind of corporate identity.

Zerubbabel as Persian Appointee
If the respective functions of Zerubbabel and Joshua are both explicable in terms of the religious tradition, there is a crucial difference between the two. Zerubbabel is a Persian appointee, and his Babylonian name probably also belies a close identification with the Babylonian court that was incorporated into the Persian empire. By placing the two figures side by side and describing them in terms that make it all but impossible to discern the relative importance of each, the narrative continues to convey a tension between Jewish aspiration and

accommodation to the Persian regime. Indeed, the fact that Haggai addresses both Joshua and Zerubbabel in the first instance indicates his perception that Zerubbabel is not able to exercise the type of responsibility traditionally associated with that of the monarch over both palace and temple. That role now requires both governor and priest together.

But this very tension is inherent in the figure of Zerubbabel himself. For as well as being the Persian-appointed governor of Judah, he is also 'son of Shealtiel'. Although there are some technical difficulties with this assignation, as noted in the Introduction, whichever way it is calculated Zerubbabel is a member of the line of David. Darius has apparently weighed the risk of an independence movement based on the Davidide Zerubbabel against the advantages of installing a figure whose authority may be legitimated in Judean terms, and decided that the risk was worth it. Again, the interaction of accommodation with the Persian authorities may be seen with the final focus on 'Zerubbabel my servant' of 2.23. All this is foreshadowed by the juxtaposition of 'governor of Judah' and 'son of Shealtiel' around the person of Zerubbabel.

Haggai

Haggai the Prophet

Before meeting either Joshua or Zerubbabel, however, the reader encounters 'Haggai the prophet'. In terms of the discourse analysis adopted by this commentary, there is a notable difference between the presentation of Haggai and the presentation of Joshua and Zerubbabel. Of the latter two I have noted that, after their introduction in this first section, they are encountered in lower levels of the discourse as the story is told about them. In contrast, Haggai, apart from when he participates in a conversation with the priests in 2.11-14, appears largely in the first level of discourse, at the introduction to each section. This gives him a unique role in the narrative. Although it is a matter of text-historical fact that the oracles and the narrative have probably been worked on by another hand, the received form of the story belongs to Haggai and to 'the word of the Lord' for whom Haggai is acting as agent. They are masters of the structure and hence of the progress of the message.

In support of Haggai's role comes a particular understanding of Haggai's person and work. First, he is given no patronymic, although it is hard to conceive that the information would not have been available to the narrator. He is not legitimated by genealogy in the way that Zerubbabel and Joshua are. That Joshua is the son of Jehozadak places him in the Zadokite succession and that Zerubbabel is the son of Shealtiel places him in the Davidic succession. The particularities of the context require that. The legitimation of Haggai is to be found in the simple ascription 'the prophet', *hanavi'*. Just as mentions of Zerubbabel and Joshua are usually accompanied by their patronymic in the Haggai narrative, so mentions of Haggai are almost always accompanied by the prophetic descriptor. That is the context within which he is to be understood.

This becomes even more noticeable in comparison with other prophetic figures in the Old Testament. Only two of the other writing prophets are described as 'the prophet' in the material that introduces the anthologies named after them. One is Habakkuk (Hab. 1.1); the other is Zechariah (Zech. 1.1), whose work is twinned with that of Haggai by this device among a number of others. But after the introductory formulae, Zechariah does not have the ascription attached to him nearly as persistently as does Haggai. As for the rest of the writing prophets, their prophetic status derives from their work as visionaries and conveyers of the word of the Lord. This absence of the prophetic descriptor for most of the classical prophetic figures, along with Amos's vehement refusal to be so described (Amos 7.14), is part of a larger debate on how those people who were subsequently identified as prophets by their anthologizers would have been perceived by their contemporaries and by themselves. It seems that in the early years of the Second Temple period there was no difficulty in ascribing prophetic status to Haggai and Zechariah by what must have been their near contemporaries. Whatever the case may be in that particular debate, the description of Haggai is sufficiently different to be remarkable and emphatic. It is also striking in the face of the promise of Deuteronomy 18, where the same definite expression 'the prophet' is used to promise the coming of a special successor to Moses. This is part of the context in which the compilers of the prophetic anthologies have apparently taken great care to describe their prophets in those terms. That makes this ascription attached to Haggai yet more worthy of remark.

Making that comment of Haggai in contrast to the other writing prophets, though, masks other aspects of the Old Testament prophetic tradition. From time to time particular individuals are described as 'the prophet'. Indeed, Jeremiah is routinely so described in the narratives about him (see, among many examples, Jer. 29.29; 36.26). The Chronicler also regularly refers to particular figures as 'the prophet' (2 Chron. 12.5; 21.12; 32.32; 34.22, for instance). One feature of the conflict between Jeremiah and Hananiah (Jer. 28) is that each of the protagonists is called 'the prophet'. This highlights the struggle as one concerning prophetic authority.

The Link with Nathan
A more interesting example for my present purposes is 'Nathan the prophet', who oversaw the transition from David to Solomon and was thus a key figure in the United Kingdom of Israel. He is often described as 'Nathan the prophet', and not only in the work of the Chronicler. In fact, the similarity of reference between Haggai and Nathan in 2 Samuel 7 and 12 and 1 Kings 1 suggests a deliberate intertextuality at work here. Notwithstanding his courage in confronting the king, Nathan has a strong association with the Davidic dynasty. He utters the words of the eternal Davidic covenant (2 Sam. 7.8-16) from which so much hope will subsequently flow. In particular, 1 Kings 1 (especially vv. 11-40) is significant in that it twins the figures of 'Nathan the prophet' and 'Zadok the priest' in the anointing of Solomon as successor to the Davidic throne. Here, the prophet, the original Zadokite priest and the first critical transfer of Davidic succession are all working together. During the time of Haggai, another prophet, another priest of Zadokite extraction and another Davidic figure may be found all working together towards a final focus on the chosen one Zerubbabel, in the same way that the focus of 1 Kings 1 was on the anointing of Solomon. Sirach 47.1 hints that the significance of Nathan to the reign of David was preserved in the memory of Second Temple Judaism. The manner in which Haggai is described at the dawn of the Second Temple era hints that his ministry is to be as significant as

100 *Haggai 1.1-2*

was that of Nathan before him. More will be said below on the possibilities created by this link in the treatment of 'the people' in these first two verses of Haggai.

'By the Hand' of Haggai

Let us turn now from the way in which Haggai is described to the way in which he receives the word of the Lord. I have already observed a discourse pattern in the book of Haggai, whereby each section is introduced by a sentence containing 'the word of the Lord' and Haggai. In three of the first four sections of the book the Hebrew expression is not exactly captured by the translation of the NRSV, or indeed of most major translations. The expression 'the word of the Lord came by the prophet Haggai' (1.1, 3; 2.1) can be rendered more literally 'the word of the Lord *became by the hand of* Haggai the prophet'. In that expression, as in so much about Haggai, there is both continuity and discontinuity with the prophetic tradition. The concept of 'the word of the Lord' coming to the people by the offices of the prophet is not the only way of describing prophetic activity (see the vision language of Isaiah and Amos for example) but it is thoroughly conventional, and places Haggai incontrovertibly among the prophets. And the notion of the word of the Lord 'becoming' is also a commonplace, especially in Jeremiah and Ezekiel (for example Jer. 1.2, 4, 11; Ezek. 1.3; 3.16; 6.1).

The use of the verb *hyh*, which I have translated as 'become', alongside the idiom 'by the hand of' to express the intermediary function of the prophet is unique in the biblical tradition to Haggai, yet it occurs in Haggai three times. Whenever the word of the Lord 'becomes' in Ezekiel and Jeremiah, it 'becomes' *to* rather than *by the hand of* the prophet. This incidentally is the expression used at the head of the final two sections of Haggai (2.10, 20). At the same time, the phrase 'by the hand of' on its own is not particularly common. Its three occurrences in Haggai account for just under 30 percent of the Old Testament total. Of the total number of occurrences, several are alongside the verbal form of *dbr*, 'the Lord spoke', rather than the nominal form represented as 'the word of the Lord'. Disregarding these, all but one of the remaining uses concerns the word of the Lord coming 'by the hand of Moses' (Exod. 9.35; Num. 16.40 [MT 17.5]; 27.23; 2 Chron. 35.6).

The interpretation of these data is problematic, as it apparently points in two conflicting directions. On the one hand, it could indicate a loss of confidence in the prophetic role, such as has been observed in the Second Temple period and in conjunction with the rise of apocalyptic. The result was a perception that the prophetic function was no longer the preserve of individuals directly in touch with 'the word of the Lord', but was manifest in heavenly intermediaries who often also provided an interpretation. The unusual emphasis on 'by the hand of' perhaps indicates an early sign of that loss of confidence as it emphasizes the prophet as mediator. The main problem with that view is that it does not take into account the continuities already noted between Haggai and the other writing prophets, nor does it take into account the more common phrasing employed in 2.10 and 2.20.

In that respect, the link with Moses observed above is a telling one. It needs to be placed alongside several other aspects of Haggai's function that I have already drawn attention to: his links with Nathan, the emphasis on his office, and his dominant role in the discourse. Taken together, these all denote a determination to assert the call and authority of Haggai and to legitimate his ministry as arising from the wellspring of the Israelite prophetic tradition. The extraordinary confidence that this displays in Haggai may also denote a need to counter a fear that the Lord has fallen silent in the wake of the exile with an assurance that there is a prophet in their midst the lineage of whose office may be traced back to Nathan and even Moses. History would show that the fear of the narrator was not unfounded, as Haggai and the other two prophets of the restoration would prove to be the last of their line, to be succeeded by more apocalyptic modes of envisioning the work of God.

The Lord (of Hosts)

As Character and Narrator
'The word of the Lord' that comes 'by the hand of' Haggai is in one sense external to the story of Haggai. Along with Haggai, it leads the narrative by appearing in the highest level of discourse for each section. But, and this is the conundrum of all biblical narrative, 'the Lord' or 'the Lord of hosts' also

appears as a character in the lower levels of discourse. The Lord of hosts is introduced to the reader in this first oracle along with Joshua, Zerubbabel and Haggai, as well as the people in general. The Lord of hosts is thoroughly enmeshed in the Haggai narrative along with each of the other characters. The significance of this phenomenon here and in Scripture generally is of a kind with the significance of the exact dating of each oracle that I have already commented on. Apart from lending a particular character to the narrative itself, it is also a comment on the nature of the interaction between human society and the divine, specified in this story as 'the word of the Lord'. If we cannot encounter the word of the Lord except as we encounter it in our human contexts, so we can hardly experience the divine except as a character within the human society of which we are members. If it be true that God speaks to humanity, and that is the premise of the Haggai narrative, then that encounter cannot be narrated without the Lord of hosts as a participant in the story. The discourse structure highlights this also for readers and listeners.

To the earliest hearers of this story it would have been self-evident that what might loosely be called 'the divine' was conveyed in the expression 'the Lord of hosts'. But what is the significance of that particular choice of name and what content does it carry? The importance of that question lies in the fact that 'the Lord' and 'the Lord of hosts' are the only names used for God in Haggai. The only discernible pattern in the variation between the two is that 'the Lord' occurs in the phrase 'the word of the Lord' throughout the top level of discourse. As I implied above, that term indicates the divine as external to the narrative. Otherwise, when the Lord is active as a participant in the narrative, the two terms are used apparently interchangeably. 'The Lord of hosts' appears thirteen times and 'the Lord' seven times. The lack of pattern and the preponderance of the term 'the Lord of hosts' indicates to me that the variations are probably more a product of literary instinct than any consciously intended distinction of meaning. When the term 'the Lord' is employed it is likely to be a shorthand for the longer expression. So, when it is clear what the narrator has in mind by 'the Lord of hosts', the same may be applied to 'the Lord' throughout the Haggai narrative.

Usage in the Restoration Prophets

The statistics are startling. It has already been noted that the 'Lord of hosts' is the only divine name used in Haggai, apart from Yahweh. This constitutes about 5 percent of all the occurrences in the Old Testament in a book that makes up only 0.2 percent of the total text of the Old Testament. This is without taking into account the probability that 'the Lord' is also shorthand for the same concept. The two other prophets of the restoration, Zechariah and Malachi, display similarly disproportionate rates of occurrence. Zechariah accounts for 18 percent of the uses from 1.04 percent of the text and Malachi 8 percent of the uses from 0.29 percent of the text. Cumulatively, nearly a third of all uses of the divine name 'Lord of hosts' in the Old Testament come from the restoration prophets, who together constitute less than 2 percent of the text. The only other points where there are similar concentrations are in Isaiah 1–39 and the book of Jeremiah. Why was this term so attractive to the prophets of the Second Temple?

Although the theory is not without its difficulties (particularly the absence of 'Lord of hosts' from Ezekiel), there is general agreement that the term develops as an important divine title employed by the temple theology of the Jerusalem cult tradition. Where the term appears in the Psalter, it generally does so in the Zion and royal psalms (e.g. Pss. 24; 46; 84; 89, and others). It is also a feature of the covenant with David narrative of 2 Samuel 7. So, it is hardly surprising that Isaiah, with his central focus on Jerusalem and Zion, should employ that particular divine name. The matter is not so straightforward in Jeremiah, where few of the 82 occurrences in the MT also appear in the shorter LXX version of the book, and consequently is best left out of the present discussion. Given this background, it appears as if Haggai and his fellow prophets of the restoration have brought the term into the re-establishment of the temple and a focus on Zion and the Davidic covenant. For them, the Lord of hosts is the God who rules from Mt Zion and the temple in Jerusalem and who has established an everlasting covenant with David and his heirs. This is the God with whom Haggai is in communion.

A Multivalent Concept

The multivalent sense of the term 'hosts' ought not to be ignored, meaning as it does both army and heavenly powers. The 'Lord of hosts' is therefore the one who marshals both the armies of earthly sovereigns and the cosmic powers (both the multivalence of the term and the parallelism of concept between earthly and heavenly powers is exemplified in Isa. 13.4-5; 24.21). It can be argued that Deutero-Isaiah uses the concept in developing a creation theology, and employs it as a specific element in the polemic against the idolatry encountered by the people of the exile (Isa. 44.6, 9-20). If that is the case, the Lord of hosts would have become an important element in the exilic hope, and one that Haggai and Zechariah would have carried back into the promised land after the decree of Cyrus in 538 BCE. The term 'Lord of hosts' fits both this background of resistance to the idolatry of the Babylonian context and the conscious re-assertion of a Jerusalem theology on the part of the prophets of the restoration. This is not to imply that Haggai, Zechariah and Malachi necessarily employed it in a self-conscious awareness of its history or with polemical intent. By this time, it may well have come to be a general term depicting the temporal and cosmic scope of Yahweh's rule that simply came naturally. That is certainly how it came to be understood in the history of reception. The LXX regularly translates 'Lord of hosts' with the formulaic *kurios pantokrator* or 'Lord Almighty'.

The Lord of hosts of the Haggai narrative is a God whose rule is focused on Jerusalem and the religious tradition, and of whom the cluster of Mt Zion, Jerusalem and the temple signify a reign that is cosmic in scope. Whether made wittingly or unwittingly, Haggai's choice of divine name helps to focus the concerns of the narrative on God's particular work among the people as temple-builders and his more general work with respect to the nations. For a contemporary reader of Haggai in the canonical context, this combination of a particular Jerusalem theology and a universal agenda is suggestive.

The Lord of hosts engages with others in Haggai in a number of different ways, which will emerge as the narrative proceeds, but significantly the first thing he does in the story is 'he speaks'. Indeed, this is the first thing we see the Lord do in each of the sections of Haggai. This draws an unmistakeable link with the creator whose task is to bring things into being and who is also conveyed by the same divine name in Deutero-Isaiah. Change comes about through the words that Haggai brings from the Lord of hosts. In this first of the six oracles from the Lord in the book of Haggai, the Lord speaks first to Joshua and Zerubbabel and the subject of his concern is 'these people' (1.2).

The People

And so 'these people' is the final element in the cast of characters. 'The people' in Haggai come under several different descriptions. Apart from 'these/this people' (1.2; 2.14) they may also be 'the people' (1.13), '(all) the remnant of the people' (1.14; 2.2) or 'people of the land' (2.4). Leaving aside for now the problem of 'all the nations' (2.7) and 'this nation' apparently in parallel with 'this people' in 2.14, all these references may be to those who have returned and share the task of building the temple. Or the variation in terminology could indicate a distinction between the returners and the hostile Samaritans, who have remained behind during the period of the exile. If the latter is the case, are they the recipients of the oracles or not? And how do the nations fit in here? Clarity on these questions will emerge during the course of the narrative, and it is too early at this stage to foreclose on them.

For the moment it is sufficient to say of 'this people' (translated as a plural by NRSV) in 1.2 that the singular demonstrative pronoun is significant in a couple of ways. First, it indicates a collective identity, which suggests an addition to the cast so far assembled. It is not a way of referring to Joshua and Zerubbabel. Secondly, the demonstrative 'this' implies that the people in question share a common life with Joshua, Zerubbabel and Haggai. They are those who at least recognize the task to rebuild the temple, a task that their three mentors are also concerned for. The narrative introduces them as such. As the first two of those leaders returned from Babylon with a special commission, and as I surmise that Haggai was also among the returners, I infer that the Lord of hosts speaks in this oracle of those who number themselves among the returned exiles and who look to Joshua and Zerubbabel in the first instance for leadership. In later oracles that conception of 'the people' will expand.

The Words of the People (Verse 2)

With the introduction of 'these people' another layer of direct speech within the oracle is encountered. The report of what the people say is a regular feature of the Haggai narrative. Their assertion is that 'the time has not yet come to rebuild the Lord's house'. That is the sum total of this first oracle. It has this short introductory narrative section all to itself, and so apparently also plays a part in the opening exposition contained in these first two verses. More of what lies behind that phrase will emerge in the next oracle, but this bald statement is highly allusive.

Remember that these introductory verses are setting up a scenario that recalls the ministry of the prophet Nathan and events surrounding the building of the first temple and the development of a theology focused on Jerusalem and the Davidic line. The people's excuse comes as an ironic echo of the message that Nathan was compelled to deliver to David on that earlier occasion (2 Sam. 7.5-16), that it was not yet the time for the house of the Lord to be built. Furthermore, although there is no lexical coincidence, the 'panelled houses' (1.4) of the people of Haggai's day are a further ironic reflection of David's discomfort with his 'house of cedar' in the face of which the tabernacle looked a poor offering indeed (2 Sam. 7.2). Although the time had not yet come when David offered himself as temple-builder, the time has now come for the temple to be rebuilt. Just as Nathan was subsequently the one to anoint Solomon, the temple builder, so it is the task of Haggai to act as midwife for the emergent leadership of Joshua and Zerubbabel. The people's comment that 'the time has not yet come' said more than they imagined.

In an odd way also the resonances of the prophet Nathan and David, and Nathan's role in anointing Solomon, introduce a kind of reversal which has a message of its own. David is told by God that the time has not yet come, while in Haggai's time the people themselves have decided that the time has not yet come. Nathan's message of delay in 2 Samuel 7 went hand in hand with an affirmation of the house of David that did not need a building made with hands for its effectiveness (2 Sam. 7.7). At the start of the Second Temple period, Haggai's message is that the house made with hands must be built, but his identification with the prophet Nathan foreshadows at the same time that the building task cannot be an end in itself. The scene is therefore set for the identification of the community or household of God with the house of God, the temple. This identification remains only implicit in Haggai, but nevertheless sits on the cusp of a movement during the Second Temple period to endow the temple building with a communal and eschatological significance (see the comments in the Introduction).

Conclusion

It would be an exaggeration to attribute the characteristics of a modern short story to the book of Haggai, as is often done for narratives such as Ruth and Jonah. Yet, in the manner of a short story, the first section has done a masterly job of setting the structure of the Haggai narrative, introducing each of the main characters in that narrative and foreshadowing the key themes and possibilities that await a reading of this deceptively subtle piece of biblical narrative.

HAGGAI 1.3-12
(SECTION B, THE SECOND ORACLE):
'CONSIDER HOW YOU HAVE FARED'

Now all of the protagonists in the narrative have been introduced, and the plot can begin to unfold. The people themselves have only been heard from indirectly, and that situation will not change as the story proceeds. This second oracle of the Lord clarifies the issue confronting the protagonists and does so with a double focus. On one hand, it contains further implications of what the people have been saying. On the other, it contains a two-fold response to the reluctance of the people, a comment on their attitudinal failure and a command to adopt a different approach. The final section of the oracle summarizes the response of the people and of Zerubbabel and Joshua to these words of the Lord by the hand of Haggai.

Verse 3 and the Structural Question

Delineation of the Second Oracle

In two respects my delineation of this second oracle goes somewhat against the grain of other readings of the book of Haggai. I have divided off the first two verses as a distinct oracle, and I have made a division between vv. 12 and 13 instead of between vv. 11 and 12, as is normally done. Both moves derive from the decision to treat the entire book of Haggai as a coherent narrative within which are nested various oracles, and to structure the narrative around the prophetic oracle markers in the story (for further on the discourse analysis, see Appendix A, along with my comment on structure in the previous section). The more traditional approach has been to structure the narrative around the dates. Leaving aside for the moment the problem of the dates in 1.15–2.1, which will be treated in a different context, this has meant that 1.1-11 is usually treated as a single oracle. The date in 1.15 is then often applied retrospectively to the oracle beginning at v. 12.

If the structure of the narrative is dictated by the prophetic oracle markers instead, the opening sentence of the second oracle is the line, 'the word of the Lord became by the hand of the prophet Haggai' (v. 3, a literal translation of the MT). This exactly parallels the phrase in 1.1 and 2.1, and closely parallels the phrase in 2.10 and 2.20, all of which have been identified as level 1 introductions to other oracles. There remains a problem with the opening of a further oracle in 1.13, but again that will be treated in more detail in the context of that oracle. When these things are considered together, the parallels in the dialogue markers ought to outweigh the 'missing' date at the start of what I am proposing as the second oracle (v. 13). If the first oracle and the narrative in which it is embedded introduced the main characters and the presenting problem, this second oracle now moves on to specify the nature of the problem and the Lord's response to it.

Parallel Responses in Verses 12 and 14
A further outcome of the decision to structure the narrative around the dialogue markers is to read v. 12 as the conclusion to the second oracle. There are only two places in the Haggai narrative where the response of the people to the words of the Lord is included: v. 12 and v. 14. Although the thrust and emphasis of these two verses differ from each other in intriguing ways, there is enough in common between the two to argue that they are intended to function structurally in parallel with each other. In each instance, the narrative describes the response of Joshua, Zerubbabel and the people to the word of the Lord that has just come to them by the hand of Haggai. Therefore, just as v. 14 narrates the outcome of the hearing of the Lord's message in v. 13, so v. 12 narrates the behavioural outcome of the much longer oracle that began back in v. 3. This is the case regardless of how we end up treating the dating problem in 1.15–2.1 or of how we deal with the discordant way in which the third oracle (1.13-15a) is introduced.

In each case the people involved are listed: Zerubbabel, Joshua and 'the remnant of the people'. There is only a small stylistic variation in that the descriptor 'governor of Judah' does not occur in v. 12. In each instance there is a reference to 'the Lord their God', although again there is a stylistic variation with the inclusion of 'of hosts' in v. 14. And in each case also they responded in a particular way. In v. 12, they 'obeyed' and feared', while in v. 14 they 'came and worked'. In this last parallel, the variation hints at narrative possibilities which will be explored in the context of the next oracle. There is also a conceptual parallel which the NRSV translation does not pick up. The phrase translated as 'worked on the house...' (v. 14) might literally be rendered as 'they did the message/task (*ml'kh*) in the house...' This echoes the obedience of the people to the 'words' or 'message' or even 'task' of Haggai (*dbry ḥgy*) in v. 12. Although the vocabulary used to express it is different, in each case this multivalent concept of the task or message of God is present. As v. 14 describes the response to the brief oracle in v. 13, so v. 12 concludes the second oracle (vv. 3-12) with a similar description of the response to the preceding oracle.

Audience

Before leaving v. 3, I should note the problem of audience at this point in the narrative. The first oracle is addressed to two particular individuals, Zerubbabel the governor and Joshua the high priest. But the oracle itself concerns another party, 'these people'. As the second oracle proceeds, there is no indication of the audience. Does Haggai now address the two leaders again, or has he turned his attention to those of whom he spoke in the first oracle, the people themselves? The text itself is inscrutable, but there are hints that the wider audience is in mind. The most obvious is the conclusion to the oracle in v. 12, which specifies the response of 'all the remnant of the people' as well as Zerubbabel and Joshua. See the comments on v. 12 below in support of this view.

Verse 4

Now the prophet brings the word of the Lord as an expansion on the oblique comment that the people do not consider it time to build the house of the Lord. Again, the comment of the people themselves is inferred as on the unheard end of a telephone conversation. The question to the people—'Is it time for you yourselves to live in your panelled houses, while this house lies in ruins?'—provides an indirect comment on the manner in which the statement 'the time is not yet come' has been conveyed. It has been not through a directly expressed opinion but through the actions of the people; they have acted in a way that expresses their disobedience. As the reason for the Lord's displeasure had been a particular style of life, so in both instances the outcome of the word or message is an active response, as observed above.

The implication of the question, that the people have chosen one house over the other, is in fact an interpretation on the part of the one who speaks at level 1 of the oracular discourse. It is, as throughout most of the narrative, the view of the word of the Lord, a word that comes 'by the hand of Haggai the prophet'. There is not a direct dialogue between Yahweh and the people as is usually the case in prophetic disputation. The narrative remains the property of the word of the Lord. At this stage we have no idea how the people may have felt about this imputation derived from their lifestyle. We are only privy to their response to the interpretation.

'House'
The conflict between Yahweh and the people is expressed around the play on the word 'house'. There are two houses: the house of the Lord and the houses of the people. This has a three-fold effect on the narrative. Most obviously it has a contrastive effect in that it intensifies and specifies the sense of conflict between the people and Yahweh that has already been sketched in the first oracle (v. 2). It is a debate about houses.

Secondly, it says something about how the temple is conceived at this point in the narrative. The building in question is consistently referred to as the 'house of the Lord' until the first and only specific reference to the 'temple' at 2.18. Perhaps the identification of the Lord's dwelling with the domesticity of the people conveys a sense of intimacy between the people and the inhabitant of the house in question. The concept of a temple, however, is much more redolent of the transcendence and otherness of the Lord. At the same time, the term 'house of the Lord' points the people as well as subsequent readers beyond the physical and institutional realities to the purpose of it all, namely, the dwelling of God with his people.

At this early stage in the narrative the intimacy of the Lord is much more in view. It is Yahweh who speaks and addresses the people in the second person, 'is it time for you yourselves?' The result is a subtle disjunction between narrative form and narrative content. On the one hand, the form of the narrative, with the 'word of the Lord' as the persistent subject at level 1 of the discourse structure, conveys the otherness of the Lord. On the other, the content indicates a longing for intimacy on the part of the Lord. It will be the task of the upcoming narrative to resolve this disjunction.

A much later Jewish reader, the one responsible for the Targum of the Minor Prophets, solves it by consistently rendering the term 'house of the Lord' and its abbreviated form, 'house', as 'sanctuary' (*mqdš*, 1.2, 4, 9, 14; 2.3, but not 1.8; 2.7). As a result, the Targum seems deaf to the rhetorical effect in the MT of the contrast between the houses. This has a two-fold effect. The root *qdš* emphasizes the holiness of the temple and so diminishes the sense of intimacy engendered by the MT. At the same time, and secondly, it shifts the focus onto the function of the house of the Lord as the locus of the rite, again an emphasis that, although present in Haggai, will turn out not to be central to the concerns of Haggai.

A third effect of the play on the word 'house' is to put the hearer or reader in mind of an earlier conversation in the history of Israel between Yahweh and an ancestor of Zerubbabel (2 Sam. 7.1-4), a conversation in which exactly the same contrast was drawn. In the earlier case, the contrast was between David's 'house of cedar' and the house of the Lord. The coincidence of vocabulary is not exact but the conceptual contrast is striking. On that earlier occasion, David himself drew the discomfiting link and asked to rectify it by building a house for the Lord. He was told that the time had not yet come to 'build a house for my name'. Here the panelled houses are equally discomfiting but the unease is felt by Yahweh. There is no hint that the people themselves are aware of the problem. And this time the people apparently think that the time for such a building is not yet, while Yahweh, in a reversal of that other occasion, has other plans.

The intertextuality works by means of the similarity and contrast that is found between the contexts. It introduces the question of why the time is right to rebuild the temple as it recalls a situation when it was appropriate not to build the temple in the first place. If the readers are already slightly destabilized by the disjunction between form and content around the descriptor 'house of the Lord', they are further put off-balance by the question implicit in the intertextual contrast. How can the right time to build the house be determined, particularly when the matter is not evidently part of the consciousness of the people to whom Haggai is bringing the word of the Lord? A failure to appreciate the intertextual implications of Haggai has contributed to the bad press so often experienced by the book. Too often Haggai has been seen simply as a prophet whose task is to promote the temple building, a project whose worthiness is held in some disdain by those who are looking back from the other side of the New Testament treatment of the temple. Yet, the intertextual echoes alert the reader to the fact that the building of the temple is not an end in itself so much as a response to the fact that for some reason the time has come for it to be built. The rest of the narrative will reinforce that impression and attempt to discern the nature of the time that requires that building.

'Panelled Houses'
The 'panelled houses' probably refers to the standard vault roofed houses of the time. They are almost certainly not indicative of excessive luxury so much as a perfectly reasonable response to the conditions found by the people on their arrival in the Persian province of Judah. The offence is not that the people have houses as that their houses contrast with the house of the Lord, which still apparently 'lies in ruins'.

'In Ruins'
The Hebrew word that is translated by NRSV as 'in ruins' ($ḥrb$) has a wider sense than its immediate application to a particular building. It calls up a picture of the countryside and the state of the social infrastructure, of which ruined buildings is only one indicator, and is probably better translated as 'desolate'. This wider reference is significant in that the state of the land is described with exactly the same word in v. 11, although there it is translated by NRSV as 'drought'. The condition of the land comes to reflect the condition of the house of the Lord, but that will be discussed further in the context of v. 11.

Verses 5-6

Structure of the Oracle

These verses represent the second stage of the second oracle, introduced as they are by 'thus says the Lord of hosts'. Further stages begin in vv. 7 and 9b, each introduced by the verb 'says' with 'the Lord of hosts' as the subject, and each delineated as level 2 units in the discourse analysis (Appendix A; 'says the Lord' in v. 8 serves a different discourse function as discussed below). This second stage effectively specifies the nature of the desolation or drought to which v. 4 alludes.

Sitz im Leben of Verse 6

The desolation is a state not so much of grinding poverty or disaster as of an ongoing struggle to make the best use of limited resources. In the Introduction I noted that the dates given to these oracles represent a time after Darius consolidated his hold on the Persian empire. His regime also brought a change in administrative emphasis from conquest to loyal maintenance. Haggai's province of Yehud would have borne a burden of taxation demanded by the central empire, but at the same time the requisite administrative structures imposed to enable this would have resulted in more settled conditions within the province and probably even some tax relief in acknowledgment of the temple project. Hence it was a period of political calm if not prosperity, a time of sowing and reaping and going about the daily business of life, in the manner expressed in these verses.

However, an understanding of the *Sitz im Leben* leading up to the time of these verses early in the reign of Darius is informed by two important debates concerning Judah in the late neo-Babylonian and early Persian periods: the question of the 'myth of the empty land', and the debate over who is to be included in the group named by the Haggai narrative as the 'remnant of the people' (1.12, 14; 2.2) and 'this people'. The two debates are related.

Who is 'the Remnant of the People'?

To take the second question first, there are those who argue that 'the remnant of the people' and 'this people' denote the returnees from Babylon as distinct from the people who have remained on the land. Others argue that the category includes both returnees and the Samaritan population who remained on the land during the period of the exile. An understanding of the *Sitz im Leben* of these verses will be determined by which side of that debate is taken. I will argue below at v. 12 for the latter understanding; the people responding to the prophet Haggai and to the leadership of Joshua and Zerubbabel include both returnees and Samaritan residents.

Loss of Infrastructure
That being the case, the description of the conditions underlying the picture painted by the prophet in v. 6 must apply to both groups of people. I have already made a suggestion as to the experience of the returnees in my comments above on the early years of the reign of Darius. But for the other group, those who remained on the land, this is where the question of the 'myth of the empty land' comes into play. Responses to this phrase on the part of readers determine their perception of the conditions faced by the people being addressed by Haggai. The debate concerns the extent of depopulation within Judah and of the deterioration of social infrastructure during the period known as the 'exile'. There is no doubt that the deportation of many Jews and particularly aristocratic Jews would have impacted the social order of Judah to some extent. There is also evidence that there were some changes of settlement patterns during the period of the exile, not least a movement out of Jerusalem, although the city was almost certainly not rendered entirely uninhabitable in the wake of Nebuchadnezzar's siege. However, there was an ongoing material culture in the region, the argument goes, and the caricature of an 'empty land' is in fact a construct founded on scholarly reading of the biblical text. Other interpreters of the admittedly sparse physical evidence from the exilic period prefer to give more credence to the biblical evidence in tandem with archeological and inscriptional material. In the opinions of such interpreters, there was a significant dislocation as a result of the Babylonian conquest. Some parts of the land were rendered uninhabitable while others were left relatively unscathed and functioned as a haven for the inhabitants. Furthermore, the destruction of the temple and the resulting disenfranchisement of the institutions of the monarchy and the priesthood is

reflected in the very scarcity of material indicating their existence. It was what one commentator has called a 'dark age', in which it is inconceivable that life would have gone on as normal.

There is also an intermediate argument. Physical evidence of life in neo-Babylonian and early Achaemenid Judah is scarce, and the interpretation of what there is is subject to vigorous debate. It may be that in parts of the region rural and small town life went on with a significant population base. At the same time, though, it seems likely that the demise of the key institutions of Judean governance and religion, along with the siege of the city of Jerusalem, would have had a devastating effect. A major and lasting social discontinuity seems likely regardless of details of population movement. An interesting question to ask, then, is whether or not those who remained behind in Judah could have restored the temple and the Judean instruments of government without the involvement of those returning from the exile under the aegis of Cyrus. It seems unlikely given the absence of a coherent structure and a corresponding loss of temple and royal ideology.

Loss and Return of the Temple Vessels
There is a further factor to consider. Both Jeremiah (Jer. 52.17-23) and Daniel (Dan. 5.2) note the impact on the collective memory of the loss of the temple treasures, subsequently installed in the temple of Nebuchadnezzar. Ezra–Nehemiah then highlight their return as almost as important as the restoration of the population of Judah (Ezra 1.7). In terms of the ideology of the period in question, the temple could not have been built without some indication of Yahweh's appeasement and presence with the people, a presence that had in some way been compromised by the loss of the temple vessels. It was the return of the vessels and the encyclical by Cyrus (Ezra 1.2-4) that provided the necessary proof. Without them, a restoration was out of the question. With them, the restoration of both the temple and the religious and governmental infrastructure became possible.

Given all of this, an ideological struggle between the returnees and the local Samaritans seems unlikely (see below on v. 12). Rather, the scenario painted by Haggai in v. 6 would have struck a chord with both groups and reflects what is known of these years in Achaemenid Judah. For the returnees it would have begun as a metaphorical chord, echoing the sense of incompleteness that was central to the exile experience. The ongoing presence of a flourishing Jewish community in the wider Persian and later Greek empire indicates that this sense was not necessarily physical, yet it was nevertheless real. However physically comfortable the people may have been, while Jerusalem lay 'empty', shorn of its ideological significance, the sense of futility that comes with a loss of *raison d'être* is well expressed by each of the metaphors employed. The necessity for the work of Haggai suggests that the metaphors may well also have become physical reality, as the people of Judah struggled to initiate the rebuilding project. During the uncertain days after the death of Cyrus and prior to the reforms of Darius (530–522 BCE) the early days back on the land would not have been easy. For those who had never been away, the material evidence suggests that making a living had been difficult in an atmosphere of dislocation, and is apparently no easier with the return to their company of those who had been living in Babylonia.

Verse 6 as Programmatic

As will be seen below, the placement of v. 7 emphasizes the content of v. 6 as programmatic for what is to follow in the narrative of Haggai the prophet. In effect, it indicates the state of affairs to which the temple building and associated promises are a response. So it is worth pausing to consider the nature of those conditions. There are three aspects of the description of v. 6 that are relevant.

First, it foreshadows the debilitating effects of adequacy. The people are not starving (they eat) nor is there a drought (they drink), their situation is sustainable in that they can plan for the next agricultural cycle (they sow much), and they have a level of employment (they earn wages). There is no crisis. But nor is there contentment, for there is never quite enough. The lexical structure of the verse emphasizes this. It begins with a finite perfect statement, 'you have sown much', and is followed by several infinitive absolute forms in a series of parallel comments on the result of this plentiful sowing: brought in little, eaten but without satisfaction, drunk but without joy and donned clothes but without warmth. All of these together build a vivid picture of the failure of satisfaction to match the level of effort made. If each of those expressions is basically a literal response to the agricultural cycle, the final clause with its departure from the pattern of infinitive absolute forms moves to a more metaphorical expression, 'you earn wages to put them into a bag with holes'. This is conveyed by the switch to a participial expression and the less literal irony of depositing money in a purse that will not hold it. The effect is that the people find it hard to lift their eyes beyond the material.

Secondly, the oracles of Haggai are a reminder that the concerns of v. 6, to which could also be added the 'panelled houses' of v. 4, are not destinations in their own right. Something more is required; the return from exile is not enough on its own. In the terms set by Haggai, the missing element is 'the Lord's house'. His words are a general reminder that the human spirit is never satisfied by the physical requirements of food, clothing, shelter and employment. And they are a further particular reminder of Qohelet's insight that God has set *'olam* (NRSV, 'a sense of past and future') in the hearts of humanity (Eccl. 3.11).

If the emphasis on v. 6 foreshadows something of the intent of Haggai's oracles, it also provides an early glimpse into the impact of the form taken by Haggai's message. It does so by the subtle blend of the literal and the metaphorical that emerges from the narrative's setting of these oracles. I have already considered the literal circumstances of the people to whom this oracle is addressed, and have seen that they are well reflected in the words of v. 6. I have also suggested that these words confront the imponderables of the human spirit. This double focus is expressed in their literary form also. On the one hand, the first four statements are literal expressions of the circumstances. On the other, their metaphorical potential is confirmed by the final element, which is not primarily a literal statement: 'you that earn wages earn wages to put them into a bag with holes'.

This interaction of the literal and the metaphorical reflects and becomes part of what will emerge as a key feature of the message of Haggai. Various terminologies can be used to express it. One might be the interaction between a people's physical circumstances and their intangible aspirations;

another would be the tension between the institutional form of religion and relationship with the divine. The former distinction is in the background of the book of Haggai. The latter will move increasingly into the foreground, for it is encapsulated in the imperative to rebuild the temple.

This is evident from the scholarly debate over the motivation behind the perceived importance of the temple. Some adopt a minimalist view and perceive the importance of the temple as primarily a matter of economics, while others discern a more worthy motivation. More will be said on this when the fourth oracle (2.1-9) is discussed. Whatever the case, there is a key relationship between the building of the physical temple and its transcendent significance. The interaction between the metaphorical and the literal in the description of the people's condition is a harbinger of these things.

Verses 7-9a

Narrative Function of Verse 7

The opening phrase 'Thus says the Lord of hosts (*yhwh tṣb't*)' functions in two different directions. At one level, it opens the second of three episodes within this second oracle, each beginning with 'the Lord of hosts' as the subject (vv. 5, 7, 9). Each of these is a second level statement in the discourse analysis, and each introduces a new development within the oracle. In that respect these verses advance the discussion begun with the observations about the present state of the people's experience (v. 6).

At the same time, the contents of v. 7 parallel those of v. 5. Just as at the start of the earlier episode, the first instruction is to 'Consider how you have fared' (literally 'set your hearts upon your ways'). However, what follows in v. 8 is not a continuation of this instruction in the way that v. 6 is a continuation of the same instruction in v. 5. In the earlier episode the instruction to 'set your heart' is followed by a reflection on the current futility of things, an indication of the matter on which the people's heart needs to be set. In this episode the same instruction is followed by an apparent *non sequitur*, a set of building instructions. It is not a *non sequitur*, however, if v. 7 is read as the concluding element in an *inclusio* incorporating the material in vv. 5-7. In that respect, there is a subtle progression within the narrative served by v. 7, with both a pointer onwards to the response to the conditions of the land and the people, and a retrospective emphasis on those same conditions.

A Metaphorical Harvest

The discontinuity between vv. 6 and 8 highlighted by the *inclusio* closed in v. 7, and the parallelism of the phrase 'Consider how you have fared' (vv. 5 and 7), invites a comparison of the contents of vv. 6 and 8, each of which responds to the invitation to 'consider how you have fared'.

As already noted, v. 6 contains a series of ironic contrasts between the hope invested in the sowing and the reality of the reaping. In response comes a series of three plural imperatives in v. 8: 'go up', 'bring' and 'build'. These three imperatives respond to the infinitive absolutes identified in v. 6, the specifications of dissatisfaction. There is an explicit link with them through the hiphil form of the verb *bn'*, which in this form means 'bring' and is often used to refer to the action of harvesting a crop. This is the first infinitive in v. 6 used to indicate that they have 'brought in' or harvested little. Now, in response, Yahweh is asking them to 'bring in' wood which they have gone up to the hills to collect. After the futility of their own harvest, they are to participate in a harvest of a different kind, of wood for building the house of the Lord. Instead of eating, drinking and being clothed, the naturally expected outcome of most harvests, they are to build a house as the outcome of this harvesting of wood from the hills.

As with many questions of the physical and geographical features of the province of Judah, there is some debate as to the literal implications of the instruction to 'go up to the hills' to procure building materials. Much of the stone work of the ruined temple is likely to have been either partially intact or still available as rubble, so quarrying was not immediately necessary as a precursor to the temple construction. However, the timber content of the temple was almost certainly destroyed by fire, or, as is natural in such situations, scavenged and recycled by the local populace who inhabited the land during the several generations in which the temple awaited its restoration. The type of timber necessary for such an ambitious construction was probably not fully available in the surrounding hills. For those focused on a primarily literal understanding of Haggai's project, this is something of a problem. One suggestion is that the timber in question was for the necessary building equipment, and hence readily available locally, rather than for the structure of the temple itself. However, in light of the suggestion that the literary link between vv. 6 and 8 conjures up a metaphorical harvest in v. 8, then the issue is not critical. Indeed, the disjunction between Haggai's instruction and local realities is itself an argument in favour of the metaphorical understanding. The intention of this instruction is that the people should acquire what needs to be acquired to start the rebuilding, and that they should think of this initial work as a type of harvest.

'Consider How You Have Fared'
The lexical link of the harvest provides the clue for this. Once that link is established, other conceptual connections between vv. 6 and 8 come into focus. Instead of the dashed expectations of v. 6, the reaping in v. 8 yields the rebuilt house of the Lord. There is an irony in this that must have been as obvious to Haggai's hearers as it is to a modern reader. If a concentrated focus on their own needs on the part of the people has failed to alter their straitened circumstances, how will this diversion of energy result in a more satisfactory harvest? Within that question lies the challenge laid down by Haggai. That is what he means when he says 'consider how you have fared'. The cryptic reference to 'the house' in the context of the harvest metaphor (v. 8) prompts the reader to reconsider the significance of the 'panelled houses' with respect to the inadequate harvest of v. 6. Part of the referent of that metaphor is that the focus on their own dwellings has not been effective. In contrast, this harvest is a result of a figurative sowing in the form of concentrating on the right house.

'Build'
This is reinforced by the multivalence of the verb 'to build'. It has an entirely straightforward sense of constructing an edifice or developing some kind of institution. This is the first sense of the word as used in v. 8. However, it also carries a well-established sense, particularly with Israel as its object, of building up a household, and in particular the household of a

nation. This is part of the message of Jeremiah to the exiles, and is explicit in Jer. 24.6; 31.4; 33.7; and 42.10. In these verses the image of building a house is also in parallel with the agricultural metaphor for the establishment of the people on their own land (especially Jer. 24.6; 42.10). While not claiming an explicit intertextuality at this point, I suggest that there are echoes of this message in the background as Haggai reverses the direction of the verb and speaks to the returned exiles of the building that they are doing. The promise made through Jeremiah of a rebuilt people has now come to fruition through the actions of the Persian empire; what building will the rebuilt people themselves now engage in? This is further reinforced by the use of a common agricultural metaphor on the part of both Jeremiah and Haggai. As the promise of God through Jeremiah to rebuild a nation is expressed metaphorically in terms of a planting on the land, so the challenge through Haggai to invest in the right building project is expressed metaphorically as a challenge to gather a potentially fruitful harvest.

This link is further grist to the argument that the interest in the temple in Haggai is not an end in itself but is part of the realization of a dream nurtured in the exile. In the Introduction, I suggested that the thought world inhabited by Haggai is likely to have included a growing concept of the temple as both eschatological in scope and as expressed in community. If that is so, then it is all the more likely that there are metaphorical echoes in this particular oracle.

Yahweh's Perspective

The outcome of the harvest provides a further conceptual contrast between vv. 6 and 8. The outcome in v. 6 has been insufficient to eat and drink, loss of warm clothing and the frittering away of hard-earned assets. The outcome of the harvest of v. 8 is Yahweh's pleasure and honour. To a modern reader, there is a discordant change in direction at this point, in that the desired shift in focus on the part of the people is expressed entirely from the perspective of Yahweh. The Lord is the beneficiary of the people's investment in the house of the Lord instead of in their own. Given that the failure is expressed in terms of the experience of the people (v. 6), the narrative leads us to expect a more humanist point of view, but that is not to be.

This perspective is confirmed by the insertion of the phrase 'says the Lord' at the end of v. 8. This narrative marker is not part of the series of verbs in vv. 5, 7 and 9, each with 'the Lord of hosts' as their subject, and so does not mark out a new section of discourse. There are two main reasons for this. The first is that a pattern is broken in this oracle by the employment of the abbreviated subject 'Lord'. This is not a compelling reason on its own and is an argument that is not consistently applied to this reading of the book of Haggai, as elsewhere the shortened subject seems to be employed simply as a shorthand for 'Lord of hosts'. However, in this case the point being made is corroborated by the manner in which 'says the Lord' is embedded in a longer train of thought that continues into v. 9a. The purpose of the clause here seems to be not so much to mark out a new section of discourse as to emphasize the Yahwist perspective at this moment. This is the perspective of the narrative as a whole, in that the level 1 discourse markers all have 'the word of the Lord' as their subject.

The resolution of the discordant note thus introduced, at least in literary terms if not necessarily theologically, comes in v. 9a, to which I turn below. However, the irony of the focus on Yahweh in v. 8b is, from another point of view, not so discordant as one might at first think, and indeed it is a further key to understanding the motivation of the book of Haggai. In the first place, it foreshadows the possibility that any sort of human offering can be acceptable to Yahweh, a possibility that will be further worked out in the fourth oracle (2.1-9). In that respect, it gives the lie to those who would confine the significance of the temple to the economic or ideological realm. Real human actions do in fact engage with divine responses. The temple is therefore important for the reasons expressed by the narrative. At the same time, it is in tune with the notion discussed above that Achaemenid Judah could not have conceived of proceeding with the building of the temple without an assurance of Yahweh's presence and approval. That assurance is now confirmed in the phrase translated by the NRSV as 'so that I may take pleasure in it and be honoured'.

'Take Pleasure in' and 'Be Honoured' as Cohortative Forms

To illustrate the foregoing point, it is necessary to discuss both the form that these verbs take and their meaning. The verb 'take pleasure' is in the cohortative form. The second verb in this phrase, 'be honoured', in the *kethib* (the written form of the MT) represents a rare niphal subjunctive form of the verb. This has been corrected in the *qere* (the accepted of reading the MT) to the more readily accessible cohortative form. Technically, it is possible that those who prefer the archaic subjunctive preserved in the *kethib* are correct, although that is a matter for debate. However, in literary terms the cohortative 'be honoured' forms a natural pair with the cohortative 'take pleasure', and both verbs share the same subject, the first person of Yahweh. The balance of the evidence seems to point in that direction, and so my comments assume the cohortative form of 'be honoured' preserved in the *qere*.

The cohortative is a first person verbal form that normally carries a volitional sense. It is multi-hued in its possibilities, but two particular uses, at least in its singular form, may be noted. Where the speaker needs the consent of the addressee of the verb, it carries the sense of a request. Where the power relation is such that consent is not an issue, it is more likely to contain a strong expression of the will of the speaker. The ambivalence thus created is powerful in this context. It means that the phrase can be read in two different ways. First, in line with the thrust of the message from the Lord of hosts by the hand of Haggai, it may be an expression of hope that the temple be built so that Yahweh may experience pleasure and honour. Secondly, it may be an emphatic statement of Yahweh's response to the people's obedience in building the temple. Since both possibilities are relevant to the context, it is a reasonable reading strategy to permit both senses of the cohortative to coalesce at this point. The phrase 'so that I may take pleasure in it and be honoured' thereby becomes both a hope with respect to and a promise towards the people on the part of Yahweh. Read in that light the phrase is a reassurance to the people of God in Judah of the Lord's approval and presence. Therefore it is safe and necessary to proceed with building the house of the Lord. However, given the ambiguity of the cohortative, it is more than a power relation statement.

It is also an expression that Yahweh in some sense needs his people to respond to him by building the temple. So, the dissonance detected at the start of this argument is now to some extent resolved, as the pleasure and honour of God reflect back towards the people.

'Take Pleasure in'
Those comments have been based largely on the form of the verbs in question, but have taken no account of the lexical possibilities of the verbs themselves. Of the 54 occurrences of the root *rtsh* ('to be pleased, to take pleasure in'), a cluster of a dozen or so instances are essentially secular in character (e.g. Gen. 33.10; Ps. 49.13 [MT 14]; Prov. 3.12). Apart from them, though, the verb is overwhelmingly employed with God's people, or the key institutions that help to define that people, as its object. I note for instance the 'stones of Zion' (Ps. 102.14 [MT 15]), the land (Ps 85.1 [MT 2]), the sabbath years (e.g. Lev. 26.34), and numerous examples of the people (Est. 10.3; Jer. 14.10; Ezek. 20.40 are several among a number). The biggest single usage, however, is with reference to sacrifices within the Israelite cult that are acceptable or not to God. There are a cluster of references in Lev. 23.22-27 as well as elsewhere in Leviticus, and also a number in the prophetic literature (e.g. Ezek. 43.27; Hos. 8.13; Amos 5.22; Mic. 6.7). Malachi, the close companion to Haggai, also contains three such uses (Mal. 1.8, 10, 13), where the cultic acceptability of blemished offerings is in question.

In contrast, the usage in v. 8 is unique in two ways. First, it is the only time that the term *rtsh* is used with respect to the temple building itself. Secondly, it is the only time in the Hebrew Bible that the term is harnessed to the verb 'to honour' (*kbd*) by a shared grammatical object, namely, the temple. The application of the verb to the temple itself reinforces the cultic context that has been emerging from this discussion. The use of *rtsh* is a giant hint that in the prophet's mind the building of the temple is in the nature of a sacrifice. This concept is a natural companion to the proposal that the building of the temple is likened to gathering a bountiful harvest. As a successful harvest culminates in the offerings of first fruits, so the successful completion of the temple is the offerings from that particular harvest. At the same time, this usage within what is not a strictly sacrificial context has the effect of drawing together the ordinary life of the people, as expressed in the harvest metaphor, and the cultic life of the people, as expressed in the hints at a sacrificial backdrop contained in the terminology of v. 8b.

'Be Honoured'
This effect is reinforced by the linking of 'take pleasure in' with 'be honoured'. To see how this is the case, consider the meanings of the root *kbd*, the verb which lies behind the translation 'be honoured'. This multivalent root mostly carries a secular sense of 'weighty' or 'heavy', with connotations that are sometimes negative and sometimes positive. However, there are various figurative uses of the term that cluster around the concept of honour or glory. This is particularly the case with the niphal and piel forms of the verb. Despite the prevalence of the term, outside Hag. 1.8 there are only nine occurrences of the verb in a niphal finite form. Only one of them, in 2 Sam. 6.20, is arguably used in a secular sense, as Miriam accuses David of honouring himself by means of his unseemly dancing in front of the ark of the covenant and his subsequent appropriation of the priestly role in distributing the sacrifice. Of the remainder, God is the subject of the verb six times (Exod. 14.4, 17, 18; Lev. 10.3; Isa. 26.15; Ezek. 28.22), the servant once (Isa. 49.5) and the Lord's servant once (Isa. 49.5). There is an overwhelming interest in the honour of God in the way the niphal form of the verb is used. And on each of these occasions the honour or glory is seen in particular actions that God has taken. In the cluster of Exodus references, the action has been the hardening of Pharaoh's heart, Isa. 26.15 and 43.4 make reference to the increase of God's glory among the nations, and Ezek. 28.22 speaks in general terms of the judgment of God being executed. Only in Lev. 10.2-3 is there an explicit connection with sacrificial matters, where the fire of God consumes those who dare to make an unworthy sacrifice.

This survey of the usage of *kbd* suggests that the niphal form in v. 8 is in keeping with the possibility of God being glorified or honoured through the actions of others. It also raises the possibility that rebuilding the temple, the action through which God will 'be honoured', is not necessarily thought of exclusively as a cultic action. I have noted above that its pairing with 'take pleasure in' is unique in Classical Hebrew. The result is a paradox between a focus on the relationship between God and the people as mediated through cultic activity on the part of the people and through divine activity on the part of Yahweh. The temple rebuilding is both an offering on the part of the people in which God takes pleasure, and an action on the part of God by which he is honoured. It draws together the ordinary and the cultic life of the people. This is also of a kind with the link between the intimate and the transcendent in relationship between God and God's people sensed earlier in the text.

I noted above the potentially discordant note, at least to a postmodern reader, of the apparent purpose of the people's activity, that God may take pleasure and be glorified. Yet, when the possibilities of v. 8 are considered, it emerges that there is a strongly relational sense to the form of expression. There is also unarguably a Yahwist perspective, in tune with the responsibility for the narrative taken by 'the word of the Lord'.

Verse 9a
This section of the oracle is now concluded with a summary phrase. The first clause, 'you looked for much', is a neat echo of the opening clause in v. 6, which speaks of the people 'sowing much', and as such represents the hope invested in future possibility that is central to the act of sowing in anticipation of a harvest. The emphatic 'and, lo, it came to little' also echoes the outcome in v. 6, that the people 'harvested little'. The terms 'much' and 'little' are an exact reflection of their equivalents in v. 6.

The next clause, 'when you brought it home', also serves as a summary of the message so far, for it continues and concludes the play on words around the concept of a harvest. The verb 'bring' reflects the harvest of v. 6 and also the metaphorical harvest of materials to build the temple of v. 8 that I have already explored. Then there is an ironic reflection on the theme of 'house' that has been so important to the dialogue so far, for it is exactly the same term used to describe both the house of the Lord and the houses of the people.

The final clause in this section of the oracle functions both to summarize what has preceded it, and to foreshadow a clarification. It summarizes in that it reflects the divine perspective of the narrative also noted above, that the restoration of the house of the Lord results in honour and glory for the Lord of hosts (v. 7). Viewed from the same perspective, it is now stated that the failure of the wrong sort of harvest is not merely an impersonal cause and effect response to the loss of focus on the temple rebuilding. It is brought about by the divine will; the Lord 'blew it away'. This makes explicit what has so far only been implicit. It also looks forward to the final section of the oracle in which the agency of Yahweh is further elucidated.

Verses 9b-11

A Structural Question

The second half of v. 9 opens a further section in this oracle. There is a break in the pattern in several respects. The use of the expression *n'm yhwh*, translated by NRSV as 'says the Lord', is unique in this particular oracle although it is used extensively in ch. 2. The question 'why?' immediately before the oracular phrase is also unusual. From the *silluq* punctuation in MT it might be argued that the clause is a continuation of the thought in the first half of the verse, analogous to 'says the Lord' at the end of v. 8. However, there are a couple of reasons why the second half of v. 9 should be designated as an introduction to another unit in the oracle. The first clue is that the subject is the full 'Lord of hosts' designation in common with the openings of vv. 5 and 7. This contrasts with the shorthand form in v. 8, which is as an embedded clause emphasizing the divine perspective of the oracle. In corroboration of that point, I note also that embedding the oracular clause ('says the Lord of hosts') within the opening phrase is not unique to this particular section. The same phenomenon was present at the start of v. 5. For these reasons, vv. 9b-11 are treated as the final main section within the oracle, excluding v. 12, on which see below.

A Summary Reference and a Link

As an answer to the question, the prophet opens with a summary reference to what has gone before, and then further develops a link that has so far only been implicit. The summary is found in the recalled contrast, a contrast introduced in v. 4, between the different houses, 'my house' and 'your own houses'. The recollection is strengthened by repetition also from v. 4 of the term translated as 'lies in ruins', in Hebrew *ḥrb*. The contrast is also strengthened by a variation. Whereas in v. 4 the contrasted houses of the people were merely things in which they lived, here they are shelters to which they 'hurry off'. The verb *rvts* is well translated by 'hurry'. It speaks of an intentional and even urgent action. If the sin of the people was painted primarily as one of omission in v. 4, here it is more one of commission. As Yahweh through the prophet Haggai warms to his theme, the culpability of the people emerges more strongly and the divine perspective is increasingly apparent.

Accordingly, a new note of causality is now introduced. The cause and effect relationship between the desolate house of God and the people's experience of unsatisfactory harvest is only implicit earlier in the oracle. Now the term *'l-kn* ('Therefore') at the start of v. 10 makes the cause and effect clear. It is because the people have turned their backs on the house of the Lord that the experience of desolation is shifted from the temple to the people themselves. This is made clear by the play on words in v. 11 with the word 'drought', which translates the Hebrew *ḥrb*. The same term is used of the ruins of Yahweh's house in both v. 4 and v. 9.

'Withhold'

At the same time the agency of this desolation emerges, at first slowly and then more explicitly. This is first noticeable in the verb 'withhold' (v. 10). The term itself suggests deliberate action, although its subject at this stage is the heavens and the earth. In that respect it is somewhat euphemistic. The possible literal sense of the euphemism is hinted at in naming 'the heavens', *šmym*, as an agent, for it is generally accepted that by the Persian period this term has become a common shorthand for the God of Israel. From the start of v. 11, the Lord of hosts in the first person explicitly takes responsibility for the drought/desolation and all its effects.

Verse 11

Most English versions do not capture the emphatic Hebrew construction of the MT of v. 11. It is dominated by a single undifferentiated list with each item prefixed by and attached by *maqqeph* to the preposition *'l*. Literally, it reads thus: 'And I called drought upon the land and upon the hills and upon the grain and upon the new wine and upon the fresh oil and upon what the earth brings forth and upon humankind and upon the animal life and upon all the toil of their hands'. The list gradually proceeds through a similar but more explicit progression than that observed in v. 6. From the generality of the earth and the hills, it moves through the provision of food and drink and on to the more general comment, 'what the soil produces'. This last named is of a piece with the reference to clothing in v. 6. The summary statement in v. 6 on wages is also reflected in v. 11 by the reference to 'all their labours' (more literally 'all the toil of their hands'). The term translated by NRSV as 'labours' may carry the sense of meaningless work, and so reflects the metaphor of a bag with holes in it (v. 6).

The play on words from the creation tradition between the soil, *'dmh* and humankind, *'dm*, occurs in the middle of this list in the phrase 'upon what the earth brings forth and upon humankind'. This recalls the dynamic of the relationship between human beings and the soil from which they were created, so powerfully evoked in Gen. 2.7. There the dynamic is such that the human is both the culmination of creation and also implicated within it. The effect is similar in the words of Haggai. As a result the fate of these drought-stricken human beings enslaved by their futile labour is a sign of something even more significantly amiss within the cosmic design; something that in the thought world of the day only a restored temple was capable of addressing.

Verse 12

Zerubbabel and Joshua

As I have already argued, this verse concludes the second oracle. It represents the response of the hearers to the word of the Lord by Haggai, and in so doing is structurally analogous to v. 14 in the next oracle.

The first named respondents are Zerubbabel and Joshua. In this case the patronymic of each is included. There is one respect in which this particular reference is unique, however—namely, that the function of Zerubbabel as governor of Judah is not given. The break in pattern is notable, and there is no evidence of textual disturbance to suggest that it is other than deliberate. But does it have any significance? Although Hebrew narrative is generally more reliant on and patient of repetition than English and less concerned for variation as a stylistic device, the prerogative of the Hebrew authors to introduce variation for its own sake is mostly seriously undervalued by commentators. I suggest that the missing title may be attributed as much to the caprice of the author as to any particular intent in meaning.

It is, however, part of the debate already noted concerning the relative importance of Zerubbabel and Joshua in the schemes of Haggai and Zechariah 1–8. As I have explored in the Introduction and in my comments on v. 2, an oscillation occurs within the Haggai/Zechariah 1–8 tradition. On the one hand, the book of Haggai moves towards a clear focus on Zerubbabel at the expense of Joshua. On the other, Zechariah 1–8 moves towards an accretion of royal roles around the figure of the high priest, Joshua. I have concluded that the two figures should be read as representing a collective of the royal and priestly ideals. That collective continues in the reference to both figures in v. 12.

'All the Remnant of the People'
This time, though, the collective comes with the additional element, 'all the remnant of the people'. For two reasons 'all the remnant of the people' should be read as part of the audience of the entire oracle. First, the NRSV implies a primacy of Zerubbabel and Joshua over 'the remnant of the people' by translating the *waw* at the head of 'all the remnant' as 'with', thus creating the impression that the people follow behind Zerubbabel and Joshua. That implication is not present in the Hebrew. The collective singular verb *šmʿ* ('obeyed') stands at the head of the sentence, and is followed by the collective subject. The three elements of that subject, Zerubbabel, Joshua and the remnant, are grammatically undifferentiated.

The second clue in this direction goes back to the opening oracle, which says, 'These people say the time has not yet come to rebuild the Lord's house'. In speaking simply to Zerubbabel and Joshua, as he is doing in the first oracle, Yahweh refers to the people in the third person. In the second oracle Yahweh addresses a group directly in the second person about the matter of their houses. The flow of the narrative implies that this is the same group who are being spoken about in the first oracle—namely, the people. In support of this, Zerubbabel and Joshua are not named directly as recipients of this second oracle beginning at v. 3. On balance, then, the audience of the entire oracle is most likely to have been the whole group who respond in v. 12 to the words of the Lord. This progression is also implied in the different subjects of the two verbs of response that appear in the verse. First the collective group 'obeyed', and then 'the people feared'. For the second verb there is no differentiation between people and leaders at all. This incidentally is another argument both for inclusion of v. 12 into the narrative of the second oracle, and for differentiating vv. 1-2 as a separate oracle in its own right.

A question still remains, however, as to who is included in the phrase 'the remnant of the people'. There is a danger of investing the word 'remnant' with a theological content that it is not intended to bear in this particular context. The word can simply mean 'the rest', and thus refer to the unnamed section of the audience. In that case, it ought not to be taken to imply a special section of the people on the land, as some have argued. As already noted, the debate concerns whether or not the remnant should be read to mean the returning exiles as opposed to the resident local populace. This debate becomes more acute for the interpretation of the fourth and fifth oracles (2.1-19), but deserves a mention here. I have argued above that the experience described in this oracle, along with the assumptions about the temple and the presence of God behind it, is likely to have applied to the whole populace of Judah, those who have returned and those who were there all along. Therefore the response described in v. 12 should be taken to apply to that whole populace. As a result, the more likely understanding of 'remnant' in this verse is the 'secular' one, the undifferentiated mass of the people who with their two leaders heard the word of the Lord.

'Obeyed' and 'Feared'

As I have implied already, there are two key verbs of response in this verse, 'obeyed' and 'feared'. Both words are ambivalent, although the ambivalence has been reduced by the NRSV choice of 'obeyed' as a translation of *shm‘*, that great Hebrew verb of response. It is certainly the case that 'to hear' (*šm‘*) strongly implies to obey in the Classical Hebrew, but a response of obeying as a result of hearing cannot be assumed. There are many instances in which the commonplace verb *šm‘* simply refers to the physical action of registering a sound or a message. Even in the Shema itself (Deut. 5.1), the hearing is followed by specific responses that must be made. The narrative here contains the strong implication that a response of obedience is likely to follow, but as yet that is not assured. The second oracle thereby concludes with the question hanging: What will be the response to the heard word of the Lord?

This effect is reinforced by the second verb, 'feared' (*yr’*). Like *šm‘*, this common verb carries both a straightforward everyday meaning and a theological sense. It may simply refer to the human emotion, but it may also imply a sense of reverence or awe likely to be accompanied by a response of worship or praise. Again, what the verb is foreshadowing will emerge during the course of the rest of the narrative. There is also a cultic section of the semantic field occupied by *yr’* which forms a tantalizing part of the backdrop to this scene. This is illustrated in several places in the book of Malachi, particularly at Mal. 2.5 and 3.5 where the fear of the Lord is expounded in the context of the establishment of the temple. This adds further to the interaction explored above between the cultic and the everyday lives of the people.

Prophecy and the Prophet

There is also a telling comment on the nature of prophecy and the function of the prophet in this final verse of the second oracle. I have noted that in the post-exilic prophets there is a slight loosening of the bonds that normally equate the words of Yahweh with the words of the prophet, and a strengthening of the sense of agency on the part of the prophet. For example, we have seen that the word of the Lord came literally 'by the hand of the prophet Haggai' (1.1, 3). Now an epexegetical (explanatory) *waw* links two concepts, 'the voice of the Lord' and the 'words of the prophet'. This is followed by an intriguing ambiguity reflected in the NRSV translation 'as the Lord their God had sent him'. Although the voice of the Lord is the ultimate source of the message, albeit through the agency of Haggai, the object of God's sending is not the words or voice of the Lord, but the prophet himself. This is a further subtle reinforcement of the interaction of the human and the divine. The personal presence of the prophet remains to the fore, but in some way this presence becomes the message of God to his people.

HAGGAI 1.13-15A
(SECTION C, THE THIRD ORACLE):
'I AM WITH YOU'

This section contains what I will argue is the briefest of the oracles of Haggai, constituting in the Hebrew just two words, the copular phrase 'I am with you' (*'ny 'tkm*) in v. 13. Yet the importance of this brief message cannot be overstated. It constitutes an advance on the nature of the relationship between the people and Yahweh since the previous oracle, and at the same time is a response by Yahweh to the obedience of the people at the end of that same. This oracle in turn will culminate in further obedience, which itself will be a development in praxis. The people will move from obedience to action, or, from another perspective, from understanding to concrete obedience.

Structural Questions and Verse 15a

The Case for a Retrospective Date

Usually v. 12 is seen as the first verse in the section of narrative culminating at v. 15a. However, in the previous section I argued from the structure of the discourse that the narrative on the second oracle of Haggai ends at v. 12 with the response of obedience on the part of the 'remnant of the people', and that v. 13 is the start of the next oracle. I argued that among several reasons for thinking this was the parallel between the response of the people in v. 12 and the response of the people in v. 14. Each is a response of obedience to a word spoken by Haggai as messenger of Yahweh, and therefore each points to a parallel structure between the two oracles.

Part of the reason for a reluctance to concede that v. 13 is the start of a new oracle is the absence of a date, whereas each of the other oracles begins with a date. Indeed, this is only one of two pieces of level 1 discourse that has no date (see Appendix A). However, I have already argued that 1.2 should be treated as a distinct oracle within the Haggai narrative as a result of which 1.3 becomes the introduction to the second oracle. That second oracle also is not dated, yet the strong discourse parallels with the other prophetic ascription formulae in Haggai outweighed the absence of the date. The same could be said to apply here. 'Then Haggai, the messenger of the Lord, spoke' functions as a level 1 statement in the discourse analysis that I have proposed, and hence an introduction to a new oracle within the narrative.

If there is no date at the start of the oracle, however, this is not to say that the oracle is not dated. Rather, the date comes at the end in v. 15a, indicating that the obedient response of the people to the oracle begun in v. 13 took place 'on the twenty-fourth day of the month, in the sixth month'. The prophetic narrative then moves into the fourth oracle dated 'in the second year of King Darius, in the seventh month, on the twenty-first day of the month' (1.15b–2.1). Admittedly, to read it thus goes somewhat against the grain of the Leningrad Codex preservation of Masoretic manuscript division and accentuation, but it does make sense of the consonantal text.

Juxtaposition of Dates

There has been extensive discussion on the juxtaposition of the two dates, much of which revolves around the integrity or otherwise of the text. There are several points to be made in support of my proposal that the date in v. 15a should be read retrospectively. I note first that it is in tune with the coherence of the narrative shape and direction as indicated in the discourse analysis. That point on its own cannot be decisive, as it is vulnerable to the accusation of circular argumentation, but several other corroborating points can also be made. First, a survey of each of the level 1 introductions to the oracles in Haggai reveals considerable variation among them. Sometimes 'the year of Darius's precedes the month and day (1.1; 2.1) and sometimes it is preceded by the month and the day (2.10). Sometimes the regnal year is left out of the date entirely (1.15a; 2.20) and sometimes it is not (1.1, 15b; 2.10). On one occasion, I have argued, a date is not given at all (1.3). This level of variation suggests that a date at the end instead of the beginning of the oracle may simply be another variation to the pattern. There are times when we should allow the author some rhetorical variation, and this is such a time.

A Parallel Dating Pattern

Notwithstanding the variations noted above, there is a parallel pattern evident when the first three and the second three oracles (roughly coinciding with chs. 1 and 2) are placed next to each other. The first oracle in each pair begins with a date patterned, 'In the second year of King Darius, in the ___ month on the ___ day of the month' (1.1, 15b). And the dates of the third and final oracle in each pair, while varying in form slightly from one another, both abbreviate the date to exclude the regnal year (1.15a; 2.20). This is a further argument in support of the dating formula in 1.15a as a conclusion to the third oracle in the Haggai narrative.

Haggai within the Narrative

Further support of the oracular introduction in v. 13 starting a new section is found also in the name and attribution of Haggai. With the exception of the account of the dialogue with the priest in 2.1-9, the name of Haggai only appears in level 1 of the discourse, as an introduction to an oracle. This renders it inherently likely that that is the case in v. 13 also. At the same time, each such appearance, with the exception of the culminating oracle in 2.20-23, contains some kind of descriptor of the prophet. Normally he is described as 'prophet', *nby'*, while here he is described as 'messenger', *ml'k*. For the purposes of discourse analysis, I suggest that the two terms may be thought of as equivalent, although I will argue below that the difference does carry a narrative significance. This approach achieves a satisfactory explanation of the juxtaposition of the two dates which is in tune with narrative patterns within the text.

Verse 13

Messenger, Message and Work

The form of introduction of this oracle indicates a subtle variation. The prevailing ownership of the narrative has up until now been with Yahweh. So far the word of the Lord has always come, in a literal translation of the Hebrew, 'by the hand of the prophet Haggai' (1.1, 3) and will do so again in 2.1. Haggai has functioned within the story so far as little more than a conduit for the message of Yahweh. But there has been a hint of a further narrative layer in the interjection of the phrase 'says the Lord' at several points in the first two oracles (1.5, 7, 8). This makes us as readers aware that although these are the words of God, they are being spoken by a human agent, and so we are conscious of the persona of Haggai, however vague his outline has so far been. Now there is a change as Haggai becomes the subject of the active verb in the sentence, 'Haggai...spoke to the people'. Accordingly, he has a different ascription attached. He is now the 'messenger' of the Lord.

There is a literary effect of which the narrator takes full advantage. Not only is Haggai the 'messenger' (*ml'k*) but he also conveys the 'message' (*ml'kwt*). The response of the people, according to the NRSV, is that the hearers of the message 'worked on the house of the Lord of hosts'. More literally translated, 'they did the work (*ml'kh*) in the house of the Lord of hosts'. The English is not able to capture the play on words between the three terms, 'message', 'messenger' and 'work'. Most lexicographers assume that all three derive from the same triliteral, *ml'k*. Even if that is not the case, the writer has indulged in a significant pun at this point. The effect is to announce that the work of the people is a direct result of the message of Yahweh, and is in fact its fulfilment. Theirs is a response to the message that 'I am with you', just as theirs was a response in v. 12 to the preceding oracle commanding them to harvest the materials necessary for the temple rebuilding.

Haggai's Status as Messenger

If Haggai's status as 'messenger' gives him an enhanced ownership of the message itself, it also introduces a tension around the understanding of prophecy in the newly post-exilic period in which Haggai did his work. The term *ml'k* at this stage probably occupies a semantic field that embraced both human and non-earthly messengers. Later in the Second Temple period it came to mean heavenly rather than earthly conveyers of the message. Early translations of the material indicate this trend. The Targum of the Minor Prophets reserves the word *ml'k* for heavenly messengers, and so in terms of its own lexical assumptions is compelled to translate 'messenger' in 1.13 as 'prophet'. Haggai is clearly a human figure so could not, in the Targumic mindset, be a *ml'k*. The LXX approaches the problem from a different angle and somewhat uncomprehendingly translates 'messenger' as 'angel' (*angelos*), an unlikely reading for a human figure. Each decision, the Aramaic and the Greek, represents the Second Temple differentiation between earthly and heavenly messengers.

This shift in understanding also coincides with the rise of apocalyptic and its accompanying move away from unmediated prophetic words in favour of messages mediated by heavenly messengers to the apocalyptic visionary. The application of the term 'messenger' to Haggai should therefore not be read merely as a synonym for prophet. It is a term that also functions to boost confidence in the veracity of the message, given a dawning uncertainty regarding the authority of the prophetic figures in their own right. This is corroborated by the situation concerning Malachi, Haggai's companion among the restoration prophets. It has been argued that Malachi represents not so much a proper name as a figure identified as 'my messenger' (*ml'ky*). That this figure is nowhere described as a 'prophet', in the way that both Haggai and Zechariah are, lends weight to this argument. The only prophet mentioned in the book of Malachi is Elijah, who stands at the fountainhead of the great tradition of classical prophecy. That Elijah is so distinguished from this anonymous messenger of Yahweh described as 'Malachi' is further evidence of this shift in understanding of which Haggai is a part.

In Answer to a Question
The message spoken by the messenger is the simple but profoundly significant phrase, *'ny 'tkm*, 'I am with you'. The significance lies as much in the context in which these words are heard as in their substance. In commenting on the previous oracle I remarked on the debate over the 'myth of the empty land'. There I suggested that the loss of key symbols in the Davidic and temple ideologies would have had a devastating effect as much on those who remained on the land as on those deported to other parts of the Babylonian empire during the

exile. For such people, the loss of their God's approval would have been of paramount importance. The question facing Haggai's audience is therefore whether or not this approval has been restored. Is a return to the hopes invested in the land and the temple as well as in the Davidic ideology a real possibility or not? The previous oracle has taken the people some way to an answer to that question with the affirmation that God would 'take pleasure in [the rebuilt temple] and be honoured' (1.8), but that affirmation had a future cast to it. Although Zerubbabel, Joshua and the people responded positively to the possibility at the conclusion of the second oracle (1.12), it still remains to be seen whether or not the Lord's pleasure will in fact eventuate. Will their obedience truly be well founded and efficacious?

The People
That is the unspoken question lurking behind this brief third oracle. And the answer comes as an assurance which emerges in two significant ways. First, the text indicates that the audience was the 'people' (*'m*). This polyvalent term can be used, particularly in the post-exilic period, to refer to any ethnic group, but it carries a strong sense of self-definition. It may also be contrasted with the *goyim*, those who are not of the 'people', and so different from the 'people' (*'m*) of God. It is a term routinely used of those with whom Yahweh made a covenant (e.g. Exod. 6.7; Hos. 5.9-10; Amos 7.15). Its persistence as the term of choice for the covenant people encourages the reader to see the people in question as in relationship with the God who promises to be pleased with their obedience. This relationship, which has so far formed the backdrop to the narrative, moves towards the front of the stage in v. 14 with the understated yet significant attachment of the possessive pronoun to 'God', giving 'their God'. I will explore that significance further below.

Covenant Echoes
If the covenant significance of the term 'people' is largely implicit, the simple message itself, 'I am with you', is more explicit. On the one hand, it specifies that God is indeed pleased and honoured, as he said he would be. The expression taps into the yearning for assurance that the people are not

called out to work alone and without the company of the God they worship. This yearning has its roots in the institution of the Sinaic covenant, and especially in the strange events of Exodus 32–34. Whatever else may have been going on in that mysterious encounter between God and Moses at Exod. 33.12-23, it was in answer to the question posed by Moses, 'how shall it be known that I have found favour in your sight, I and your people, unless you go with us?' (33.16). Just prior to this, Moses had in fact received the promise that '[God's] presence will go with you' (33.14).

The choice of words at this point is not accidental, as it intensifies the covenant echoes implied in this brief oracle. The word *'tkm*, 'with you', is not as common as we might suppose in the Classical Hebrew corpus, and when it does occur it regularly does so in the context of covenant talk. This is the case in Gen. 9.11 and the covenant with Noah, and Judg. 2.1 and 2 Kgs 17.38 with respect to the Mosaic covenant. A variation on the phrase occurs at Deut. 4.23, again in the context of the cutting of the covenant, this time using a different preposition (*'mkm*) but to the same effect. The reminders of covenant that echo behind the words of this oracle are further earthed by a resonance with 1 Chron. 22.18, in which the Lord promises to be with Solomon in his building of the first sanctuary. Thus, the phrase 'I am with you' does much more than assure the people of God's ongoing presence with them. It is also a reassertion of the covenant, and an echo of the link between the covenant and the sanctuary that the people are now called upon to rebuild. In the previous oracle, the prophet conceptualized the task as that of rebuilding an existing ruined building (1.8); and a further link will be encountered in the next oracle when the 'former glory' of the old temple is recalled (2.3). It is therefore inherently likely that the promises made to Solomon at the initial building of the temple are echoed at its rebuilding in the re-established province of Judah. Against a background of dysfunction and uncertainty at the loss of their undergirding ideology, the people may now be confident that God is indeed pleased and honoured by the task to which they are about to set themselves. The temple may be rebuilt.

Verse 14

The Response
The response to this assurance is as dramatic as the response to the previous oracle: 'They came and worked on the house of the Lord of hosts, their God'. In this description, a gradual development of a sense of call may be seen as we contrast this verse with the equivalent response verse at the end of the previous oracle (1.12). There, the people 'heard' (NRSV 'obeyed') the voice of the Lord their God (1.12); now, they work on the house of the Lord of hosts their God. The difference between the two stages may be found in the fact that 'the Lord stirred up the spirit' of the leaders and people. I return below to an examination of that concept.

Apart from the literary effect already noted of the phrase '*śh ml'kh* ('they did the work'), it is interesting to note that the same term is used of those who worked to repair the temple in the time of Josiah (2 Kgs 22.5-6). This reinforces the point made above that this temple is not conceived so much as a new second temple but as a restoration of the original temple. This is another one of the implicit links with the older temple that is emerging.

Their God
But first, the recurrence of the expression 'their God' is a point of connection with the contents of the oracle itself. Just as the epithet 'I am with you' is pregnant with covenantal significance, so is the expression 'their God'. This occurs in two ways, one explicit and one implicit. Explicitly, it recalls other occasions where the possessive pronoun has been attached to God. More frequently, this is found when God is speaking and refers to himself as 'your God' (Exod. 6.7; Isa. 51.15-16; Ezek. 20.20; Hos. 1.9; Ruth 1.16) but the effect is the same. And the instances are redolent with meaning, as in the struggle for release from Pharaoh, the words of promise of the prophets and the poignant story of Ruth. All focus in different ways on the covenant relationship, and each echo reinforces the point of the oracle that God is with the people.

Implicitly, the term recalls the natural companion to 'their God' or 'your God', and that is the term 'my people'. The two come together at at least two significant moments in the memory of the returning Jews. The first is in the story of the plagues and the deliverance from Egypt. At a time when Pharaoh is referring to 'your God' in addressing the Hebrew slaves (Exod. 8.25), Moses delivers the message from God that Pharaoh is to release 'my people' (Exod. 7–12). The commitment of God to those who are now rebuilding his temple is thereby located in that central event in the people's memory. The second occasion is in the message of the prophet Hosea who negatively links together 'your God' and 'my people' through the name of his second child by Gomer (Hos. 1.9). The child is named Lo-Ammi, 'not my people', and carries within himself the message from God that 'you are not my people and I am not your God'. The final outcome of the book of Hosea is that, although this is true for the moment, finally the people and the God of Israel remain yoked in some way (Hos. 14). The response of the people to the message of Haggai is made in that context and is an enduring expression of that fact. Haggai's close companion in the work of restoration, Zechariah, expresses a similar confidence, more explicitly in a vision of Jerusalem in which 'They shall be my people and I will be their God' (Zech. 8.8).

Those Who Respond
Those who are doing the work and are being assured of God's presence with them are exactly the same group as those who responded with obedience in v. 12. The only difference is that this time the titles of Zerubbabel and Joshua, governor and high priest respectively, are included. I argued in the previous section that this difference between vv. 12 and 14 should be taken as a stylistic variation and a deeper significance should not be sought. Once again, 'the remnant of the people', as I argued at v. 12, should be taken to be the entire populace who are hearing both this and the previous oracle. It is unlikely that the term indicates a distinction between the incomers and the settlers on the land. Once again, the leaders and the people together are affected, as an ongoing reminder that any work of God needs both leadership and a grassroots involvement.

The narrative reinforces this by the specific inclusion of the 'remnant of the people' with the leaders as those who have their spirits 'stirred up' (on which phrase see below). The syntax of the verse has a subtle double effect. On the one hand, the order of the corporate subject continues to place stress on the two leaders and particularly Zerubbabel. On the other, the inclusion of the people in a composite subject of a singular verb means that God's dealings have, to employ a convenient anachronism, become democratized. The whole people may be confident of God's presence and therefore respond to God's call. This itself is a message on leadership. As the leaders respond, so the people are enabled to respond; at the same time, the leaders on their own are not a sufficient response, for the people's obedience is also necessary.

'The Lord Stirred up the Spirit'
That the Lord 'stirred up the spirit' of the recipients of Haggai's message is significant in two ways. First, it introduces into the narrative an oscillation between the active response of the people and the initiative of the divine sovereign. In the context of a growing obedience comes the action by God to enable that obedience. In that respect this is in tune with the progression from hearing/obeying the voice of the Lord in the previous oracle (1.2) to actually doing the work (v. 14). In the previous oracle, the obedience is entirely the responsibility of the people as subject of the verb. On this occasion, the activation of that obedience on the work of the temple is harnessed by God stirring up the spirit of the participants. Thus do the two forces of human obedience and divine enabling work together in the field of godly achievement.

But it would not do justice to the phrase simply to individualize it. Observation of its use in the exilic and Persian contexts is instructive. The Lord stirs up the spirit of the Medes against Babylon (Jer. 51.11), the spirit of various kings of Assyria against Israel (1 Chron. 5.26), the anger of the Philistines and the Arabs against King Jehoram (2 Chron. 21.16) and the spirit of Cyrus to issue the edict for the return of the Hebrews from exile in Babylon (Ezra 1.1). On each of these occasions the spirit of a Gentile is stirred and on each occasion the context is political. There is only one instance outside of this reference in Haggai of the spirit of Israelite people being stirred up, and that is in the response of the heads of families to the edict of Cyrus which led to the restoration of the people to Judah (Ezra 1.5). By employing this phrase, the narrator alerts readers to the political and temporal undertones of the development of the temple. While those who argue for a primary economic or political motivation behind these oracles overstate their case, there is no doubt that the restoration of the temple is in part a political response to the return to the province of Judah and the re-establishment of the people's sense of nationhood. Its reassurance of God's presence in the restoration project has an outcome in the political life of the people.

'House of the Lord of Hosts'
The expression 'the house of the Lord of hosts' is unique in Haggai in that it is the only point at which this unabbreviated title for God is used in construct relationship to 'the house'. The result is a culmination to the oracles so far. The obedience of the people is now consummated. The succeeding series of oracles in ch. 2 in effect work out the significance of that obedience. From here on the 'house of God' will not be mentioned again in those terms. The focus will be on the people and the land, now that the commitment to the temple has been secured.

Verse 15a

And so it comes to pass some 23 days after Haggai first spoke the message of the Lord of hosts that, buoyed by a new-found confidence in God's presence, the people and their leaders begin work on the restoration of the temple. For detailed comment on the retrospective application of the date, and the separation of v. 15a from v. 15b structurally, see above on v. 13 and in the next section on 1.15b–2.1.

HAGGAI 1.15B–2.9
(SECTION D, THE FOURTH ORACLE):
'THE LATTER SPLENDOUR'

The fourth oracle of the Haggai narrative opens a major new section. The last part of the previous oracle stated that the people and their leaders came and 'worked on the house of the Lord of hosts, their God' (1.14). This new section of narrative, running through to the end of ch. 2 and incorporating the final three oracles, details the significance of the people's work, addresses questions implicit in the whole enterprise of rebuilding the house of the Lord and reveals God's response to the people's response. Accordingly, there is a shift in the pattern of the discourse. Up until now the narrative has functioned largely at two levels and the chief participant has been Yahweh (through his agent Haggai) with the people and their leaders as occasional respondents (see Appendix A). Now it moves into a more complex discourse structure, with up to four levels of discourse in the remaining three oracles. The subject continues to be Yahweh, but the participation of the subject within the narrative is enhanced. The result is a greater level of engagement with the audience of the oracles in that there is greater scope for inference.

Verses 1.15b–2.1

There is some debate over the dating material in 1.15–2.1. See the previous section for the argument that v. 15a refers back to the third oracle while the material beginning 'In the second year of King Darius's contains the date for the fourth oracle that runs through to v. 9. That being the case, and as a corollary to that argument, there is an exact replication of the dating formula from 1.1. These are the only two occasions in the book where the dates are formed in this particular way. The literary effect of this is two-fold. First, it marks out for the reader the start of a major new section, and implicitly the end of the first major section. Secondly, it indicates progress from the conclusion of the previous oracle that the people came 'and worked on the house of the Lord of hosts'. That progress will gradually unfold over the next three oracles.

The conflation of the two dates in 1.15–2.1 has occasioned much text-critical comment. I have suggested that there is a literary coherence in the progression through the oracles based around the dating formulae. In that spirit, it is possible to discern a literary effect in the current form of the dates. The clause 'in the second year of King Darius's can be read both retrospectively and prospectively, and thus as applicable to both the third and fourth oracles. This adds to the effect of continuity as the third oracle slides into the fourth through the mechanism of the blended date.

There is also repetition of the introductory formula. Just as was the case in the opening of the Haggai narrative, 'the word of the Lord was in the hand of Haggai the prophet'. However, there is a difference. On that earlier occasion the word was 'to' Zerubbabel and Joshua (1.1). On this occasion the audience is not named, principally because it is by now well established. In that sense the abbreviation of the introductory formula is a further hint at the continuity between chs. 1 and 2, alongside the slightly more active role for Haggai that is emerging and the slightly different narrative structure that is in store for ch. 2. The fourth oracle brings both continuity and discontinuity.

Verse 2

The differences are immediately evident at the start of v. 2. First, in contrast to the opening oracle of ch. 1, this oracle is not issued directly 'by the hand' of the prophet. Rather, the prophet himself is enjoined to speak to Zerubbabel, Joshua and the people through the imperative 'speak' and the connected untranslatable particle of entreaty (*n'*).

That God should address Haggai in these terms suggests a second difference. The prophet now participates with Yahweh in conversation where previously he has primarily been a conduit. Haggai is now responsible for a communicative layer in the discourse. The particle *n'* regularly occurs in the prophetic literature when God is dealing with his people, and its effect often is to highlight the role of Yahweh as participant in the narrative and conversely the contingent responsibility of those with whom Yahweh converses (e.g. Isa. 1.18; 5.3, 5; 19.12; 47.12, 13). The effect is the same here. The trend glimpsed in the previous oracle of Haggai's enhanced role in the narrative as 'messenger' (1.13) is now being worked out.

Haggai's audience remains the same as in the previous two oracles, Zerubbabel, Joshua and the people. Together they continue to form a collective object; the title and patronymic of the governor and high priest continue to occur; Zerubbabel continues to receive an implied priority in the narrative; and the term 'the remnant of the people' continues to be used as before to express all the people of the land affected by the temple rebuilding project.

Verse 3

A Series of Questions

As the oracle proper begins, the prophet remains the silent participant as the Lord himself indicates the content of the message. Once again, in an echo of the second oracle, the problem to which the oracle responds is encapsulated in a question. The presenting problem in the first series of oracles was organized around the question: 'Is it time for you...to live in panelled houses?' (1.4). The rest of the first chapter was spent exploring the answer to that question and its consequences. An important stage in that exploration was the further question, 'why' the people should rebuild the temple (1.9). Now there are a series of questions raised by the narrative: 'Who is left among you that saw this house in its former glory? How does it look to you now? Is it not in your sight as nothing?' At the level of literary form, this continues the effect of a new section paralleling ch. 1.

Much has been made of the question–answer format in the book of Haggai. One fruitful line of enquiry is that it reflects the Deuteronomistic tradition that has produced such forms as the one found in 1 Kgs 9.8-9. There the historian, probably in the exilic period, calls forth as mute witness to the disobedience of the people the sight of the ruined temple. The questions of Haggai echo that tradition, but they also contradict it in that they represent an advance. In the new post-exilic context, they now function for the people both as an echo of the explanation for the disaster that has befallen them and as an assurance that the time has come for them to move forward safely and experience again the blessing of Yahweh.

A further rhetorical effect wrought by the questions posed here is to maintain a strong sense of audience for subsequent readers. The narrative primarily belongs to Yahweh, with some increasing involvement from Haggai the messenger over these last couple of oracles; the recipients of the message have no explicit voice. Nevertheless, to a degree unusual in classical prophetic literature, readers remain aware of those recipients. This began back with the question concerning panelled houses (1.4), and continued with the rehearsal in 1.6 of the woes of the people. Indeed, there are a couple of syntactic hints in the last two of the three questions that a contrastive dialogue is being set up between the way the people see things and the way that Yahweh sees them. This comes about first through the participial effect of a continuous present in the second question. A literal translation renders it thus: 'And how are you seeing it now?' The result is a portrayal of the people's perspective. This is reinforced in the next question, which contains the clause 'in your eyes' placed emphatically at the end of the verse. The hesitations about the glory of the temple are very much from the point of the view of the people. The contrasting perspective of the divine is about to emerge.

The explicit inclusion of 'the people' as part of the audience along with their leaders also continues the effect. Now the voice of that audience is heard again by means of these questions. Not only do we sense their despair and anxiety, but we also glimpse the march of the generations as we hear the reference to memory of an earlier time.

The People's Memory
Where the first chapter began with the houses of the people, this one assumes the shift in focus that has been achieved by those same people. They are now at work on the house of their God, and so the inevitable comparison arises between what they see now and what once stood on the site. This sets the scene for the reflection on covenant life connected with the

temple that dominates the rest of the book of Haggai. As a rhetorical link there is a play on words in the Hebrew between the 'remnant' (*š'ryt*) of the people' (v. 2) and those who are 'left' (*nš'r*, v. 3) who may have seen the temple prior to its destruction. These superimposed images shift the scene from oracular introduction to the actual message of Yahweh.

At a more literal level, the superimposition raises the possibility that the 'remnant' which Haggai had in mind was no more than that small group of people who survived the Babylonian experience and now are able to bring to the rebuilding project a distant memory from youth of the temple prior to its destruction in 587 BCE. As I noted in the Introduction, there is some speculation that the question of v. 3 is fuelled by a prophet who himself once saw the temple in its original form. There is no way of assessing that possibility, and an answer either way is not critical to a literary appreciation of these verses. What is relevant is that there were some among the people for whom the earlier temple is a physical memory.

This is a different perspective on the term 'remnant' in the book of Haggai than the one often purveyed. I have argued previously that a division between the local Samaritan populace and the returning Judeans is not likely to be reflected in the term. This is all the more the case given that the recipients of this oracle are both 'the remnant of the people' (v. 2) and the 'people of the land' (v. 4), a term sometimes taken to refer to the local populace as opposed to the newly resident Judeans. There seems to be no such distinction evident in the text of this fourth oracle, except as a possible literary echo of a small number of people whose lives spanned the exile experience.

Given a space of nearly seventy years between Nebuchadnezzar's destruction of the temple and its rebuilding under Darius I, Haggai's oracle can hardly be relying on a literal and accurate memory for the force of his message. More relevant to the reception of the message is the likelihood that a collective memory has grown up among those who experienced the exile from Judea, a memory that included some idealization of the splendour of the temple. This would have been partly fuelled by the natural processes of nostalgia and partly by the active interest in and hope for the restoration of the temple that was nurtured during the exile. This is supremely expressed by Ezekiel in his final vision of the temple (Ezek. 40–48), but is a recurrent theme throughout his prophecies (e.g. 8; 11; 25.3). It is surely not a coincidence that Haggai's 'house of the Lord' (*byt yhwh*) terminology exactly reflects Ezekiel's. This would have had a further effect of idealizing the temple. A sense of the former glories of the temple would have been all the more poignantly felt in that the emerging rebuilt temple at this stage was indeed a pale reflection of what once was. All of these dynamics lie behind the question that Haggai poses about the former glory of the temple.

With that in mind, we might wonder also how Haggai's question about the temple's former glory may have impacted those who had never departed from the land. I suggest that the same effects of nostalgia would have been in operation over the two or three generations since the destruction of the temple. It is not difficult to imagine that those who lived in regular sight of the ruined stones, and who perhaps themselves had quarried the site for recycled building materials, would have built an idealized image of the way the building used to be. This would have been reinforced by those who remembered the days prior to the temple's destruction. They may not have invested the image with the same religious content, but Haggai's questions would nevertheless have also been the people's questions.

The 'Former'

The term 'former' functions as a descriptor of the glory of 'this house'. Although recent academic study of this era of history has labelled it the Second Temple period, there is no apparent sense in Haggai's expression of the words of the Lord that the building in question is a 'second' temple. The Hebrew syntax is explicit that the building currently being worked on once possessed a 'former glory'. This is consonant with the message of the second oracle which perceived the house of the Lord of hosts as being 'in ruins' (1.4, 9). Haggai is talking about the restoration of the ruined house; not its replacement. This is reinforced by the Hebrew metaphor expressed by the English translation 'in ruins'. The metaphor is of 'desolation' (*ḥrb*), the same term applied to the drought stricken land mentioned in the same oracle (1.11). The land is not to be replaced but restored to fruitfulness; so the temple is not to be destroyed and replaced but restored (on the term 'restoration', see n. 15 in the Introduction). As has also been seen, there is a close link between this concept and the agricultural cycle in the thought of the second oracle.

'Glory'

The comparison between the older and the restored forms of the temple is made in terms of its 'glory'. This theme has already been hinted at in the second oracle where the motivation for rebuilding was to be that the Lord may be pleased and 'be honoured' (1.8). The verb *kbd* used in that instance was the root from which the word translated as 'glory' (*kbwd*) is derived. There the term was used with a strong sense of the honour of the Lord. This honour is upheld both through the actions of Yahweh himself (as, for example, in Exod. 14.4, 17, 18 with respect to the plagues in Egypt) and through the actions of others on Yahweh's behalf. Only in a derived sense is this honour or glory connected to sacrificial or cultic matters. In referring to the 'glory' of the temple at this point, the Lord through the prophet is making a judgment on the extent to which it honours the Lord. The rhetorical questions in v. 3 assume that in the minds of the listeners there is little apparent honouring of God in the temple as it now is, either in that it conveys little sense of the activity or presence of God or in that there is little honouring of God evident on the part of the people.

The Targum on the Minor Prophets associates this honour or glory in the temple much more closely to a tangible sense of the presence of God. This is evident by its use of the term *shekinah* in 1.8 to translate the 'glory' (*kbwd*) of the MT. This term strongly locates the presence of God within the temple itself while the MT, and indeed also the LXX, are content to see the temple as indicative of God's honour through the people's activity. In that sense, the Targum invests the text with a cultic focus that remains merely implicit in the MT. The glory of God is something that is evidenced by the rebuilding of the temple in the MT, rather than by the temple itself as the Targum implies. The difference serves to highlight an important aspect of this reading of the MT of Haggai, namely, a focus on what the building is saying about the people of God and their relationship with Yahweh.

But to return to the worry of lost honour, by this stage, less than four weeks after the revival of the project, a depressing sense of the size of the task and an awareness of how poor the initial efforts look has probably set in. It is not entirely clear if this loss of honour relates to the state of the ruined building itself or to the rather inadequate attempts of the newly established community to restore it. In one sense, the ambiguity is appropriate, for both possibilities are effectively addressed by the Haggai oracle. It has been seen that the second oracle assures the people of God's approval of the project to rebuild. This oracle continues that line of thought in addressing the problem of the ruin, but it also looks forward to the possibility that even if the rebuilding is accomplished, the result may not be worthy of the original temple or, by implication, of the Lord's pleasure. That is why the prophet goes on to address the question of the 'latter splendour' (v. 9) in contrast to the 'former glory'. The rhetorical effect of this question to the people is to link the two concerns, the failure represented by the ruined building and the potential risk of restoring it in an inadequate fashion. The Lord through Haggai has addressed the former concern, and will shortly have more to say on the latter by way of encouragement.

'As Nothing'
As well as the question relating to the 'glory' of the temple, Yahweh asks the people if what they see is 'as nothing' (*k'yn*). The term *'yn* on its own is a negative particle that can be used in a number of quite mundane ways, and as such does not normally attract any particular significance. In that sense, it may be said in this context to indicate merely a contrastive effect between the lack perceived by the people and the glory itself. However, in this case it is attached to the comparative preposition *k*. Care should be taken not to put too much weight on this, but the form with this particular preposition is relatively rare, occurring on only five other occasions (Isa. 40.17; 41.11, 12; Pss. 39.5 [MT 6]; 73.2). The Isaiah references are instructive, for on each occasion they are used to contrast the honour of God or his people with those who would set themselves up in opposition to that honour, whether they be the nations who claim god-like status (Isa. 40.17) or those who pose a threat to the people of God (Isa. 41.11, 12). The issue is

similar here, and it is possible that Haggai's audience would have appreciated echoes of the prophetic voice that came to them during their sojourn in Babylon. It is a further reminder that the prophet's interest in the temple is not driven as much by a concern for the physically located presence of God as by a concern for the honour of God and his people with respect to the building project.

Verses 4-5

The pattern continues of challenge and encouragement. In the second oracle the Lord commanded a harvest of temple building with the motivation that 'I may take pleasure in it and be honoured' (1.8). Thus he answered the unspoken question as to the legitimacy of the people's actions in the light of the covenant curses that seemed to have befallen them in the loss of their land and temple. Now he responds to the people's concern over the inadequacy of the building with both an exhortation to take courage and a further promise of support.

A Textual Issue

The editor of the *BHS* raises the possibility that the MT includes a number of later scribal additions in v. 4, although he adduces no manuscript evidence in support. If he had his way, v. 4 would read like this: 'Yet now take courage, O Zerubbabel; take courage, O Joshua; work for I am with you, says the Lord'. In fact, the literary coherence of these verses as preserved in the MT and as illustrated below suggests the integrity of the received text.

The Audience

The people addressed continue to be the same trio of governor, high priest and people that introduced the oracle. The only difference here is that the patronymic and title of Zerubbabel has been omitted. Any number of points have been made about this omission, and usually they reflect the concomitant arguments about audience on the part of those who make them. As already noted, there is some primacy for Zerubbabel that seems to arise during the progress of the Haggai narrative, but the reason for the omission at this point remains inscrutable. It is as likely to be a feature of style, either for variation or for summary, as anything else. Certainly, to take it as evidence of a reducing focus on Zerubbabel denies much else in the progress of the narrative.

Of more interest is the third segment of the audience of Haggai's words, 'the people of the land'. Thus far those who hear the oracles along with their leaders have been described as 'these people' (1.2) and 'the remnant of the people' (1.12, 14; 2.2). Now we have a new descriptor, the same as that used in Ezra 4.4 and Neh. 10.30, in each case of a body of people who are hostile to the returning exiles and their restoration projects. If that is the intention here also, then it is a surprising usage. Up until now Haggai has been concerned with 'the people' or even 'the remnant of the people', which some have argued depicts those who have returned as against the adversarial 'people of the land' described by Ezra and Nehemiah. However, that argument breaks down in this context, as here both terms are used synonymously. 'The people of the land' (*'am ha'aretz*) in this oracle seems to reflect the older use of the term in the Deuteronomistic History to depict the local Israelite citizenry (e.g. 2 Kgs 11.14-20; 15.5; 16.15; 21.24), which has been retained by the Chronicler (e.g. 2 Chron. 23.13-21; 26.21; 33.25; 36.1). This terminology is also depicted in the exilic utterances of Jeremiah (e.g. Jer. 34.19; 52.25) and Ezekiel (e.g. 7.27; 22.29; 33.2). Significantly, the term is often used of the people's involvement in some of the epoch-making affairs of state (see, e.g., 2 Kgs 11.14-20; 21.24; 2 Chron. 23.13-21; 33.25; 36.1). By using this term, the Haggai narrative recalls those moments of significance and implies an expectation that the actions of the people in restoring the temple will turn out to be equally significant.

The term 'people of the land' is also used occasionally in the pentateuchal material of the local populace, sometimes Canaanite (Gen. 23.12; Num. 14.9) and sometimes Egyptian (Gen. 42.6; Exod. 5.5). It is in that sense that Ezra and Nehemiah apparently use the term, and perhaps Haggai echoes that here. If so, this further reinforces the point that a clear distinction between the local populace and the returning exiles cannot be part of an understanding of the audience of these oracles. Indeed, the choice of such a multivalent term is further support for the notion that both groups of people are represented in Haggai's audience. As I have argued, the message of restoration was relevant to each in different ways, and the restoration of the temple provides a response to each set of needs. That the message is explicitly directed at '*all* the people of the land' further distinguishes Haggai's use of the term from that of Ezra and Nehemiah.

'Yet Now'
As for the message itself as it continues in v. 4, remember the possibility argued above that the questions in v. 3 reflect both the tragedy of the temple's ruin and nervousness about the adequacy of the restoration attempts. The questions reflect the perspective of the people. Now v. 4 brings the divine perspective in response, and it opens in the MT with the adverbial particle *w'th*. Especially with the *waw* attached, the term normally conveys a strong link with what has just preceded it. Sometimes that link is consequential and sometimes it is contrastive. Both senses are in operation here. What follows is a response to the fears expressed in the rhetorical questions of v. 3, but it is also a kind of contradictory assertion of God's presence with the people despite the evidence in their minds of his absence. Once again the people are reassured that they are not alone.

'Take Courage'
The reassurance begins with an emphatic exhortation to 'take courage'. The emphasis comes through the repetitive attachment of the singular imperative form to each member of the audience in turn. Often in Hebrew syntax a single occurrence of the verb will suffice for several elements in a collective subject. In this case, the verb is repeated as a deliberately emphatic rhetorical effect.

The qal imperative, *ḥzq*, has not been well translated by the NRSV as 'take courage'; that sense is more likely to be found in the hithpael form. The implication of the NRSV translation is that the message is one of comfort, perhaps along the lines of encouragement to the people not to fear. However, the intent of the Hebrew is more hortatory than that. The people and their leaders are being asked to stand firm, to prevail, to be strong. This is to be expected if the 'people of the land' as audience has been correctly understood. As such, they have been used to appearing at key moments in the history of their nation and land and exercising their influence. Now they are to do so again as they rebuild the temple. So, the command is not merely that they be brave, but that they be strong and effecttive. This is a natural continuation of the call to work to the end that Yahweh may be pleased and honoured (1.8). The three-fold repetition of the verb reinforces that.

'I Am with You'

Both the grounds for courage and the reason to act are that 'I [the Lord] am with you'. This is an exact echo of the oracle in 1.13 which prompted the people to work on the house of the Lord. As in that earlier context, this phrase links building the original sanctuary with rebuilding the ruined sanctuary and in so doing recalls the important theme of covenant. In the previous oracle this was done in the context of the command to start building. In this oracle, the link is made in the context of questions about the adequacy of the building task. The people have already been assured that God is both with them and honoured by the task they are accomplishing. Now that is conveyed again as they eye the rather inadequate restoration of the ruin. And again the history of God's dealings with the people is recalled in the intertextual echo of covenant conversations. By linking this to the command to 'take courage', the significance of which has been explored above, the narrator reinforces the portentous nature of the moment.

'Says the Lord'

As if to emphasize the point, v. 4 contains an important cluster of the oracular indicator normally translated as 'says the Lord (of hosts)' ($n'm\ yhwh\ [tṣb't]$). Two out of the three indicators are attached to the commands to take courage while the third is attached to the assurance that 'I am with you' and completes the set with the added emphasis of the full title of 'the Lord of hosts' rather than the abbreviated form used with the first two. The form $n'm$ occurs as a verb only once (in Jer. 23.31). The noun form patterned after the qal passive participle, which appears in the formula here in Hag. 2.4 and often in the prophetic books, is much more common. Although most English versions usually translate $n'm$ as if it were a finite verb, the phrase in which it occurs is more properly rendered 'a judgment/utterance of Yahweh'. It normally appears, as it does in this verse, as extraneous to the syntactical flow of the utterances. Its function is therefore emphatic in some way, probably to draw attention to the origin and authority of what is being said. That is certainly the case here. Both the requirement to be strong ('take courage') and the assurance of God's presence come with an emphatic evocation of the God of the covenant.

A Textual Issue in Verse 5

If this has so far only been implicit in the intertextual echoes of the prophetic oracle, it is now made explicit by the prophet's turn of phrase at the start of v. 5. First, however, it is necessary to establish a position on the textual puzzle created by the absence in the LXX of the entire first line of the MT, 'according to the promise that I made you when you came out of Egypt'. Other early versions also follow the LXX. In contrast, the MT verse begins awkwardly with an object indicator that appears to have no verb governing it. The result is a strong case for some textual disturbance at this point. The NRSV masks the problem with the phrase 'according to' which does not reflect the MT. A variety of solutions have been offered, none of which are entirely satisfactory. One of the governing commitments of this commentary is to give the benefit of doubt to the received text where possible. Accordingly, I suggest that the principle of *lectio difficilior* (the assumption that the more difficult reading is likely to be more authentic by the fact of its preservation) may apply in this instance, and that the translation offered by Meyers and Meyers provides a way forward. They connect the command in v. 4, 'to work' (also translatable as 'to do' or 'to act'), with the object, 'the promise that I made', at the start of v. 5, and suppose that the statement 'for I am with you' has been interposed between imperative verb and object as a kind of parenthesis. In my literal translation of this suggestion, the result is thus: 'Do (for I am with you [an oracle of the Lord of hosts]) the word which I cut with you when you came out of Egypt'. While the result is a little strained and certainly unusual in terms of Hebrew word order, it is not impossible and it does make sense of the received text. This on its own would not be sufficient warrant for the solution suggested, but there is also a literary argument that asks for the preservation of the beginning of v. 5.

'The Word that I Cut'

Before turning to that, however, there is another technical issue to address, this time concerning translation. The literal translation given above of the first phrase in v. 5, 'the word which I cut', draws out an effect in the Hebrew which is not strongly enough evoked by the NRSV (following its parent, the RSV), 'the promise that I made'. The NIV (in tune here with the AV) renders the phrase in question as 'what I covenanted with you'. At least in respect of its appreciation of the covenantal echoes of the verb 'cut' (*krt*), the NIV has captured the strong implication of the Hebrew, although in making it explicit has destroyed the subtlety of effect inherent in the Hebrew.

There is an important inference evoked by the clause, 'the word which I cut with you'. The term *krt*, 'cut', is regularly employed to describe ordinary actions, such as cutting down a tree, or cutting off, or more metaphorically rooting out. More often, though, it is used with 'covenant' (*bryt*), as its object. 'To cut a covenant' is a well-recognized idiom to describe the fact that a covenant was traditionally sealed by the ritual cutting up of an animal. An example of this is seen in Gen. 15.18 where the Lord made a covenant with Abram. The first person qal perfect form, such as is present in Hag. 2.5, almost always occurs with Yahweh as subject and 'covenant' as object. The only exception is in this phrase, 'the word which I cut'. The echo of the covenant-making activity of God is inescapable in this context. As such, it is a natural development of the covenant echoes in the phrase 'I am with you'. The resulting literary coherence therefore becomes an argument for the retention of the first line of v. 5 as authentic despite the syntactic awkwardness that is present.

As this echo is in the context of a command relating to the current activity of rebuilding, so there is a further historical echo into the contemporary situation of Haggai and his audience. Just as there is a sense in which they are participating in the same movement of God that resulted in the original temple, so now they are in some way continuing to participate in the covenant-making activity of God. They are part of a common thread with their history, rather than a radical discontinuity.

'Out of Egypt'

There is a further echo of the history of God's dealings with Israel in the reference to their coming out of Egypt. Again, this is a classical form of expression evoking the memory of those days. In using it, Haggai follows in the strong tradition of his predecessors, most evident in earlier members of the Book of Twelve. Hosea, Amos and Micah in particular all do their work in the eighth-century crises and all recall God's action in bringing Israel out of/up from the land of Egypt. Only in Mic. 7.15 is Haggai's idiom, 'coming out of' Egypt, replicated exactly; the close relative, 'coming up from' Egypt, is more common (Hos. 2.15; Amos 2.10; 3.1; 9.7; Mic. 6.4). In each instance the phrase recalls God's goodness and faithfulness to the people. In each also there is an implied rebuke that contrasts God's faithfulness with the people's unfaithfulness. In the different restoration context the element of rebuke is not so relevant, but the memory of God's faithfulness reinforces the message that God is with them.

Although the reader may find in the idiom an echo of warning that this time God's presence should not be ignored, that is not the primary point of the reference to Egypt. Of more immediate concern to the hearers of the oracle is the worry either that their efforts are not pleasing to God or that the resulting building is not an adequate reflection of God's glory. To each concern comes this further reinforcement that they need not 'fear', to add to the assurance that the God who once brought them out of Egypt is with them and that he is of a mind to be pleased and honoured by their efforts.

'My Spirit Abides'

Immediately prior to the command not to fear is the striking assertion that 'my spirit abides among you'. If one reads the opening *waw* attached to 'my spirit' as a sequential conjunction, then the presence of God's spirit among the people functions as a reason to do the work that they have been commanded to do (v. 4). The reason for doing the work and the assurance that God is with them continue to pile up on one another. At a literary level, the phrase provides a link back to the narrative section of the previous oracle in which we are told that the Lord 'stirred up the spirit' of Zerubbabel, Joshua and the people. The response of the people as their spirits are stirred up now finds its echo in the divine spirit.

But there is much more to be said about this phrase. It is striking in that the turn of phrase employed here is found nowhere else in the prophetic corpus or indeed in the Old Testament. There is plenty about 'my spirit' or the spirit of Yahweh/God. There is also an awareness of God's spirit being with or upon or in the midst of one person or a group of people, yet this is almost always expressed with a preposition as part of a copular phrase. What is unique here is the verb '*md*, translated by NRSV as 'abides'. As a result, this is a stronger statement than that found anywhere else in the Old Testament of a permanent presence of the spirit of Yahweh among the people. What exactly the author and his hearers/readers may have understood by that is explored further below, but, as a first observation, the strength and permanence of the verb is striking.

An examination of the phrases 'spirit of Yahweh' and 'spirit of God', along with the term *ruach* or 'spirit' with a possessive pronoun linking it to Yahweh, is instructive. Most obviously, it carries a generic sense of the presence of God (Ps. 139.7; Isa. 40.13). It also has a less common sense of God as creator spirit. In that respect, the possibilities of Gen. 1.2 occasionally surface in the Psalms (Ps. 104.30) or wisdom literature (Job 34.14). An extrapolation of the idea of creator spirit leads to identification of the creative spirit in craftsmen (Exod. 31.3; 35.31). The concept of the spirit is also commonly linked with the prophetic impulse. This is either in the sense of individuals conveying the words of God under the influence of the spirit (1 Sam. 10.6, 10; 1 Kgs 18.12; Neh. 9.30) or of some visionary experience that has a prophetic function (Ezek. 11.24; 37.1). Most famously, this sense occurs in the promised democratization of the prophetic impulse of which Joel spoke (Joel 2.28, 29). Occasionally, there is a more subtle development of the notion of the spirit enabling action to be undertaken on behalf of God or in obedience to God. For instance, God's spirit is resident in the Isaianic servant (Isa. 42.1) and is invoked by Ezekiel as an aid to the people's faithfulness on the land (Ezek. 36.27). Interestingly, this last example alerts readers to the theme of the spirit as a force that gathers people in the land and enables them to live there. This is found principally in the exilic utterances of Ezekiel (Ezek. 36.27; 37.14; 39.29), but also has an echo in Isaiah of Jerusalem (Isa. 34.16). The

Ezekiel examples are all numbered among the relatively few occurrences of *ruach* with the first person singular possessive suffix with reference to Yahweh ('my spirit'), such as is present here in v. 5.

Putting all this together, readers may sense a number of echoes in the hearts of those who hear these words and seek to be obedient in the land that has been restored to them. The echoes of Ezekiel, who offered hope during the wait for this to happen, are uppermost. Haggai's oracles then come as an affirmation of Ezekiel's prophecy; their restoration to the land and to the institutions of that land is indeed a fulfilment of the hopes of the exile. At the same time the prophetic impulse would almost certainly have been implicitly invoked by this phrase; the presence of God's spirit abiding among the people and with their leaders reassures that the words which they obey are genuine prophetic utterances, and their ongoing work in rebuilding a temple and a community of faith is undergirded by the settled presence of God's prophetic spirit among them.

As a result, the oracle retrospectively applies the assurance that 'my spirit abides among you'. There is also a forward-looking aspect in two respects. The echo of God as creator spirit is relevant to God's restorative work in creation (v. 6) as a response to the desolation of the land identified in the second oracle (1.11). And the echo of God as the one who gathers people to the land links forward to the anticipated shaking of the nations (v. 7).

Earlier it was noted that the reference to the spirit of the people (1.14) both invoked a political significance for the obedience of the people and their leaders and conveyed a sense of the sovereignty of God behind the obedience of the people. By means of the literary link between God's abiding spirit and the spirit of the people, those people have been caught up into the work of God's spirit re-creating, gathering, declaring and enabling faithful living on the land.

Verses 6-8

The Lord of Hosts
The most intense concentration of the full divine name, 'Lord of hosts', that there is in the book of Haggai is found in these

few verses and running through to the end of the oracle. Given its prevalence throughout Haggai, one could argue that even the name *yhwh* is in fact an abbreviation of the fuller name (see my comments on 1.2 regarding this name). But just here it is spelt out in full each time. Given that the name, among other things, conveys the fullness of the divine sway throughout God's creation, it is appropriate that it should receive this emphasis at the point in the text where the question of the glory of God is most explicitly addressed. The literary effect of the repetition is to highlight the authority with which this assertion of the glory of God comes.

Prophetic Aspect
At this point in the oracle a future cast creeps into the language, although in the aspectual nature of the Hebrew verb system that is less explicit in the MT than in the English translation. Accordingly, it is a future cast that flows from what has so far been uttered by God and experienced by the people as recipients of the prophetic narrative. This is evident from the introductory *ky*, translated as 'for', which connects what is to follow with what has preceded, and it is an early hint that the basis of the command 'do not fear' (v. 5) is both God's experienced presence and God's future action.

The future aspect begins with the idiom translated as 'once again, in a little while'. The phrase itself is problematic. One possibility is that the word *'ḥt*, meaning 'one' or 'once', has intruded into the standard idiom that has the sense 'again in a little while'. The result could be read as a contradiction in terms, one element denoting a one-off event and another describing an ongoing effect. A variation on the phrase in the LXX has suggested to many commentators some textual disturbance at this point. However, on the assumption that this phrase is intended as a poetic effect, it is a compressed and to some extent paradoxical expression but one which does make sense in literary terms. The Haggai narrative has been struggling to understand the continuity of God's work in the context of the radical discontinuity introduced by the destruction of the temple and the exile. Now it uses a temporal expression that combines continuity and discontinuity. Yahweh will yet again work in the way that has so far characterized him, but will do so in a manner that is unique. Both elements are present in the clause too tidily translated by NRSV as 'once again'. Quite apart from any of this, the term introduces a sense of anticipation and imminence into the narrative that has so far not been as evident. The reader and hearer are asked to take notice.

'I Will Shake'
The use of the predicative participle with the personal pronoun at the start of v. 6, translated by NRSV as 'I will shake', is a further indication that this future action is rooted in present events. The ambiguity of the turn of phrase permits the future translation but could equally be rendered 'I am shaking'. The subsequent *waw* plus the imperfect construction of the key verbs in v. 7, 'I will shake' and 'I will fill', supports the English translator's choice. Nevertheless, to the Hebrew ear the future referred to is likely to have been understood very much in terms of the present. As will be seen below, this is consistent with the trend of thought that emerges from the vocabulary used in the oracle. The *waw* consecutive forms of the subsequent verbs, 'I will shake [all the nations]' and 'I will fill', should then be read as the outworking or consequence of the introductory predicate participle 'I will shake [the heavens]'. There is a sense in which the cosmic shaking will have a historical outcome within the nations and with respect to the house of the Lord that is being rebuilt.

The term 'shake' (*r'š*) either in nominal or verbal form occurs mostly in the prophets and to some extent in the writings, and so Haggai is drawing on a vein of prophetic tradition in the form of expression here. It may refer to the physical phenomena of earthquakes and other similar natural upheavals (Amos 1.1), but as it is used in the prophets it generally has a more portentous impact. As has been the case on more than one occasion in reading Haggai, the prophet echoes the work of his exilic predecessors, Jeremiah and Ezekiel. Both prophets regularly use this term in the context of God's glory and judgment (among many examples see Ezek. 3.12; 38.19; Jer. 10.10, 22; 47.3). And both often use it to describe the effect of God's judgment on various of Israel's neighbours (Edom, Jer. 49.21; Babylon, Jer. 51.29; Tyre, Ezek. 26.15; Egypt, Ezek. 31.16). It is therefore a natural term for Haggai to use as he describes the impact of God's glory as he acts among the nations. Yet, unlike his predecessors, who also use the term to foreshadow the coming judgment against Israel, Haggai has re-directed the metaphor. Now it heralds a gathering of the nations into Israel. This difference typifies the shift in focus achieved by Haggai and Zechariah as they move beyond the judgment of God and concentrate on the reconstruction of the people of God. Perhaps Haggai has picked up a clue again from Jeremiah (Jer. 4.27) who in the context of the quaking of judgment promises that God 'will not make a full end'. Now he sees the evidence of that.

For some commentators the metaphor of shaking indicates a shift towards a more apocalyptic conceptualization of Israel's enemies, less rootedness in temporal affairs and a more distant future focus. However, it is difficult to see how this could be the case here. As has emerged so far in this reading, Haggai has maintained an unrelieved focus on the moment and its significance. This focus will follow through until the end of the final oracle, when 'on that day' Zerubbabel will be chosen 'like a signet ring' (2.23). There is much more to be said about that phrase in the context of comment on the final oracle, but for now it is sufficient to note that right to the end of his prophetic narrative Haggai is working with contemporary events and people in mind. This must induce caution about ascribing an eschatology to the narrative that is not closely moored to contemporary events.

Notwithstanding that, Haggai's expression does introduce a portentous tone into the narrative. There is a significance that listeners and readers cannot yet fully glimpse. Haggai is working within the wider eschatological tradition that looked to the intervention of Yahweh in ways that will have a cosmic impact (see n. 22 in the Introduction for the sense in which I am using the word 'eschatology' and its derivatives). Yet this is not an intervention for the distant future; it is something that Haggai's hearers begin to see as they experience the glory of God through the rebuilding of the temple. This is reinforced by the object of the shaking discussed above, 'the heavens and the earth and the sea and the dry land', which foreshadowed the Second Temple period conceptualization of the eschatological significance of the temple such that it transcended its physical realities.

That Which Will Be Shaken

Yahweh promises to 'shake' a number of things. At a literary level the continuity referred to above is expressed in the fact that the Lord will shake the 'dry land'. This feminine noun is assumed to come from the root, 'be dry/dried up' (ḥrb), hence 'dry land'. The masculine noun already encountered meaning 'desolation' or 'ruin' or 'drought' is probably derived from a different but orthographically identical root, 'be waste/desolate' (1.4, 9, 11), and has a feminine counterpart with the same meaning and the same consonants as the noun meaning 'dry land'. The result is a pun that links the compromised land and temple with what Yahweh is promising to shake. The reference to the 'dry land' is additional to the commonplace reference in ancient cosmology to the entire cosmic order, 'the heavens and the earth and the sea'. The unusual addition of 'dry land' emphasizes the literary link back to the province of Judah and the temple. At the same time, the eschatological significance of the temple is foreshadowed by the reference to the entire created order.

Haggai also brings the promise of God to 'shake all the nations'. In doing so he continues to reflect the exilic prophecies of Jeremiah and Ezekiel, who use the verb $r^{\varsigma}š$ as a metaphor for the effects of God's judgment on both the natural order and on the nations or peoples affected (e.g. Jer. 4.24; 8.16; 10.10; Ezek. 26.10; 38.20). In this respect, it conveys that rebuilding the temple will have an impact on the nations that surround the reconstituted people of God in Judah.

'The Treasure of All Nations Shall Come'

The result of this impact is that 'the treasure of all nations shall come'. This phrase is a *crux interpretum* in the book of Haggai. The interpreter needs first to determine what may be intended by the term translated by NRSV as 'the treasure', then to ask who 'the nations' might be and finally to wonder what this 'treasure of the nations' may be doing when they 'will come'. An examination of the various uses and forms of the term ḥmdh ('treasure/desirable object or person') indicates that it most commonly concerns some kind of physical reality. Sometimes it simply means 'valuable' (Ezra 8.27). Occasionally, the value is not so much in its commercial cost as in its significance to the one who speaks about it. For example, the 'land' is precious or pleasant (Zech. 7.14; Ps. 106.24). A person may also be precious, as in the description of Saul as 'Israel's desire' (1 Sam. 9.20) or Daniel as 'greatly beloved' (Dan. 9.23). Ezekiel achieves a poignant connection of these two uses in the prophetic message arising from the death of his wife. She who is the 'delight of his eyes' (Ezek. 24.21) becomes a symbol of the sanctuary, described as the delight of the people's eyes (Ezek. 24.25). The two ideas come together in the concern for the precious temple vessels, whose commercial value as objects made of precious metals helps to invest their less material significance as consecrated objects of status in the temple worship (2 Chron. 32.27).

Any or all of these echoes might be expected to reverberate in Haggai's usage. In the context of the discussion concerning the adequacy of the temple building, an interest in objects of commercial value which will boost the splendour of the temple is clearly part of the equation. Given the expectation of imminent divine portents that the verb 'shaking' partly implies, this 'treasure' might also be expected to hold significance for the people beyond its physical value. It is also part of the indication of divine approval.

Some have highlighted this transcendent aspect, noted the singular term, literally 'a treasure', taken one strand of meaning that describes a person as a 'treasure' or 'beloved one' and then invested the term with a messianic significance. This is represented in the AV translation 'desire of nations', the roots of which go back at least as far the Vulgate translation and which is still alive in some recent English version translations (for example NIV, 'the desired of all nations').

Against this, I note the grammatical oddity that the singular subject 'treasure' preserved in MT takes a plural verb 'will come'. That is not a strong argument on its own as Classical Hebrew, much more so than the Indo-European linguistic tradition, is routinely capable of ignoring rules of agreement. However, the LXX translates the singular 'treasure' of MT with a neuter plural substantive, *eklekta*, 'the chosen things'. This suggests either that the translator interprets the phrase in physical terms or that he/she is representing a plural tradition of pronunciation of the consonantal text. In either case, this evidence must be taken seriously. The context of temple splendour already noted above strengthens the case for the plural represented in the LXX. As a further point, the poetic effect of the first line of v. 7 makes it inherently likely that the 'treasures' are something that emerge from 'the nations'. A literal English rendering of that line reads thus: 'And I will shake [object indicator] all the nations and [they] will come/bring the treasures of all the nations'. The repetition of 'all the nations' (*kl-hgym*) as the final element in each stich suggests that the 'treasure' is more than something that happens to the nations; it emerges from the nations. In that light the nations themselves are likely to produce the treasure as an outcome of the shaking that they will experience from Yahweh.

The image taps into some rich strands of Israelite hope, of which both Haggai and his audience would have been aware. At the most obvious level, it recalls the fate of the temple vessels that became a metaphor for the experience of the people who use them in worship. Jeremiah recalls with horror their loss to Nebuchadnezzar and his treasury (Jer. 52.17-23), Daniel continues to echo the insult to God's name felt by the exiles (Dan. 5) and a key moment in the return from exile is when Ezra is given these self-same vessels to return to their rightful home (Ezra 1.7). As a literal historical statement, in 520 BCE when these oracles are dated the nations have yielded treasure for the greater splendour of the temple. This seems a more likely account of the immediate echoes than the traditions of booty from the holy war and tribute paid by vassal states.

At the same time, this prophetic oracle is not merely temporal. In tune with the eschatological echoes that the prophet has already invoked by his choice of the verb 'to shake', there is a hint of the notion that grew during the exile of a day when the wealth of the nations would be released to Israel, and the nations themselves would stream towards Zion (e.g. Isa. 2.2-3; 56.1-8). This perhaps lies behind the statement that 'the treasures of all nations shall come'. It is true that Haggai's focus remains on the immediate problem of the quality of the temple and its acceptability before God; and it is true that the re-establishment of the institutional temple would be a huge fillip to the local economy. But it is also true that the release of the temple vessels is a first instalment in a much bigger process that is hinted at but not specified.

'The Nations Shall Come'

This is reinforced both by the term used for the 'nations' and by the fact that their treasures 'shall come'. To consider the verb first, the idea of the nations coming (the Hebrew verb is *bw'*) is in tune with the picture of an eschatological gathering into Israel noted above. Secondly, as also noted above, the term *goyim* for 'the nations' is emphasized by the structure of the first line in v. 7. There are two main terms used in the Old Testament to express ethnicity, *gwy* and *'m*. The former is likely to refer to the non-Israelite nations while the latter is likely to refer to Israel, and usually does so particularly in a covenantal context. The distinction is not absolutely observed, and there is some evidence of its breakdown in the Deutero-Isaianic exilic tradition. Even allowing for that exilic prophet's agenda of destabilizing the Israelite sense of superiority over its neighbours, the Deutero-Isaiah usage indicates that the two terms could on occasion be used synonymously (e.g. Isa. 42.6; 49.22; 58.2; 66.8). Nevertheless, in this context the consistent reference to Haggai's audience as the *'m* ('people') means that the reference to 'the nations' (*gwym*) brings an emphasis on the gathering of foreign wealth into the temple.

'Splendour'

As already indicated, in the grammatical structure of vv. 6-7 the divine shaking of the cosmos has two outcomes relevant to the concerns of the prophet and his hearers. First, God will shake all the nations, and the significance of that turn of phrase has been considered. Secondly, and in parallel with that action, God will 'fill this house with splendour'. The term translated by NRSV as 'splendour' is *kbwd*, the term elsewhere translated as 'glory' or 'honour'. This promise therefore comes as an echo and a response to previous oracles. It reflects the hope of the second oracle (1.8) that the people's action in rebuilding the temple would bring honour to Yahweh. It also reflects the further question about the 'former glory' of the temple (v. 3). The answer is that the house will be filled with God's glory/'splendour'. It is interesting to note that in previous oracles God's glory is seen as an outcome of the efforts of the people in rebuilding the temple. Now God's glory in his house is a direct result of divine action. Part of the answer to the poverty-stricken nature of the second attempt at a temple is the promise that the people are not required to do it on their own; they are participants in an event of eschatological significance. Thus the delicate oscillation between human and divine initiative continues to express itself.

There is a subtle interaction between the two events of v. 7, the shaking and filling. There is not a simple causative relationship between the two as some have argued. To read it thus is to miss the poetics in the syntax. Rather, they are parallel but closely related events. The reduction of this vision to economics depends on the assumption of causation; that the splendour or glory of God is a result of all the treasure that the temple attracts. A preferable way to read is that both the glorification of God in the temple and the influx of treasure are the result of God shaking the entire created order. The wealth that results is a visible and compelling sign of God at work, but that work and that glory is greater than simply the temple treasures. Thus continues the interplay between the institution and the charism in the relationship between Yahweh and his people.

Silver and Gold Are Mine

This does not mean the sign is unimportant, however. The emphatic statement of v. 8, 'the silver is mine, and the gold is mine', ensures that the treasure of the nations is understood at least partly in material terms. It also reinforces the sense of immediacy to this oracle already noted.

Verse 9

The conclusion to Haggai's fourth oracle is a ringing response to the questions raised in v. 3. Knowing that the Lord is with them, and sensing Yahweh's own imminent intervention in the temple building, the people are now assured that the rebuilt temple should not be regarded 'as nothing' (v. 3). Indeed, if they think that their efforts are puny in contrast to Solomon's, they should think again. The opposite will in fact be the case.

From what we know about the rebuilt temple, this statement owes more to poetic exuberance than to a sober assessment of the facts. The reader might well ask: Wherein lies this 'greater' splendour? In the terms of the oracle itself, this hope is based on two developments that move beyond the function and perception of the original temple. First, it is now part of an eschatological vision in a way that the earlier temple was not. Within the Judaism of the Second Temple period, there gradually developed a vision of the temple as in some sense the very cornerstone of the created universe. The beginning of this process may be discerned in Ezekiel's vision of the temple (Ezek. 40–48), and is found in more developed form in the Temple Scroll preserved by the Qumran community (see my comments on the temple in the Introduction). Haggai here is drawing on a tradition that has been planted and nurtured in the soil of the exile experience.

Secondly, in line with the Deutero-Isaianic vision of the nations among an augmented Israel referred to above, this renewed temple is to receive international homage and tribute on a scale beyond anything experienced by the first temple even in the utopian days of Solomon. This is found at such moments as the expression that God's servant Israel will function as 'a covenant to the people, a light to the nations' (Isa. 42.6), and in the much more material expectation that 'the wealth of Egypt and the merchandise of Ethiopia...shall come over to you and be yours' (Isa. 45.14). In the minds of Haggai and his listeners, the redevelopment of the temple begins to create the conditions under which these visions of the exile may receive their fulfilment.

The intentional repetition of the demonstrative pronoun by the prophet enhances the effect of immediacy, as the greater splendour will be for 'this house' and prosperity will be experienced in 'this place'. At the same time, its repetition serves to link the 'house' with the 'place', implying that the prosperity experienced will flow beyond the temple into the 'place', which I take to mean the wider context within which the temple will function. In that respect, the link between 'house' and 'place' looks both forward and back in that it echoes the second oracle's identification of the people's material want with lack of attention to the temple (1.4-6) and it foreshadows the promise of material prosperity with which the next oracle concludes (2.19).

However, the term 'prosperity' is an unfortunate representation of the Hebrew *shalom*. The NIV and other translation traditions do better with the translation 'peace', but even this does not quite capture the sense of the Hebrew. 'Prosperity' is an inadequate translation as it focuses on commercial wellbeing, which is a subset of the outcomes of *shalom* but is considerably less than the entirety of *shalom*. The promise of this oracle is that God's glory will be expressed as the fulfilment of all human dreams of harmony, wholeness, prosperity and wellbeing in the widest sense of the term. The concept is in tune with the way this whole oracle has balanced delicately between the eschatological and the immediate in its expectations, for it can imply a future hope and a cosmic vision while also responding to a temporal need.

A long LXX addition at the end of v. 9 is presumably a gloss on the idea of *shalom*. It may be translated thus: 'and peace of soul for protecting [or strengthening] those who are bringing about the building of the temple'. This narrowing of *shalom* to the idea of reward for the builders seems out of touch with the balance between the eschatological and the immediate that has been a feature of the oracles of Haggai to this point (see the Introduction for further on this LXX plus).

HAGGAI 2.10-19
(SECTION E, THE FIFTH ORACLE):
A PROPER OFFERING

This is the fifth and penultimate prophetic oracle in the Haggai narrative. Because of its apparent incongruity with the material surrounding it, if the purpose of this oracle within the Haggai narrative as a whole can be discerned, then considerable progress will have been made towards grasping the scope and significance of Haggai's vision. Indeed, I suggest that the very sense of dissonance and paradox that this oracle imposes is itself integral to the message of Haggai, both for the people of his own day and for subsequent readers.

There are several strands to a sense of dissonance encountered in these verses. Within the Haggai narrative the priestly concern for purity is unique to this oracle. This is apparently at odds with themes of honour and shame that have so far motivated the narrative. This focus on the particular in itself seems to a modern (or postmodern) reader to be unfortunately at odds with the breadth of vision that has so far been in evidence. Notwithstanding the final part of the oracle, there seems to be a distressing focus on the mundane. This in itself introduces the conundrum that the people have been enjoined to build the house of the Lord so that the Lord may be honoured, but now find that they have been doing so with unclean hands (v. 14); what they have to offer as a building is compromised from the start because of the uncleanness of the builders. One of the challenges of this section will be to consider this apparent Catch-22 situation.

In terms of the discourse, also, there is a departure from the pattern that has so far obtained. Up until now the discourse analysis has not gone below three levels. We have encountered Yahweh and the prophet and the objects of their oracles, namely, the people and their leaders, Joshua and

Zerubbabel. The opinions of the people have remained implicit while their response of obedience has become more and more explicit. There is embedded in this oracle a further conversation between Haggai himself and the priests which introduces a fourth level of discourse (see Appendix A).

Verses 10-11

A Significant Date

This oracle is dated on the 'twenty-fourth day of the ninth month', still in the 'second year of Darius'. This means that it comes some two months after the previous message, and exactly three months since the people 'came and worked on the house of the Lord of hosts' (1.14) on the twenty-fourth day of the sixth month. It is therefore unlikely that work would have progressed much beyond the initial stages of gathering the necessary materials for rebuilding and planning their deployment (see 1.8). Any sense of a completed edifice emerging would have still been in the future. Nevertheless, the oracle contains a number of hints that there was something special about this day. Verse 15 asks the people to note 'this day' as some kind of a watershed moment, and v. 18 equates the date with a foundation laying. The effect is reinforced by the recurrence of the date in the body of the oracle (vv. 10, 18). I will discuss in more detail in the context of v. 18 exactly what, as expressed in the NRSV translation, the 'foundation of the Lord's temple' may have entailed, but suffice to say at this point that some special stage was marked and confirmed in the rebuilding of the temple, a stage that was to produce a lasting memory.

Introduction to the Oracle

There is a small shift in the idiom used to introduce the prophetic oracle. Apart from the variation in 1.13 around the term 'messenger' considered earlier, the previous oracles were all introduced with the phrase that may be literally expressed, 'was by the hand of the prophet Haggai'. The primary effect of this idiom was to emphasize Haggai's function as a conduit of the word of the Lord as distinct from the prophet's own involvement in the oracle itself. Now the word of the Lord literally 'was to Haggai the prophet saying...'; the idiom 'by the hand of' has been omitted. It is possible that this is simply shorthand for the earlier oracular introductions; it is also possible that the effect is to enhance the involvement of Haggai himself in his own oracles as the narrative moves towards its culmination, an involvement that was identified as incipient in the description of Haggai as 'messenger' (1.13). Gradually the prophet is emerging into clearer focus as a participant in the narrative. This time he is part of the story as he engages in conversation with the priests.

The Place of the Fifth Oracle in the Haggai Narrative
The fact that the final oracle will be introduced in exactly the same manner on the same date with the added note that it is a 'second' word from the Lord (2.20) is also significant. There are several literary features which will be explored in the context of a discussion of 2.20-23 that expand on the link implied by the date. However, the significance for the present discussion relates to the charge that this fifth oracle is a literary and theological interloper in the Haggai narrative. It is said to be so for the reasons of dissonance and paradox already noted in the introductory comments above. In addition, there is a natural connection between the cosmic shaking promised by each of those oracles and the linked concepts of 'treasure' at 2.7 and the 'signet ring' of the final oracle (2.23; for further on this link see on 2.23). This is used to reinforce the view that the intervening conversation about purity is somehow out of place. However, the uniqueness of the oracular introduction to each of the last two oracles militates against such a conclusion. The narrator clearly intends the readers to associate these last two oracles in some way. On these grounds alone, the call to Haggai to 'ask the priests for a ruling' cannot be dismissed as out of place; it is necessary to wrestle with the material to discern what the connections may be with the rest of the Haggai narrative.

Despite the anxiety of some that the charge of impurity is out of tune with the promise that the Lord will be pleased and honoured by the rebuilding of the temple, a basic response by the contemporaries of Haggai could be that this is merely one expression of the paradox of faith, of that complex notion of being the people of God. We live constantly between the two truths that God is honoured by our obedience and our work, and that our efforts are never the product of unalloyed hearts and in that respect never quite good enough. God is always the initiator yet always also the respondent to human striving and obedience. This phenomenon means that, even to twenty-first century eyes, the paradox introduced by the requirement for a priestly ruling must be permitted. On the grounds of a shared humanity across the centuries, the Haggai narrative cannot be accused of inconsistency at this point. Further, this paradox is in tune with the tension around the continuity or discontinuity of the second temple with the first. In the discussion of the previous oracle, I noted that the prophet emphasizes the continuity or renewal of the temple, while at the same time hinting at something different or innately new or discontinuous. The question of purity and impurity is partly an extension of this question of continuity or discontinuity.

But there are also arguments for the integrity of this oracle from within the thought world of Haggai and his hearers. Indeed, I suggest that this integrity is in tune with the possibilities sensed much earlier in the narrative around the metaphorical understanding of the temple building as a harvest (see on 1.6-8) and the concept of the Lord being pleased and honoured (see on 1.8). There Yahweh's pleasure and honour were the result of the people offering a harvest in the form of building the temple. At the same time, a word study of the verbs translated as 'take pleasure in' and 'be honoured' suggested that the narrative was both linking the temple project with cultic possibilities and seeing it as somehow transcending the cultic context. This is part of the reason why up to this point in the narrative the term for the temple has consistently been 'the house of the Lord'. Now there appears to be a narrative shift occurring in the progression of thought. This shift is partly signalled by the shift in terminology. What has so far been referred to as 'the house of the Lord' is now explicitly named as 'the Lord's temple' (vv. 15, 18). It is not a coincidence that this terminology is introduced at the point where purity concerns are also introduced.

The Temple Concept
Two particular aspects of the thought world in which these words were first heard help to clarify the integrity of this oracle within the Haggai narrative. The first is an appreciation

of the manner in which the conceptualization of the temple was changing during the Second Temple period. The process had begun in Ezekiel's great temple vision (Ezek. 40–48), in which two interesting moves were made. First, the description of the temple was linked to the re-allocation of the land as an inheritance to the people of Israel (Ezek. 47–48). Secondly, the glory of God in the temple was linked to the end of the defilement of the whole house of Israel (Ezek. 43.1-9). Both of these links are key tributaries to conceptual developments through the Second Temple period, whereby the sacredness of the temple bursts its limits and spreads across the whole land of Israel. Generally speaking, insufficient energy has gone into relating this background to the train of thought in Haggai, for exactly the same moves are being made by the inclusion of this purity oracle within a narrative that is primarily focused on the honour of God and God's people. The concept of purity is now applied to the whole life of the people of God with the temple as a central symbol of this fact. At the same time, the link between purity and honour that is so explicit in Ezekiel is here simply assumed. It is entirely natural that at some point while talking about the honour or glory of God (*kbd*) the matter of purity should be raised. How it is dealt with will emerge in the discussion that follows.

Holiness
This point may be further reinforced by an awareness of the way in which Hebrew thinking handles the concepts of holiness and the sacred. Unlike the Greek and Latin linguistic domains, of which English speakers are the inheritors, the Hebrew does not make a sharp distinction between the concepts of holiness and of the sacred. Both are encapsulated in the term *qdš*. That single term is opposed by two slightly differing concepts that could be described as the profane and the impure. The Western linguistic division of concepts contrasts impurity with purity and profanity with a sense of the sacred. The Hebrew worldview opposes both impurity and profanity with the concept of *qdš*. Where holiness is, there is also purity, and purity is worked out in the context of everyday human life. It is therefore not surprising to find purity concerns introduced into the narrative; on the contrary, it would have been surprising if they had not appeared. Their

application to the entire experience of life back in the province of Judah is also to be expected given the propensity to see the temple as somehow foundational to the experience of life in the land.

Prophet and Priest
A related feature of this oracle is the conversation between prophet and priest. Although an oppositional distinction between the prophetic and priestly institutions ought not to be overdrawn, it is the case that there is not much interaction between the two in the writing prophets. Although prophets talk about priests and have adversarial encounters with them, such as that between Amos and Amaziah (Amos 7.10-17), this conversation between Haggai and the priests is unique in the prophetic corpus. It is perhaps not a coincidence that it occurs during the restoration period when the temple, despite being a poor reflection of the Solomonic building, begins to take on a stronger role as a template for life within the covenant. Within such a movement one might expect to see the necessity for a prophet to consult with the priestly outlook.

As a related point, this may also reflect the beginnings of the textualization of prophecy. Up until the Second Temple period prophecy had largely been an oral phenomenon, with the texts of prophetic material having later been collected and anthologized towards particular ends. The shaping of Haggai into a coherent narrative indicates that his prophecies may have been conceived from early on in their composition process as literary text. This textualization of the prophetic impulse would go on to express itself in the years ahead primarily through the vehicle of apocalyptic. In such an environment, a conversation between priests, whose role is at least partly as keepers of tradition, and prophet is intrinsically more likely to happen.

Haggai asks of the priests literally that they give him a *torah* ('ruling'). In making that request, he reflects the ancient view of the priesthood as the keeper of the law given by Moses and its teachers, while also anticipating the movement under Ezra and Nehemiah to reconfirm the law as the heartbeat of the new community's life. At the same time, he reflects the intellectual tradition of wisdom, with its close implicit identification with *torah*, which was to flower and become more accessible to later readers from the Second Temple onwards.

Torah and Wisdom
This may be seen in the dual developments of *torah* and wisdom as agents of God in the cosmos. With respect to wisdom, Prov. 3.19 speaks of the Lord 'founding' the earth 'by wisdom'. The preposition *b* prefixed to 'wisdom' is used in an instrumental sense, thus conveying a sense of wisdom as agent. It is interesting to note that the verb translated as 'founded' in Prov. 3.19 is the same verb (*ysd*) used by Haggai to speak of the foundation of the temple (v. 18), reinforcing the link between this oracle and the wisdom tradition of the period. More explicit still on the role of wisdom in the world is the programmatic Prov. 8.22-31, which speaks of wisdom's presence at the creation of the world and culminates in the comment that wisdom was 'beside [God] like a master worker'. While the interpretation of the term translated by NRSV as 'master worker' is problematic, the sense of wisdom as agent is clear. By the Second Temple period there are also some explicit and implicit links between wisdom and *torah*. Explicitly, in a different collection within the book of Proverbs, listeners are reminded that the '*torah* of the wise' is the 'fountain of life' (Prov. 13.14). Implicitly, the link between *torah* and life drawn by such verses as Ps. 119.92-93, 105 points towards the importance of wisdom as the foundation of a well-lived life. It is no coincidence, as will be discussed further below, that the failure of creation to be productive is linked in this oracle to questions of *torah*.

When Haggai asks the priests for a *torah*, then, he is at one level tapping into some deep-seated links in the cognitive environment of his listeners between the quality of life and the pervasive importance to that life of *torah* and wisdom. Incidentally, this interaction of wisdom with the prophetic is also a feature of the apocalyptic mode of divine communication that would increasingly become a dominating carrier of the wisdom tradition during the era of the Second Temple.

This involvement of Haggai with the priests has sometimes been taken as an indication that he himself is of a priestly family. The figures of Jeremiah (Jer. 1.1) and Ezekiel (Ezek. 1.3) indicate that prophets could have priestly links, but that is not inevitable or necessary, and to conclude that Haggai was such a prophet asks too much of the evidence. Indeed, one could as easily argue that if Haggai had to ask the priests for a *torah*, then he could not have been one of them. We are left merely with speculation that does little to advance our understanding of the story. Much more significant is the literary and thematic linkage between this encounter with the priests and the rest of the book.

Verses 12-13

The Function of Haggai's Questions

Haggai then poses two questions, and in so doing for the first time becomes a full participant in his own oracle. In a sense, especially with the first question, Haggai is asking the priests to fulfil their function as interpreters and declarers of the *torah*. That was unremarkable. And however simple the questions may have been, they were quite legitimate. At the same time, any good Israelite would have been able to take a good guess at the likely answers, and the priests' simple declarations confirm their guesses; indirect contact with holiness of itself is not able to transmit holiness, while impurity does indirectly infect the pure. Such strangeness as the people may have felt would have been in the incongruity of the prophet even having to ask the questions. As a conversational gambit, when a question with a self-evident answer is asked, the effect is normally to wonder what the subsequent point of the question will be. So it is here. And the point will become clear in the second half of this oracle.

I suggest that these questions function in two ways at this point in the narrative. First, and at a most basic level, they continue a rhetorical device that has featured throughout the narrative of Haggai. In the second oracle, the prophet raises the problem by means of the question about panelled houses (1.4), and then follows up with a diagnosis introduced by asking why the people's harvests have been so unproductive (1.9). In the fourth oracle, Haggai brings the worries of the heart to the surface with questions about the former glory of the temple (2.3). It is therefore quite in character for him to bring this related theme of *torah* into the narrative by the same rhetorical device. The same effect is also achieved by implying the responses of somebody other than the prophet and the Lord in the narrative. This will be followed up with further questions in the latter part of the oracle.

If the questions are explicable in terms of the rhetorical habit of the book, these particular ones also add a new twist to the narrative. So far, as indicated, the questions have had the effect of keeping the audience present in the story even though they do not actually speak. Now they are addressed to a different party and the answer is given by somebody other than the Lord or the Lord through Haggai. The shift in subject matter has the effect of bringing a particular focus onto the more universal concerns of the honour of God and the significance of the temple. The form of discourse now echoes that trend by bringing more sharply into focus some of the people who have so far only been seen through imagining the other side of the conversation. Now it becomes evident that Haggai the prophet and messenger is also part of the group who receive God's message.

The First Question
Each of the questions refers to a different aspect of holiness and purity or impurity. The first question concerns consecrated meat that has been offered as some type of sacrifice. As Haggai's example does not require that the person carrying the meat be a priest, he is probably referring to a sacrifice that the offerers themselves could consume. The offering described in Lev. 7.14-18 fits this bill, a special offering made in thanksgiving for something or on the fulfilment of vows or simply as a freewill offering to God. As such an offering could also be eaten the day after the sacrifice, it could obviously be taken from the immediate premises of sacrifice and would need to be treated with considerable care until such time as it was eaten. Leviticus 7.19 makes clear that such flesh loses its consecrated or holy status if there is contact with anything unclean. It is not able to transmit holiness indirectly via the 'fold of the garment' (Lev. 6.27). The idea of the holy and the integrity of things and places that are designated as holy must be rigorously maintained as different from the profane. There is no easy flow between the holy and the profane.

It is appropriate that the sacrifice in question was one sometimes offered in the hope of God's bestowal of blessing

182 *Haggai 2.10-19*

and fertility. The absence of blessing in the form of productive land has been the presenting problem since the start of the Haggai narrative, and it is not accidental that the topic is revisited in this oracle (vv. 15-17) in the context of sacrifice. Through this example the principle is established, a principle that runs like a thread through Judaism, that holiness cannot be indirectly acquired; rather, it is the regular responsibility of the individual to maintain it.

The Second Question
Haggai then shifts the field of thought away from sacrificial matters and concerns of holiness to the closely related concepts of purity and impurity. Once again, the authority of the writings that would come to be known as the Pentateuch is recruited by Haggai (through the priests) to make his point. The reference here is to Num. 19.11-13 where the laws of defilement relating to contact with dead bodies are expounded. As the rules and rituals of purification relating to contact between life and death were among the most conscientiously observed in early and Second Temple Judaism, the answer to Haggai's second question would have been even more obvious than for the first question. As there is no simple affirmative particle in Hebrew, the priests emphasize in their answer that indeed 'it becomes unclean'. Although holiness cannot be acquired indirectly, as the first question to the priests indicates, when it comes to impurity the opposite is true; uncleanness can pollute what surrounds it (Num. 19.22), to differing degrees according to the type of defilement in question. At no point is this more keenly felt than in the matter of handling dead bodies, and this is the very scenario that Haggai deploys. He could hardly have argued more strongly that impurity is communicable.

If the principle in question is obvious and obviously stated, however, what is less clear is the actual location of the impurity. The text asks what happens when an unclean person touches 'any of these' (kl-$'lh$), but there is some ambiguity around the referent of the demonstrative. I am taking it to refer back to the foods ('bread, or stew, or wine, or oil, or any kind of food', v. 12) that encounter the fold of the garment yet do not become holy through indirect contact with the holy things that have previously been carried in that garment.

Conceptually, these foods may not be holy, but nor are they in and of themselves unclean. However, if a person who is ritually impure through contact with a dead body touches those same items, the items themselves become impure. What cannot be consecrated by indirect means can be rendered impure by indirect means. The demonstrative pronoun 'these' is easy to pass over, and most commentators do, but it serves the important function of binding the two questions together as both applicable to the foods touched by the fold of the garment in v. 12. As will be seen below, the interpretation that begins in v. 14 must similarly be understood in a way that applies both of Haggai's questions in the same direction.

Verse 14

Location of the Analogy

Haggai has asked two questions, both of which have attracted unambiguous answers. Their applicability to the context in which they are asked, the recently commenced reconstruction project, is less obvious than the questions themselves. As a paratactic language, Hebrew uses relatively few logical indicators between clauses. Perhaps the strongest logical indicators are the particles that make use of the preposition k, of which kn is one. Haggai makes clear that there is an interpretation as he repeats the deictic particle kn three times, translated by NRSV as 'so' on the first and third occurrences but left untranslated on the second occasion. The effect may be expressed with a literal translation thus: '*so* with this people, and *so* with this nation, says the Lord, and *so* with every work of their hands'. The repetition emphasizes the analogy between the people and their work on the temple and the *torah* rulings of the previous two verses. How, then, does this analogy work?

'Therefore'

The keys to answering this are to clarify what the intended referent of the adverb 'there' ($šm$) may be, and to establish the relationship between 'what they offer there' the final clause of the verse, and the preceding three phrases all introduced by the particle kn. To take the second point first, I am reading the people, the nation (on which terms see further below) and the work of their hands as a collective concept bound together by the repetition of *kein* just examined. The relationship of all of that with 'what they offer' is determined by the nature of the *waw* ('and' in NRSV) that connects the final clause to the three preceding ones. The challenge of understanding the parataxis of Hebrew, at least to a native English speaker or anybody else who thinks in a syntactic language, is nowhere more evident than in the number of uses to which the ubiquitous *waw* may be put. Several of those uses express some kind of causal relationship between clauses, and I propose that is the case in the present instance. This might be expressed by reading the final *waw* as 'therefore'. As a result, conceptually all that the people offer is unclean because they are like the food that is able neither to achieve indirect holiness nor to be protected from the infectious nature of impurity.

'There'

If it is possible to establish the likely referent of 'there' in the clause 'what they offer *there*', then further progress will result. The argument that the efficacy of a local sacrificial site, activated prior to the restoration of the temple, is being condemned is ultimately unconvincing. Not only does it lack reference in the text itself, it fails to appreciate the wider vision that Haggai's oracles bring to the project of reconstruction. The latter half of the oracle, which explores the outcome of the interpretation (see below), focuses on the building project itself and the impact of the state of the building on the people's entire experience of the land. It seems much more likely that 'there' should be taken as the site and the fact of the incomplete temple, and the additional fact that this state of affairs is ongoing due to the procrastination that the Haggai narrative addresses.

The expression, 'what they offer', is therefore everything that is going on with respect to the restoration of the house of the Lord. This is in tune with the thrust of the second oracle, where the call to rebuild had echoes of sacrificial language resonating around it and at the same time was conceived metaphorically as a kind of harvest offering to God. There is a continuation of the interwoven themes of sacrifice, harvest and call to service in the broadest sense rather than a narrow focus on a technically illegitimate sacrificial offering. The cult itself has hovered in the background so far in the oracles. On this occasion it moves into the foreground for the first time, but it continues to serve the wider theme of faithfulness as the people of God. In that respect it is not dissonant with its surrounding material.

The State of 'What They Offer'
Having established that the *torah* parable relates to the work and attitudes of the people in rebuilding the temple, the question remains as to exactly what the parable of the two questions (vv. 12-13) says about the legitimacy of that work and those attitudes. The answer lies in the applicability of both questions to the 'people' and the 'work of their hands'. In interpreting the significance of this statement, there has often been a tendency to focus on the second of Haggai's questions to the priests without taking sufficient account of the first. Yet it is necessary to discern the relevance to the temple building project of both questions, one indicating that holiness cannot be mediated and the other that impurity can be. Both questions in the parable itself are about the same objects, the food mentioned in v. 12. In both cases the food comes into contact with an intermediary agent; in the first instance the agent is the garment that has carried the consecrated meat, while in the second it is the person who has had contact with a dead body. The question in each instance revolves around the efficacy of that intermediary, in the one case to transmit holiness and in the other to transfer impurity.

It is important to remember that the state of the temple has had a paradoxical effect on the people up to this point. On the one hand, it stands as an ongoing rebuke to their unfaithfulness, while on the other it calls them on to make a proper offering to God in the form of the restoration of its former glory. In the same way, the ruin of the temple and the early stages of its work continue to function with this double focus in the mind of Haggai as he consults the priests with his two questions. On the one hand, the temple and its former glory may be thought of as the holy meat in the first question. The intermediary is the fact that the people have not been conscientious in carrying out its restoration. As a result, the holiness within their midst that the temple may represent cannot be automatically mediated. At the same time, the ruined temple is also represented by the dead body in the second question to the priests. Again, the intermediary has been the people's inactivity while the people themselves are those who remain unclean because of this unclean presence among them in the form of the continuing ruin of the temple. The phrase 'what they offer there is unclean' therefore has a kind of double focus. It is both a reminder not to expect to live on the memory of the former glory of the temple, and a reprimand about the offence perpetrated by the presence of the ruin.

This interpretation is dependent on an observation made by many commentators that there is a progression of outlook through this oracle from the past to the present to the future. This early section of the oracle is looking to the past, and as such it is not condemning recently commenced rebuilding activity so much as observing what has been. As well as being a reassurance that the absence of holiness is not a terminal condition, it is a powerful reminder of the consequences of not maintaining the momentum that has recently begun. The next move in the oracle will be a shift in the time perspective as signalled by the 'and now' at the start of v. 15.

'People' and 'Nation'

This verse also raises the question of exactly to whom all this may be applied, given that both 'people' (*'m*) and 'nation' (*gwy*) are mentioned. Some have suggested that the distinction between these terms reflects the split between the returning exiles and the Samaritan presence that has remained resident on the land, drawing on the picture painted by Ezra–Nehemiah of tension between the two groups. However, as already indicated, such a distinction is not reflected in the text so far, and so it is unlikely to be behind this mention of 'people' and 'nation' together (see on 1.5-6, 12). There are a number of hints in Isaiah that the semantic use of these terms to distinguish Israelite from non-Israelite is breaking down, and indeed that the tradition represented in Isaiah draws on this as a deliberate effect in its expansive vision for the people of God. For instance, the two terms are used in parallel with each other in reference to Israel in Isa. 1.4; 9.2 and 65.1, and in parallel with each other in reference to other peoples in Isa. 2.4; 42.6 and 49.22. On these grounds alone, care should be taken not to draw a distinction between the two terms. Notwithstanding my earlier comments on the covenant significance of the term '*m* ('people'), Haggai is most likely to be using 'people' and 'nation' in parallel with each other in the present context.

A LXX Gloss

The LXX has additional material at the end of v. 14 that has been variously translated. One translation reads thus: 'because of their early burdens, they shall be pained because of their toils [or wickedness]; and you have hated him that reproved in the gates'. There is no other textual support for this addition, and it seems reasonable to consider it to be a gloss. The motivation for such a gloss remains obscure although many have noted an echo of classical prophecy's condemnation of the cult on ethical grounds (e.g. Amos 5.10). If that is the case, it would be an expansion on the nature of the uncleanness detected by Haggai (for further on this possibility see the comments on LXX in the Introduction).

Verses 15-17

'But Now'

As noted above, the start of v. 15 signals a shift in time perspective. The first word in the verse, represented by NRSV as 'but now', is *'th*. This is a term that functions in a couple of ways. It is commonly used in prophetic literature to introduce something that Yahweh is about to do. Often there is a contrastive sense with what has just preceded the statement introduced by *'th*. The term is also used as a simple adverb of time, pointing the narrative to the present moment. Here the adverb at the head of v. 15 indicates a shift in perspective from the past into the present. At the same time, it attunes the reader or hearer to expect the subsequent message to indicate the activity of the Lord in the present moment. Before that, though, the prophet reminds his readers of the historical forces that have led to the present state of affairs. There is therefore a double focus through these verses. While they describe the present experience of Israel, they are charged with a sense that this is not the end of the story; something new is about to happen.

In using this particular adverb, the narrative maintains a rhythm that is connected to 1.5 and 2.4, where it used in the same way. On the first occasion it calls for a response to the ruins of the house of the Lord, and on the second occasion it calls for courage in the face of the inadequacy of the attempted restoration. In each instance, the operation of time in the narrative is the same; the narrative looks forward by focusing on the present.

'Consider'
There is an added connection to 1.5 in the repetition of the idiom represented in both 1.5 and v. 15 by NRSV as 'consider'. Literally this reads, 'set your hearts'. As a retrospective, the people are now asked to reconsider the matters that were canvassed in the second oracle. But the retrospective is not merely for its own sake; it has a developmental purpose. On the first occasion that the people were asked to 'set your hearts', they were to set them 'upon your ways' ('how you have fared' in the NRSV translation of 1.5). Now they are asked to 'set your hearts' on 'what will come to pass from this day on'. Their reconsideration of their circumstances now looks to the future rather than to the present.

'From This Day On'
The Hebrew expression that points to the future is more subtle than its NRSV translation, 'from this day on'. Literally it may be rendered 'from this day and upwards', employing a second adverb, *m'lh*, that is used both spatially and temporally. It remains unclear whether the Hebrew concept of 'upwards' when applied to time describes moving backwards from a defined moment or moving forward from a defined moment. The ambiguity applies here, and is compounded by the repetition of the same idiom in v. 18. The repetition of the idiom has a poetic effect at v. 18 of moving time forward (see comments below). In this first use of the phrase, what ensues indicates that the people's thoughts are being directed back over all that they have been experiencing up until this point.

Stone upon Stone
This is evident from the fact that the people's thoughts are directed by the prophet to a time 'before a stone was placed upon a stone' in the temple. In other words, to a moment before they had begun to respond in obedience to the prophet's urging them to action. At the same time, the experience in the past

still continues in the present. It is only three months since Haggai started talking to them and the difficult conditions described in 1.5-6 almost certainly continue to apply. Change could hardly be expected until at least an agricultural cycle has been completed. What follows is therefore an encouragement to keep working because a better future beckons. At this point, as discussed with respect to the previous oracle, the narrative remains firmly rooted in the historical moment while also hinting at eschatological possibilities.

'The Lord's Temple'
A further indicator of that is the sudden shift in terminology about the building that is being worked on. Up until this point in the narrative it has consistently been named as 'the house of the Lord' or, in abbreviated form, 'the house'. Some of the effects of this terminology have been noted, principally the immediacy and intimacy of relationship between the people and the one who dwells in the Lord's house. This was even the case in 2.6-9 with the sharp focus on the material splendour of the house. Now the narrative is talking about something that is also the Lord's temple. There are several effects arising from this shift in nomenclature. At the most basic level, it reminds the people that, although the relationship with Yahweh may be as intimate as with one who dwells in a house, this does not mean that the Lord may be domesticated. He is one who also inhabits a temple, one who is other. This was a message that Haggai's prophetic predecessors constantly had to hammer home through their reminders that the God of Israel is also the God of the nations (see, e.g., Amos 9.7-8; Isa. 56.3-8).

The shift in terminology also reflects thinking on the significance of the temple that began to take shape during the Second Temple period. (For more detail on this, see the Introduction on the temple context.) Suffice to say at this point that the temple begins to take on an eschatological status as a central organizing focus in the furniture of the universe. Implicitly, the shift in terminology reminds the people that their project is much more significant than a local attempt to appease a local god in the hope of improved agricultural productivity. Haggai, and probably his audience as well, are likely to have been familiar with the concepts opened up during the exile by Ezekiel and preserved in Ezekiel 40–48. The rest of the oracle deals with the temple and all the possibilities resident therein. The prophecy remains earthed in the local situation, but the shifting focus on the temple begins to move the people's thinking onto a bigger canvas. The link between the health of the land and the health of the Lord's house, first made in the second oracle, is now reinforced and given a wider significance, albeit somewhat different from the full eschatological flowering of contagious holiness and purity envisaged in Zech. 14.20-21.

A Pun on 'Set/Place'
In sending the people's thoughts back to a time before any of this had begun, the narrative takes advantage of a pun in the use of the Hebrew verb *sym*, which is impossible to reflect directly in the English. This wide-ranging verb includes both a conceptual and a physical sense of establishing or setting something up. It is used in the idiom examined earlier, 'set your hearts', which is translated simply as 'consider' by NRSV. What they are to set their hearts on is a time before 'a stone was placed upon a stone' and the verb 'placed' is the same Hebrew verb *sym*. The poetics of the wordplay reinforce the link between the state of the people's heart and the state of the temple.

The Beginning of Verse 16
Before considering the description of that state, there is a difficulty with the Hebrew text at the start of v. 16 to address. In giving the reading 'how did you fare?' the NRSV has taken a lead from the LXX translation, probably on the assumption that a different Hebrew *Vorlage* than the MT lay before the translator. This suggests an emendation of the MT text to give 'how was it with you?' or words to that effect. This or something like it is almost unanimously the view of modern commentators. Older commentators were more likely to read the MT as received with no revocalization or consonantal emendation, reading the first word of the verse, *mhywtm*, as a participle of the verb 'to be', prefixed by *mem* and carrying a third person plural possessive suffix. A literal translation would be 'before their being'. The first word in v. 16 is therefore a temporal clause referring back to v. 15b, to the time before the rebuilding began, and governing the next three

clauses. It can be represented thus: before the rebuilding, 'when one came to a heap of twenty measures', when 'one came to the winevat to draw fifty measures', and when 'I struck you...with blight and mildew and hail', when all that happened then 'you did not return to me'. This is not an easy construction, the MT vocalization is not standard and there is the evidence of the LXX reading. Nevertheless, the construction is possible, and the consonantal text as it stands preserves the sense of the narrative flow. It is as possible that the LXX is grappling with a difficult text as that it is reading a different *Vorlage*. On balance, I favour the more traditional reading of a temporal clause opening v. 16.

With that the prophet leads the people to reflect on their recent and current experience. In doing so, he reiterates the contents of his second oracle, both in the experience of diminished productivity and in the suggestion that this state of affairs relates in some way to the condition of the house of the Lord. This time, however, there are a couple of differences. First, this now applies not to the 'house of the Lord' but to the 'temple'. In a cognitive environment that increasingly connects eschatological wellbeing with the health of the temple, the link is made yet more explicit. As already argued in the context of the previous oracle, there is a more deep-seated connection than simply the economic. At the same time, Haggai connects the current experience more strongly with previous prophetic utterances in the history of the Judean people than was the case in the second oracle. In that way the expansion of significance achieved by this oracle continues.

Current and Recent Experience
This reflection of the longer corporate experience of the people happens in several ways. The first is in the reference to a loss of harvest yield. Haggai reminds the people of times when they expected literally 'a heap of twenty' and found there only ten. The word 'measures' is absent in the MT resulting in a somewhat oblique phrase, the more so in that 'heap' itself is a rare word and the verbal form from which it derives is used only once (Exod. 15.8) in quite a different context. Nevertheless, the context makes clear that the reference is to a harvest yield of grain, perhaps with a picture of harvest stooks ready for gathering. The companion picture is of a winepress that yields

only a portion of what is expected. Again, the expression is concise since the term translated by NRSV as 'measures' is *pwrh*, another rare word which probably refers to the trough or vat of a winepress. As with the field that produces only a proportion of the expected number of stooks of grain, so the pressed grapes yield only a portion of the expected amount into the vat beneath the press. Although this sentiment is not often expressed in terms of exact proportions, the loss of agricultural productivity is a pervasive theme through the prophets both prior to and during the exile. Much of this can be traced back to passages like Deuteronomy 28, which in the context of the giving of the law indicate that obedience leads to blessing on the land and disobedience has the opposite effect. Amos is one of several prophets who reflects this (see Amos 4), in that he links a famine in the land with the oppressive habits of his audience.

In fact, in Amos 4, where the prophet attributes the drought to 'blight and mildew', exactly the same term is used as in Hag. 2.17. It is not known exactly what crop diseases were meant by these words, but they formed a common hendiadys for the destruction of crops by disease and infection. The additional mention of 'hail' by Haggai is a more oblique echo of the 'pestilence after the manner of Egypt', in another probable echo of Amos (Amos 4.10). Although Haggai himself does not go as far as his eighth-century colleague, the mention of pestilence produces a faint echo of that earlier prophet's ironic appropriation of the plagues of Egypt as a punishment of the people who themselves were once delivered from slavery by means of those very plagues.

The Final Clause of Verse 17
The final clause in v. 17, 'yet you did not return to me', in fact represents the LXX. The MT is more ambivalent; it simply says, in a literal English rendering, 'there is not you to me'. Various attempts have been made to make sense of this. Perhaps the most common is to assume a missing verb which has been preserved in the *Vorlage* of the LXX translation. This entails a radical emendation of the MT of no less than three of the four consonants in the word represented by 'you' in my literal translation to give 'you...returned'. In the face of such a radical emendation, it is important to ask whether the MT in the

received form may be made sense of grammatically. My argument is that it may be, and that its very ambivalence represents a deliberate poetic effect in the present context. The phrase may be read in a reflexive sense, 'you yourselves were not to/towards me'. This gives a stronger contrast with what has just preceded the phrase. Despite all the evidence of God's hand of judgment, the very object of that judgment, 'the people', has remained deaf to the message.

The use of a complementary phrase rather than a noun and object also shifts the emphasis onto the final preposition in the phrase, 'towards/to me'. This echoes the same preposition used twice in v. 16, in the phrases 'when one came to...' This implies that there was no corresponding coming to Yahweh in response to their coming to the grain and wine and finding a reduced yield. Despite the disappointment experienced in coming to the harvest yield, there has been no coming towards Yahweh, the one responsible for that diminished yield.

The echoes of Amos 4 have been strengthened by the LXX. That translation's rendering, 'yet you did not return to me', is likely to be based on the assumption that that phrase, which reverberates through Amos 4.6, 8, 9, 10 and 11, naturally belongs in this context also. This is consonant with the LXX plus at v. 14, which also seems to echo Amos, this time Amos 5.10 with its reference to judgment in the gate. It may be that in hearing 'yet you did not return to me', the LXX has picked up one of the intertextual echoes set off by Haggai, even if the syntax of the text allows other echoes as well.

It is partly on these grounds that some have supposed v. 17 to be a later gloss. Yet it contains a strong thematic link both with v. 16 and with the sentiments of v. 19, which itself is a further echo of earlier prophecy (see comments below). On balance, it seems best to assume the integrity of the MT of this verse within the Haggai oracles.

Verses 18-19

A Future Prospect

So far in this oracle Haggai has looked to the past through the priestly questions of vv. 10-14 and has painted a picture of the present experience in vv. 15-17. The present focus was introduced by the phrase which I translated literally as 'from this day and upwards' (v. 15, NRSV reads 'from this day on'). Now the prophet turns to a future focus introduced by the identical phrase, 'from this day and upwards', and accompanied by the same instruction to 'consider', literally to 'set your hearts'. The terminology has been discussed fully above. As I indicated, in v. 18, the temporal clause introduces the future rather than the past, and as such is a nice illustration of the Hebraic habit of looking to the past in order to contemplate the future.

Just as the temporal indicator points us back to earlier in the oracle (namely, v. 15), so the specification of 'this day' as 'the twenty-fourth day of the month' recalls the date of the oracle given in v. 10. That this date is abbreviated (literally 'the twenty-fourth day of the ninth') with no reference to the year, indicates that it serves a resumptive purpose as the perspective changes towards a time yet to be encountered by the hearers.

The Day of the 'Foundation'

There is a further definition of the present moment, the moment from which a new reality begins to intrude, as the 'day that the foundation of the Lord's temple was laid'. This is more accurately translated as 'from the day that the Lord's temple was founded'. The point here is that there is no noun in the MT for 'foundation', regardless of what is suggested by the NRSV and other English translations. The nominal translation of the verbal form (so NRSV) suggests a particular physical stage in the rebuilding much more strongly than does the MT, and has led to the supposition that this verse refers to a ceremonial laying of the foundation stone. A key historical problem with this assumption is that such a ceremony in 520 BCE is apparently at odds with the ceremony of 538 BCE described by Ezra 3.10-13.

One historical response to the problem is to suggest that, in the context of the purity parable, a ceremonial cleansing of the temple or altar is envisaged. A literary, and to my mind more convincing response, is to focus on the pual verb *ysd*, that speaks of the temple of the Lord 'being founded', and to consider what exactly may be intended by that verb. There is a compelling argument that the term need not apply merely to laying foundation stones; it may also include the idea of under taking restoration work. This can be illustrated from another postexilic text, namely, 2 Chron. 24.27, in which the same verb is used to describe a 'rebuilding' or 'restoration' of the house of the Lord. The rebuilding refers back to a range of activities described earlier in the chapter (2 Chron. 24.12-15) and undertaken by a range of craftsmen, including iron and bronze workers, rather than to an explicit ceremonial event. In the 2 Chronicles context it is clear that the more general sense of rebuilding or restoring applies. If the same is the case here in v. 19, then there need be no conflict with the ceremony described in Ezra 3.10-13 some eighteen years earlier. In the same vein as the Chronicler, Haggai is referring to the point at which people picked up their tools again and resumed the work that had lapsed since the laying of a new foundation stone. From this day when the work of restoration is resumed, look forward, says the prophet.

A Historical Note
Before leaving the question of the foundation-laying or temple restoration, the perfect tense of *ysd* raises an interesting question. From a perspective within the story, it is not possible to speak of the temple as having been restored by the twenty-fourth day of the ninth month of the second year of Darius. As already noted, this was only some three months after the challenge was taken up. However, the perfect aspect of the verb in the second half of v. 18 alerts readers to the fact that for the compiler of these oracles the narrative is in the past. Earlier prophetic literature takes the form of anthologized addresses to a specific moment, and a strong sense of the present normally pervades such anthologies. They have subsequently been collected and turned into texts, which in turn transforms their contents into a record of the past, but still the perspective of the original setting prevails. The book of Haggai is different. It is not merely an anthology of oracles spoken into these few months. It is a tightly crafted narrative of a series of exactly dated oracles, developed after the event. Even though the narrative was probably formed close to the time of the prophetic oracles themselves (see my remarks in the Introduction), the narrative formed around the oracles constantly takes the reader or hearer beyond the immediate context to a

consideration of the later relevance of the story and the message it preserves. That is partly why the concluding section of this commentary tackles the question of contemporary relevance in some detail.

Agricultural Blessing
The prospective stance of vv. 18 and 19 continues to link agricultural results with the state of the Lord's house. Again, readers are reminded of the harvest failure, this time through another set of questions. The rhetorical effect of engagement is the same each time questions are used by Haggai. This time, though, they are curiously ambiguous. The questions come some three months after grain sowing around the time of the winter rains (October–November) and after the harvest of the grape, fig, pomegranate and olive. Perhaps these important fruits have shown a better yield and the grain harvest at least looks encouraging in the early stages. The final statement that 'from this day on I will bless you' then functions to confirm that this is not a coincidence but is a confirmation of the Lord's words through the prophet and an indicator of a brighter future. That is possible, but it is just as likely that part of the point of this oracle is to encourage the people once again even though the promised abundance is not going to occur overnight. If that is the case, the questions are a reminder that things are not as they might yet be. Perhaps the ambiguity is an intentional one as the people stand with their faces now turned towards the future but with an eye on the present and the past.

Whichever approach to these questions is preferred, there is at least an implicit concrete hope in the second question. Unlike the grains which require an annual planting cycle, the fruit trees in question are perennial, and although they may 'still yield nothing', at least these centrally important species remain in potential production. It could have been worse. Not only that, these trees point beyond subsistence and towards prosperity. In that there is also some encouragement.

However ambiguous the questions may be, the oracle ends with the unequivocal promise that 'From this day on I will bless you'. The conditions of the present and recent past will not continue into the future. The repetition of the *Leitmotif* 'from this day on' (literally, 'from this day and upwards'; see on

v. 15 and v. 18) brings to a conclusion the sense of movement through time that imbues this penultimate oracle.

As the prophet signs off this oracle, it is noticeable that he makes no attempt to connect the promises of vv. 18-19 with the opening reflections on the nature of purity. Whatever else this might indicate, it at least implies that my initial assumption was correct that the questions about purity are not the substantive questions. Rather, the prophet has used them as a parable from which to extrapolate out to the question of the people's work on the restoration of the temple. The promise that things are going to be different 'from this day on' indicates that the offence of an unfinished temple will no longer be an impurity within their midst, and that the potential that remains inherent in the temple will be released by the restoration of the building. At the same time, the ambiguities inherent in the questions function as a reminder that simply rebuilding on its own cannot guarantee purity; the nature of the offering that it represents is also important.

A Question of Theodicy
This raises a question of theodicy. Is the Lord obliged to bless because the people are obedient and the temple is now intact? The lessons of history during the Second Temple period, a period whose beginning is marked by the very project now under examination, is that this is by no means the case. The 'abomination of desolation' could still be imposed on the very temple itself, as foreseen by the prophet Daniel (Dan. 9.24-27) and fulfilled under the heel of Antiochus IV Epiphanes in 167 BCE. Furthermore, the temple could not protect the people from the might of the Romans as they faced its destruction and their eventual expulsion from the land. In one sense, history repeated itself as the first temple similarly could not protect the people of God from the punishment wreaked by the Babylonian exile. Although Haggai speaks into the moment and draws the link between blessing and obedience in the matter of the temple, in his mind the temple was always a sign of something much bigger, the obedience of the people in their offerings and the eschatological role that the temple has to play. It is for others to explore the problem that obedience does not always reap agricultural blessing (see, e.g., Hab. 3.17-19).

HAGGAI 2.20-23
(SECTION F, THE SIXTH ORACLE):
THE SIGNET RING

If the previous oracle was a *crux interpretum*, as I suggested in the introduction to 2.10-19, this final oracle is a puzzling conclusion to the Haggai narrative. The puzzle is created by the sudden shift of the spotlight onto the figure of Zerubbabel (see the detailed comment on Zerubbabel in the Introduction). This altered perspective seems to indulge in several discontinuities of content with the preceding oracles while painting a picture of narrative continuity. Indeed, at least one commentator has suggested that Haggai simply changed his mind at this point and decided to try a new tack around the complex questions of Israel's return to the land and God's dealing with his people. However, in the light of comment on the preceding oracles, this one is not so much a radical discontinuity as a refinement of the balance between the eschatological and the temporal that has characterized the narrative so far. At the same time, it reinforces the theme of the monarchy, only implicit in the narrative to this point, as a natural companion to the emphasis on the temple that has so far dominated the book of Haggai.

Verse 20

However discontinuous the train of thought in this final oracle may appear to be, its introduction sends a clear signal that in narrative terms it ought to be read with the one that precedes it. This signal is found principally in the date formula and prophetic ascription. There are several features of the formula that point in that direction. First, the phrase 'the word of the Lord came...to Haggai' is identical to the beginning of the previous oracle (2.10), which itself is slightly different from 1.1 and 2.1. This is an immediate hint at some commonality between the two oracles. Secondly, there are two key differences from the previous oracle's introduction which can both be described as resumptive. The reference to 'a second time' is one such, again pointing back to the previous oracle and the first time that God had spoken on that particular day. The date itself is also abbreviated, speaking as it does only of the 'the twenty-fourth day of the month'. Neither the month nor the year is named. This is unique in the Haggai narrative, and as such functions as a reference back to the full date in 2.10, further strengthening the sense that this final oracle is a continuation of the thought that has preceded it. In these ways readers are primed by the narrative to expect continuity.

Verses 21-22

Introductory Links and Contrasts

If the dating formula links us with the previous oracle, the opening command to Haggai that he 'speak to Zerubbabel governor of Judah' takes us yet further back in the narrative and recalls the start of the fourth oracle (2.2). There Haggai was enjoined to 'speak to Zerubbabel son of Shealtiel, governor of Judah, and to Joshua son of Jehozadak, the high priest'. The patronymic for Zerubbabel is not included this time, but if its omission is taken as an abbreviation, then the command to speak to Zerubbabel is a further point of narrative connection with the earlier oracles. The LXX has a plus here which includes the patronymic, either because its *Vorlage* included it prior to its abbreviation by the MT tradition or because it was harmonizing with earlier references to Zerubbabel. In any case, this is a further indication of the connectedness with the preceding oracles.

Yet this very connection highlights the absence of Joshua the high priest, who up until now has consistently been mentioned in the same breath as Zerubbabel. The sudden shift of focus onto Zerubbabel that will culminate in his being compared to the Lord's signet ring (v. 23) poses an interpretive challenge. Among other things, it entails a significant shift in the role of Zerubbabel. Up until now he has apparently been the reluctant leader who needs the impetus of the prophet to make things happen. Suddenly he is a metaphor or promise —depending on how ultimately his significance in the narrative is read—of God's blessing on the people.

The Focus on Zerubbabel

So far I have highlighted a gradual shift in focus away from Zerubbabel and Joshua as the narrative proceeds. The first two oracles are explicitly addressed to Joshua and Zerubbabel (1.1-12), with a strong implication that the people are included although they are not mentioned. The third one draws the people alongside their two leaders. The fourth oracle then addresses Zerubbabel, Joshua and 'the remnant of the people' (2.2) as a collective whole. By now the people are thoroughly implicated in the narrative. The fifth oracle (2.11-19) does not even name the audience; it is content merely to imply that the discussion is with all the people. It is in that context that the sudden focus on Zerubbabel must be considered.

At the same time, it has been becoming increasingly apparent that the erection of the temple is not an end in itself. Rather, it is an enterprise that symbolizes and encapsulates the aspirations of the whole people to know and be blessed by Yahweh. Perhaps, then, the focus on an individual in the final oracle is not the main point either. Rather, it too may be part of the gradual process of using human institutions to express the interaction between the Lord and his people. This theme will be considered in more detail in the comments on v. 23. For now, it suffices to note the possibility that the status of Zerubbabel, like the focus on the temple rebuilding, is expressive of a larger truth couched in terms of Israel's traditional institutions. In that respect I observed in the Introduction that each of the restoration prophets brings his message to a focus on a key individual (Zerubbabel, Hag. 2.23; Branch, Zech. 6; Elijah, Mal. 4.5). Together, these three represent the royal, priestly and prophetic hopes that would culminate in the Second Temple concept of the people of God as a temple community (see on the Qumran material in the Introduction).

Even if that is true, though, the absence of Joshua in this final oracle is still puzzling. In commenting on the historical context of the book of Haggai, I considered the question of the primacy of Zerubbabel or Joshua in both Haggai and Zechariah 1–8, and found that a consistent and easily categorized picture does not emerge. On the one hand, Haggai seems (and I use the word advisedly) more interested in Zerubbabel the governor while Zechariah is more interested in Joshua the high priest. On the other, Haggai has a generally negative picture of the other nations (v. 22) while Zechariah conveys a somewhat more inclusive vision (Zech. 8.20-23). We might have expected the opposite to have been the case: Zechariah's interest in the high priest to have led him to a focus on the purity of the nation, and Haggai's interest in the Davidic Zerubbabel to have led him to a focus on the primacy of Israel among the nations. At the same time, the technical arguments around Zech. 6.12-13 raise the possibility of two developing eschatological traditions in the early post-exilic period, one focusing more on the Davidic figure of Zerubbabel and the other on the Zadokite figure of Joshua. At that point, I suggested that the best tactic is to read the two synoptically and understand them coalescing into a single sense of *shalom* around both gubernatorial and high priestly authority. Haggai must be read with Zechariah 1–8 to account for the absence of Joshua from the narrative at this point.

For the moment, however, in the oracles of Haggai the focus on Zerubbabel denotes a shift in emphasis. There is some debate over the extent to which a royal ideology lies behind the promotion of Zerubbabel in the narrative. It is hard to avoid the sense that, given the Davidic status of the governor, some kind of reworking of the monarchical ideal is in progress, appropriate to the changed circumstances of Judah as a province and its people as subjects of the Persian empire. That Zerubbabel's Davidic ancestry is nowhere explicitly referred to in the narrative suggests that a political challenge to the Persian empire is not being proposed, nor is there any immediate hope apparent in the narrative of a restoration of the monarchy in its pre-exilic form. However, the re-institution of the temple, and the explicit comparison with the first temple (2.3) would naturally have prompted the observation that the institutions of monarchy and temple historically were mutually interdependent. Where now was the accompanying re-institution of the Davidic line? Part of the answer to this is the assurance that Zerubbabel is chosen and significant in the eyes of Yahweh as leader of a people now restoring their temple. As I noted with respect to developments in Zechariah 1–8, this is not the whole story, but it is sufficient for the moment and it coheres with the nature of the hope so far invested in the renewed temple in the Haggai narrative.

Links and Contrasts with the Fourth Oracle

To turn to the content of the message to Zerubbabel, there is a strong echo of the message already given in the fourth oracle (2.6-7). Notwithstanding the variation in the NRSV rendering, the phrase 'I am about to shake the heavens and the earth' (v. 21) is identical to 'I will shake the heavens and the earth' in 2.6. Both use a personal pronoun plus participle construction to convey action in progress. Each thereby implies that the actions of God do not remain in the future but are beginning now. And the action is the same in each case. The LXX plus, 'and the sea and the dry land', highlights the link further, probably as a harmonization with 2.6. If in doing so the Greek translators have accurately read the intent of the MT, then this is another example of the abbreviating seen in both the date of the oracle and the name of Zerubbabel. Just as with those examples, the abbreviated object of about to shake, 'the heavens and the earth', is intended to raise a strong echo of the earlier oracle.

The syntax of the message also recalls the earlier oracle. In each case, the opening verb is a pronoun plus participle construction, as indicated already, while the subsequent verbs in the oracle follow the *waw* plus perfect narrative pattern implying events in the future. In each case the shaking is a present reality that will result in certain actions still in the future but anticipated by the prophet (on the background significance of the verb translated as 'shaking', see comments on 2.6-8).

This grammatical link leads to a comparison of the outcome of the two prophetic statements. In the earlier one, the shaking will result in some kind of ingathering of the nations and their assets to Israel (see again comments on 2.6-8). On this occasion the shaking has a quite different impact; it results in the overthrow and destruction of kingdoms, presumably the very kingdoms whose treasure is promised in 2.6. The term translated as 'overthrow', *hpk*, can also have the sense of transforming or changing something. It need not be cataclysmic in intent although it can be. In this instance, however, paired as it is with the unambiguous verb *šmd*, which carries a dominant sense of annihilation and is here translated as 'destroy', there can be little doubt that the overthrowing is envisaged as cataclysmic.

The destruction will be of 'the strength' (*ḥzq*) of the kingdoms. This term has a physical forcefulness about it that adds to the confrontational picture being painted. Lest there be any doubt on that score, Haggai recalls some of the martial imagery that his prophetic predecessors have employed, and in doing so evokes some of the memories of Israel. Overthrow of the chariots and riders of course conjures up memories of the deliverance of Israel from the pursuing Egyptian army at the start of their exodus (Exod. 14.26-31). Subsequently, some of the prophets would liken the threat from Egypt to the threat from contemporary neighbouring powers, most often Assyria or Babylon. Note, for instance, Isa. 36.9 where the use of Egyptian chariots against the Assyrian threat is discussed, or Mic. 5.10, again in the context of an Assyrian threat. The turning of comrade's sword against comrade recalls the demise of the Assyrian Sennacherib at the hand of his own sons after his defeat by the angel of the Lord and the consequent deliverance of Hezekiah (Isa. 37.36-38). The use of *ḥzq* ('strength') is a further link back to the fourth oracle. There, when the people were enjoined repeatedly to 'take courage' (2.4), the verbal form of *ḥzq* was used.

The Kingdoms

A problem for the reader at this point is that these destructive sentiments are at odds with the expectation painted in 2.6-7 of an ongoing relationship with the nations and their wealth. As a first response, it is worth noting that the tension is not new to Haggai. Israel's attitude towards the nations has always contained these competing elements. The Isaiah scroll in particular projects a variegated vision for the nations, sometimes as entities to be destroyed, sometimes as partners with Israel in a new world and sometimes as subjects of Israel (compare Isa. 11.12-16; 45.14; 56.1-5). The first and last of those options evident in Isaiah are seen here. In one respect, readers are always compelled to maintain a creative tension between the different prophetic visions for the nations.

In this particular instance there is also a subtle difference between the earlier oracle and this one. In the fourth oracle of the Haggai narrative, the prophet concerns himself with 'all nations' (2.7) while in the present oracle he is speaking about the 'throne of kingdoms' and 'kingdoms of the nations' (v. 22). It is possible that these terms are synonymous both with each other and with the notion of 'nations' in the earlier oracle. I suggest, however, that in the present oracle the phrases 'throne of kingdoms' and 'kingdoms of nations', while more or less synonymous with each other, carry an extra nuance not found in the term 'all nations' (2.7). In short, 'kingdoms of nations' is not a synonym for 'nations'. The latter is the *gwym*, a term that speaks primarily of ethnicity, whereas 'kingdoms', *mmlkwt*, refers to the entity that gives political expression to the ethnos. Sometimes the term *gwy* carries a political sense so the distinction is not absolute, but in this context the distinction makes sense. The result is that the confrontation anticipated by this oracle is in fact against the political entities in question rather than against the peoples they represent. In that respect it is not at odds with the earlier vision of the *gwy* streaming to the house of God with their treasures. Although it has to be acknowledged that the tension here does not entirely yield to a neat synthesis, this vision for the political expressions of ethnicity, 'the kingdoms', is in tune with the focus on the political figure of Zerubbabel as against the conglomerate of the people and their leaders which has so far obtained. The lexical links with the fourth oracle should be read alongside the difference in vision between the two oracles. When that is done, the positive view of the 'treasure of all nations' (2.7) or all ethnicities is seen to be rooted in the more destructive vision for the political entities ('the kingdoms') that give them expression. In one sense, each outlook is a different side of the same coin.

I have suggested that Haggai is not proposing a direct confrontation with the Persian empire, and that the obliqueness of reference to the governor's Davidic status makes it unlikely that Zerubbabel would feature in such a confrontation. These somewhat cataclysmic references to the nations, then, should be read as part of the eschatological echoes that emerge from time to time in the Haggai narrative. The prophet accepts that for the moment the people under Zerubbabel continue as subjects of the Persian empire, but also projects a longer future in which things may well be different.

Memory and the Future
Haggai's employment of the past as a gateway to the future for the people of God is a tactic encountered in previous oracles. Memory is often a response to the present and the basis of hope for the future in the Hebrew prophetic mindset. The move by Amos to recall the exodus and conquest in his message to complacent Israel (Amos 2.9; 3.12) is one of myriad examples.

Verse 23

'On That Day'
The prophet's vision for Zerubbabel is to be implemented 'on that day', which raises the question of the referent of the demonstrative pronoun. The immediate context is the preceding description of the cataclysmic destruction of nations (vv. 21-22), which in itself is a strong echo of the earlier vision of the 'treasure of all nations' (2.7). The most natural move for the reader, then, is to connect the elevation of Zerubbabel with the shaking of the heavens and the earth. The eschatological overtones of that vision now attach themselves to the figure of Zerubbabel as 'signet ring' through the link provided by 'on that day'. This is in tune with the gradual shift in time perspective seen during the course of the previous oracle, from a focus on the past through the present and on into the future. This future aspect was expressed as something that would obtain 'from this day on...' (2.15, 19). The most natural reading of 'on that day' here is to assume that the narrative has now shifted yet further into the future.

This is all the more likely considering the freight carried by the phrase 'on that day' by the early Second Temple period. This may be illustrated by the use of the term in Zechariah 14 (vv. 4, 6, 8, 9, 13, 20, 21), which looks forward to 'that day' as a time that can only as yet be imagined when even the local geography will be transformed. However, I have noted in other contexts that Haggai often echoes his prophetic predecessors and this is the case in his use of 'on that day'. It is also the case, as observed in other contexts, that he seems to have an affinity with the pre-exilic prophets. The densest cluster of occurrences of 'on that day...' is in the oracles of Isaiah of Jerusalem. Between Isa. 2.11 and 31.7 there are no less than 44 instances and, in contrast to Zechariah 14, they introduce a variety of anticipations. On some occasions, the phrase introduces a distant idealized hope for the reign of Jerusalem (e.g. Isa. 11.10; 26.1, and the vineyard vision at 27.2, 12, 13), or the recovery of a remnant some time in the future (e.g. Isa. 11.11; 28.5). At other times, it relates to events that are more contemporary (for example the references to the Syro-Ephraimite crisis of Isa. 7.18, 21, 23). Often 'that day' is a time that relates to the interaction of Israel with the surrounding nations, either in the context of an oracle against a particular nation (for example Tyre at Isa. 23.15) or as part of a vision for Israel among the nations (see especially the interaction of Egypt, Syria and Israel at Isa. 19.16-24). At one point there is even a reference to creation mythology in the form of Leviathan (Isa. 27.1). A similar multivalence is evident among Isaiah's prophetic colleagues, who evince both a concern for events of the day and a look towards an immediate and an imagined future. The contrast in the use of the term between the eighth-century BCE crisis in the Jezreel Valley (Hos. 1.5) and the wooing of Israel (Hos. 2.16, 18, 21) is one example of such. So, the hopes introduced by the phrase 'in that day' are multifarious, and oscillate between the historical and the eschatological future.

There is also an incident in Isa. 22.20-26, where 'on that day' God calls 'my servant Eliakim son of Hilkiah'. He is to be endowed with authority and to be fastened 'like a peg in a secure place, and he will become a throne of honour to his ancestral house'. Notwithstanding the problematic nature of this particular Isaianic oracle, in which the promise invested in Eliakim is apparently withdrawn, what is of particular interest is the devolvement of a future hope onto a relatively insignificant contemporary royal official.

Hope Invested in Zerubbabel
So, if I am right that all of the above lies in the background to Haggai's reference to 'that day' (v. 23), then this final investiture of hope in Zerubbabel is in continuity with much that has gone before. It is a hope that oscillates around several poles: an expectation of pre-eminence for Judah among the

other nations, a sense that the personalities and events of the day have something to do with all this and always an expectation that looks beyond those personalities and events to an as yet only imagined future. In that sense, the expectations placed on Zerubbabel are in continuity with what has preceded in the Haggai narrative. They are grounded in the conviction that God is at work in the present; just as the re-establishment of the temple is an indicator of that work, so too is the leadership of Zerubbabel. Once that point is established, and Zerubbabel is relieved of the eschatological burden that he has so often been asked by interpreters of these verses to carry, then the oracle becomes less problematic. Since Zerubbabel is not seen by Haggai as a messianic figure, so the oracle does not need to be seen as failed prophecy.

Further, it specifies what has so far only been implied by Haggai, that the restoration of the temple must go hand in hand with the maintenance of the house of David. The appointment of Zerubbabel, a Davidide governor of Judah appointed by the Persian empire, is one further step in that process of restoration. Zerubbabel continued to be a name that was honoured at least by portions of Judaism during the Second Temple period for the role that he played (see Sir. 49.11). But the eschatological story is not yet fully told and there is more yet to come.

'My Servant'
This is further borne out by the descriptors of Zerubbabel and by the verbs of which he is the object. Taking the descriptors first, Zerubbabel is still 'son of Shealtiel' just as he has been throughout the narrative, but he is no longer described as 'governor of Judah'; he has now become 'my servant'. At one level, this is a narrative indicator of the importance of Zerubbabel as governor of Judah. In fulfilling this function, he is doing the work of God. In that respect he is in the same league as the patriarchs (Gen. 26.24), Moses (Exod. 14.31), Joshua (Josh. 24.29), David (2 Sam. 7.5) and Eliakim (Isa. 22.20-25), all of whom carried out their appointed functions as God's 'servants'.

The term comes with two other important connotations. It is from time to time attached to individuals who have a particular function that seems to transcend the context in which they are operating. Whether the servant of Deutero-Isaiah is identified as messianic or not, the vision for the servant of Isaiah 42–55 relates to an ideal future. Similarly, 'Branch' of Zech. 3.8 is described as 'my servant'. There too the servant is implicated in a vision of the future. Famously, King Nebuchadnezzar is also described by Yahweh as 'my servant' in Jer. 27.6. In his case there is apparently no transcendent significance to the term, but a clear sense that Nebuchadnezzar plays a role in the temporal plans of God for Babylon and its neighbours in the sixth century BCE. This multivalence is similar to what was observed around the phrase 'on that day'. Like that phrase, the term 'servant' earths the role of Zerubbabel in the events of his day, but brings with it a sense of God at work in those events and a strong hint of a significance that transcends the current context. Historically, we do not know what Zerubbabel went on to achieve among the Judeans. As God's servant he played an important role at a time when the temple project had lost momentum, and in so doing helped to build a future beyond the sixth century BCE.

'Signet Ring'

Zerubbabel is also described as a 'signet ring'. In fact, in Hebrew the term is literally 'signet' and refers to the royal seal with which important documents were attested and then secured. It was an assertion of the authority of the one who owned the seal. Due to the importance of the signet, it was often worn on the finger of the king, hence the assumption of the NRSV translation that 'signet ring' is intended. The reference to the 'signet on my right hand' in Jer. 22.24 supports that assumption. It was an object that was both precious and expressive of authority. It was also an object that could be regarded as a metaphor for belonging, and is so used in Song 8.6 of the somewhat more egalitarian relationship between lovers. Indeed, the same idiom is used in Song of Songs as of Zerubbabel, the verb *sym* followed by *ḥwtm* ('signet') with a preposition of simile prefixed to the noun, 'made you like a signet'. This suggests that it should be seen as a sign as much of belonging as of delegated authority. Zerubbabel is both one who is precious to Yahweh and one who for a brief period is a bearer of Yahweh's authority. However, the authority that he bears is derived and exercised on behalf of another just as is that of a servant. Once again, it is a term that is used of temporal relationships and authority, but also carries implications beyond its immediate context.

'Take', 'Make' and 'Chosen'

Three verbs are employed in this verse with Zerubbabel the signet ring as their object. The first is 'take', *lqḥ*. This has connotations of selecting or summoning somebody to a task. It need not denote any significance for the object or person taken, although in the present context it should be read with the third verb used of Zerubbabel, 'chosen' (*bḥr*). This specifies that Yahweh's 'taking' Zerubbabel is not a random or neutral action, but contains a strong element of intent appropriate to one designated as 'my servant'. Indeed the verb is used in Deutero-Isaiah of the servant of the Lord, Israel, on several occasions (Isa. 41.8; 42.1; 44.1). The sentiment expressed in the second of those references adds the rider that the servant is one 'in whom my soul delights' (Isa. 42.1). Similarly, Zerubbabel, as the servant whom God has taken and who will be like the signet ring on the finger of Yahweh, is more than a servant; he is by virtue of his selection beloved of the Lord. This is reinforced further by the second of the three verbs, 'make' (*sym*), which is better translated as 'set' or 'appoint'. It is an idiom that highlights the personal nature of the relationship between Zerubbabel as servant and Yahweh.

'Says the Lord of Hosts'

Finally, the prophet signs off his final oracle with the affirmation, 'says the Lord of hosts'. This has been the signature tune of the entire Haggai narrative, perhaps more so than for any of the other writing prophets, and it is appropriate that this should be the last word. The Lord has spoken, the second or reconstituted temple is under way and the leadership of David, whose nation-building work made the first temple possible, is being recalled and re-envisioned. It is now over to the people of Judah to work through how all that might look in the changed circumstances of the restoration, an enterprise that may be observed in the literature of Second Temple Judaism (see my comments on the interpretive context in the Introduction). It is now also over to Judah, and to Haggai's readers, to continue to bring a worthy offering of themselves and their work to Yahweh.

CONCLUSION:
THE CONTEMPORARY RELEVANCE
OF HAGGAI

Summary of Method

In the terms laid out in the Prolegomena, I have sought to read the book of Haggai primarily as a coherent narrative, both with a discrete message of its own and as an episode in the longer story of the struggle to restore Judah at the end of the sixth century BCE. The narrative has also shown strong connections with the yet longer story of the people of Israel, particularly but not exclusively as it has been mediated through the corpus of prophetic writings. As I have read the narrative, I have tried to allow it to speak in its own terms as much as possible. The tools of narrative criticism and the supporting work of historical-critical analysis have assisted in this task. Additionally, I have been guided by some of the pragmatic linguistic categories expounded in Speech-Act Theory and Relevance Theory. The concepts of locution and of inference have been particularly helpful.

These have guided us towards an awareness of the circumstances of the hearers and readers of this narrative and a corresponding alertness to the inferences that would have been taken from the words and story of the prophet Haggai in those early years after the return from exile. Relevance Theory has also supplied the category of 'implicature' (as opposed to 'implication') as a guide to this reading. Essentially, this recognizes an intentionality in what the text or its author wishes to convey, alongside an onus on the reader to discern ambiguities in the text present in what Relevance Theory calls 'weak implicatures'. Speech-Act Theory leads in a similar direction with its focus on locution, and in particular the concepts of illocutionary intent and perlocutionary effect. I have sought to make use of those categories in the proposition that divine discourse is contained within the biblical text. Therefore, as the story of the words of Yahweh to Zerubbabel, Joshua and their people, as delivered through the hand of Haggai, are read, both the intent and the effect of those words may be discerned as divine discourse. And readers of Scripture may expect also to discern a contemporary intent and effect of the divine discourse.

The deployment of those tools contains a huge assumption about the nature of text as vehicle for divine discourse. This raises the issue of the context of the contemporary reader and its impact on a reading of Haggai. I have already implicitly revealed one aspect of my context, namely, my Christian expectation that the text speaks the words of God. There are other aspects of my reading context that must be acknowledged, and part of the task of this conclusion will be to draw my contextual assumptions to the surface of discerning the relevance to our own times of the text as delivered and received in its original context. This will draw on the categories of Relevance Theory noted briefly above (see the Prolegomena for further analysis) to understand the implicatures that are discerned and the inferences that are drawn. An important part of this process will be to bridge the chasm between the times of Haggai's hearers and editors and our own times, while also respecting the intentionality of the oracles to the first context. I will do my work with half an eye on the types of relevance that have been discerned by readers between the Second Temple period and the present, as noted in the Introduction.

But first a summary of the form, content and context of the message of Haggai is in order.

Summary of the Message and Context

From Exile to Restoration

Traditionally, the era in Israelite history of the events set out in Ezra–Nehemiah has been described as the 'restoration'. This terminology raises the debate over the actuality or otherwise of the exile and the return to the land, and masks the fact that the history is more complex and nuanced than the historical line drawing produced by the biblical narrative. I have argued that the period of the Babylonian exile did result in a major disruption in the region of Judah and among the Judean people. I have assumed that to be the case particularly in the thesis that the prophet did not distinguish between the local populace and the returned exiles in his audience; his words were directed at both groups. In that respect Haggai can appropriately be described as a spokesman for the 'restoration'. He was interested in reinstating something that once did exist and had gone into abeyance. The vision of the book therefore is that the alienation of exile need not be a permanent state. There are those who have argued that the experience of Israel is fundamentally exilic and that the theology that arises from that experience is a theology of exile. The book of Haggai suggests that the exile is not the last word from Yahweh. There is a restoration at hand.

Now and Then
The possibility of restoration ushers in two important tensions within which the hearers of Haggai and the compilers of his prophetic narrative were compelled to live, one spatial and one temporal. The temporal tension is found between the poles of history and eschatology. Something has begun to happen in history. Cyrus and his Persian successors have acted, as a result of which the newly re-constituted nation has the chance to restore the key institutions of its nationhood. The people are in the land, the temple and its accoutrements have begun to be rebuilt and the leadership reflects the twin ideologies of priest and king. The prophet is concerned with the concrete expression of these things in the present, for they represent the potential for restoration.

At each point, however, they are not quite sufficient. The people are not yet at peace with their land (1.10), the temple is a poor reflection of what it once was (2.3) and Zerubbabel needs the promise of 'on that day' becoming the signet ring of Yahweh (2.23). At several points the narrative points beyond the present to greater possibilities. These possibilities are resident in the present circumstances but always just beyond them. The hint of as yet unfulfilled potential reverberates through the narrative as the prophecies of Haggai call forth both behavioural outcomes and eschatological hope. As the commentary has indicated, the former predominates in ch. 1 while the latter comes to the fore in ch. 2.

To that extent, the Haggai narrative is part of a wider anthology. The interaction between Joshua and Zerubbabel needs to be complemented by the oracles of Zechariah 1–8, while the questions of holiness and purity await a final resolution such as that expressed in Zech. 14.21. In that respect, the narrative is a set of context-specific oracles. That in itself encourages later readers to read them in a context-specific way.

In But Not of the Empire
The spatial tension lies in the comment above that 'Cyrus and his Persian successors have acted'. The dating of the oracles by the regnal year of the Persian emperor is a persistent reminder that the people are subjects of the empire. At the same time, Haggai's culminating promise is that Zerubbabel, the Davidic figure appointed by the Persian hegemony, will be Yahweh's signet ring (2.23). This tension between the nation as the people of God and as Persian subjects crackles through the narrative without a tidy solution being reached. The restoration of the temple and the promotion of Joshua as high priest and Zerubbabel as governor contain the possibility of a challenge to the empire. The expressions of hope that the treasures of the nations will pour into Jerusalem (2.7) and that the thrones of kingdoms will be overthrown (2.22) hold out the potential for economic and political independence from the empire. Yet somehow the narrative never spells out the implications of these hopes for Judah's relation to the empire. They are rooted in the context but always pointing beyond it.

In one sense, the puzzling promotion of Zerubbabel only reinforces the effect, for it implies that the present circumstances are ones in which Yahweh may be found. The governor of Judah is indeed the chosen one of Yahweh. For Haggai, that is enough motivation on its own to do the work of restoring the religious and temporal fabric of Judah. Yet, for the reader, the story is unfinished. At the very least it asks for the ongoing work of Zechariah 1–8 in developing a vision for the future that includes Joshua the high priest. On a wider canvas, it needs the exilic and post-exilic vision of God's faithfulness to the Davidic covenant. For the Christian, it raises questions that come further into focus in the ministry of Jesus.

Memory and Future

Speaking of the wider anthology, one of the features of Haggai is the extent to which he draws on the pre-exilic memories of the nation and recasts them for his own context. I have noticed regular echoes of Isaiah of Jerusalem and his eighth-century colleagues. Haggai joins them also in looking back to the foundational events of the covenant people, the law and the Exodus. The words of Jeremiah and Deutero-Isaiah also reverberate from time to time. We might have imagined that the prophets of the exile would primarily have been ringing in Haggai's ears as he undertook his work of restoration. Like them, however, he has reached further back for an appreciation of the significance of the moment. As with his prophetic colleagues, Haggai begins with memories as he confronts the present and the future. Although the covenant is not explicitly mentioned, it forms part of the backdrop to Haggai's oracles, as it does for the prophets whom he echoes.

A Time to Build/a Time Not to Build

These spatial and temporal tensions flow from the opening exposition of the problem confronting the prophet, that the people are living in their own houses while the Lord's house lies in ruins. As discussed in the body of the commentary, there is a strong intertextuality with the occasion when David compared the splendour of his own house with the Lord's tabernacle and asked to build something more splendid as a house for Yahweh. To David came the answer through the prophet Nathan that the time to build had not yet come; the privilege of building would be Solomon's (2 Sam. 7.1-17). There is a time to focus on the physical expressions of 'God with us', but the presence of God may never be contained in or guaranteed by such structures and institutions. The experience of the exile has illustrated both. The people lost the temple and their land despite the promises of God, but also discovered that God was not absent as a result. Nevertheless, at this moment, another prophet, Haggai, brings the message that to rebuild the temple is a crucial act of obedience.

A Worthy Offering

But why did Yahweh need the people to repair the temple? In one sense the only assured answer is that Yahweh required it and so it was the right thing to do, but the narrative gives us a little more to go on than that. As I explicated in the discussion on the second oracle, the gathering of materials to build the temple is likened to a harvest (1.8). The diversion of scarce resources to the temple project, even at a time when the people are struggling to fill a 'bag with holes' (1.6), is in the nature of an offering to God. At this moment in the people's history, the rebuilding project is a worthy offering. Apart from the focus on priestly concerns of purity in the penultimate oracle, one of the interesting aspects of the Haggai narrative is that a concern for the temple building does not lead to a pervasive focus on the cult. Even in the parable of purity and impurity (2.11-14), the narrative quickly moves on to other considerations. Nevertheless, the sacrificial system forms a persistent backdrop to the narrative. This reinforces the call on the people to build the temple as a worthy offering to Yahweh.

Desolate Land/Desolate Temple
The prophet draws a strong link between the failure of the land to provide for its inhabitants and the failure of the people to set their priorities and bring a worthy offering. This is couched in terms that may be understood against the background to the prophecy. It is set in a settled period within the Persian empire by which time conditions have slowly stabilized, yet still the people's experience is of a constant battle to make ends meet. In the terms laid down by Haggai, this would probably have been understood as an outcome of cultic disobedience (2.16-19). In an age in which global and local ecological concerns are becoming increasingly urgent, the link between the habits of life of a people and the land to which they look for support is suggestive.

Intimacy and Otherness
The book of Haggai encounters other inter-related paradoxes that are inherent in the covenant relationship between Yahweh and his people. The first one to note is that Yahweh is experienced as a being who encourages intimacy while also maintaining a strong sense of otherness. The intimacy of the relationship emerges in the steady nomenclature of the temple as 'the Lord's house', although the earliest interpreters by and large papered over this effect. Only late in the narrative is the

Lord's house named as 'the temple' (2.15). At the same time, a commitment to the wellbeing of the 'the Lord's house' on the part of the people is for the pleasure and honour of Yahweh (1.8). Somehow this latter concept emerges as reasonable and just as far as the people are concerned.

Self Interest and Altruism
Closely connected to this is the question of the people's motivation for rebuilding the temple. We have seen that some readers factor out any component of religious altruism on the part of the people and argue that the motivation for building the temple lies simply in its economic importance. Beyond that, it is sometimes argued, both the temple building and the promotion of Zerubbabel constitute a temporal challenge to the empire. Against this I have argued that the religious devotion on the part of the people is genuinely conceived. What the temple building represents to a significant extent is a desire to connect with the God of the covenant. That relationship is at the heart of the prophetic motivation. There is no doubt, however, that the outcome does have material benefit, not only in the restoration of an aspect of the societal infrastructure that carries an economic benefit, but also in the simple promise of agricultural blessing that accompanies it (2.19). The blessing of God is experienced in the material and the particular.

The Ordinary and the Cultic
Closely related to this is the interaction between what, for want of a better set of terms, I am calling the cultic and the ordinary. The narrative is deeply concerned with the experience of the people on the land: their wages, their productivity, their sense of involvement with a worthwhile project. Despite the fact that the entire story is focused around the building of a temple, it is surprising how little the explicitly cultic intrudes on this story. Even the oracle that discusses matters of holiness and purity treats these categories as a parable of the relationship between the temple itself and agricultural bounty or the lack thereof (2.15). That the narrative concludes with a vision of the role of Zerubbabel and the destruction of kingdoms is a large clue that readers are not to remain focused narrowly on the material functions of the temple (2.22-23); they are a signal for something much bigger. Yet the temple

does remain central to the narrative. As observed in the body of the commentary, the cultic remains part of the backdrop to the action. The narrator does not intend to factor it out. These two aspects remain in tension.

The Charismatic and the Institutional
This also highlights a broader tension, of which post-exilic Israel's concern for the temple is but one example; that is, the tension between the charismatic and the institutional in the religious life of the people. The vision of the oracles of Haggai is not ultimately for the construction of a building that will never look quite as good as its Solomonic predecessor. The construction of that building is essential at this point in the life of the re-emergent nation, for, despite its inadequacy, this restored temple will achieve a 'splendour greater than the former', the spirit will abide among the people in a way not previously witnessed, and the promises which emerge from the foundational experience of the Exodus are assured (2.5-9). These are the important things, and all of them connect the prophecies with the covenant in some way. They are matters which might be denoted as 'charismatic' in that they point towards a relationship of grace that is bigger than any of the externals and remain true and possible despite the externals. Yet they are worked out in a specific institutional context at a specific point in time with even an intertextual hint of political relevance in the endowment of the spirit. This is the nature of religious experience. Contextless faith is ultimately impossible in the prophetic vision.

Leaders and People
A further tension emerges in the narrative between the roles of leaders and their people in the matter of being the people of God. In my comment on the final oracle of the book, I noted the gradual shift in focus from the leaders who received the instructions to build the temple to the people they were leading until by the time of the fifth oracle the two are indistinguishable. Then the final oracle suddenly shifts the spotlight, not back onto Joshua and Zerubbabel together, but to Zerubbabel alone. As with much of the classical prophetic material, a first response is called for from the leaders of the people. There is

much said in the writing prophets about the inadequacies or otherwise of prophets, priests and kings (arguably all encapsulated in the damning indictment of false shepherds in Ezek. 34), although, in tune with a changed restoration tone, Haggai is more mild mannered than most of his predecessors. What is remarkable is the shift of focus onto the people. They are the bearers of the spirit and they respond in obedience as much as do their leaders (1.14). A democratization seems to have occurred in the light of which the shift back onto Zerubbabel is a puzzle. It is probably best to read this as an intended paradox borne out by human experience. From at least the time of the Deuteronomist (which I trace to the Josaianic reforms of late seventh century BCE), personal responsibility of the type implicit in the blessings and curses of Deuteronomy 28–30 has been sought by the prophets, yet the realization of a communal vision is always more than the sum total of personal commitments. Its achievement also requires leadership and a focus of hope and unity. Zerubbabel, God's chosen signet ring, is part of the answer to that need to galvanize the people's obedience into a bigger project.

The Nature of Holiness

I have indicated above that the oracles of Haggai need to be read both as a discrete narrative and within their wider literary context. In terms of the wider literary context, there are two things that the Haggai narrative does not do. First, by the end of his oracles Haggai has not quite articulated a universal vision, despite the emerging interest in the nations. The parable of the fifth oracle makes clear that the priestly paradigm retains some of its privilege. Despite what has been said about the temple not being an end in itself, the religious system that it draws around itself is still important. While the questions asked by Haggai in 2.10-14 and the concepts behind them seem strange to Western ears, they would not have seemed either strange or out of place to Haggai's hearers. They would have been obvious statements to the effect that any correlation of purity between the temple and the people cannot be mediated. This has two effects: one is to remind the people that they need the temple to be pleasing to God in their midst, and the second is that they need to be doing the building in a state of purity.

For the moment this is an important accompaniment to the paradoxes outlined above. The particular and the concrete remain important in the exercise of faith.

Evil and Suffering
The oracles of Haggai also fall some way short of an attempt at a theodicy. Perhaps this is because the prophet is too wise to attempt one, knowing that an ultimate solution is likely to be unattainable. Probably, though, it arises from his concern to explore the relationship between the currently unsatisfactory human experience of life in the land and the possibility of pleasing God. At this moment, the answer is to be found in a whole-hearted attempt at rebuilding the temple with the possibility that this momentary faithfulness is a marker post on a much longer journey. Ultimately, the prophet promises, there is a link between faithfulness and blessing. Short of 'ultimately', though, that link cannot always be relied upon, and it is the task of the writers of books such as Job and Ecclesiastes, and even occasionally the prophets (e.g. Amos 4.7; 5.15; Hos. 11.9) to confront that fact. But that exploration lies beyond the scope of this story.

Messianic, Eschatological, Contemporary?
Another way of drawing all this together is to consider the extent to which the oracles of Haggai are messianic, eschatological and/or contemporary. I have made the point consistently that the book of Haggai can only be thought of as messianic in a derived sense. The two references that are most often interpreted as messianic are the phrase 'treasure of all nations' (2.7) and the picture of Zerubbabel as 'signet ring' (2.23). In the case of the former, the phrase should be understood in temporal terms, and if there is an eschatological slant to it, this should not be thought of as messianic.

The argument is a little different in the case of the final reference to Zerubbabel. While this does denote a special status for Zerubbabel, that status need not be messianic. It does constitute a continuation of the Davidic hope but it is anchored firmly to the present circumstances. Although Zerubbabel continued to command respect at least within elements of Second Temple Judaism, he does not seem to have attained messianic status in his own right (Sir. 49). With respect to messianism, the most that can be said is that Zerubbabel is one marker in the Davidic trajectory, but even this should not be overstated lest the message of Haggai to his own day be distorted.

With respect to matters eschatological, the approach taken in this commentary has been to understand the 'eschatological' as concerning both events in the future around which hope coalesces and an all-embracing sense of the cosmic significance of the temple and all that it represents. Taking that approach, little has been found in the oracles of Haggai that point to a final end. There is, however, a clear expectation of a better future and a confidence that the temple occupies a place at the centre of the cosmos. This hope gathers around several key and well-attested themes: the temple, agricultural bounty, sovereignty of some sort among the nations and the appearance of a key leadership figure. In that respect, Haggai is eschatological, but again care has been taken not to overstate that and thereby inadvertently attribute an entirely futurist cast to the book.

Throughout, I have insisted that the oracles of Haggai arise from the context in which the people find themselves early in the Second Temple period, and they aim to address the conditions that prevail in that immediate context. They expect a change from apathy to obedience on the part of the people; they expect that that change will be fuelled by the activity of the spirit of the Lord among the people and their leaders; they expect an immediate consequence of attention to the temple rebuilding project; and they expect the fledgling nation to know an enhanced level of prosperity as a result. Yet, just as the eschatological cast to aspects of the prophetic language should not be overstated, neither should the contemporary nature of these oracles. This is more than a utilitarian vision. There are regular hints that Haggai's vision, deeply committed to and rooted in his and his hearers' circumstances, is always somehow bigger than those circumstances and times. As indicated on a number of occasions, there is a constant oscillation between the historical and the eschatological of which any reading for contemporary relevance must take account.

A Contemporary Readerly Context

All of the above seems to this particular reader to portray the world of the text. Now the context in which the text has been read by this commentary will be considered from three main angles: first, from a position within my own particular community of faith, secondly as somebody who inhabits the Western hegemony, and thirdly as a citizen of an increasingly fragile globe. Each perspective brings with it its own kaleidoscope of effects and these will also be explored.

With the New Testament

As indicated, I read as a Christian, which means that I bring my expectation of divine discourse to a canon that includes the New Testament. I have adopted the interpretation that sees the aspirations of the temple as idealized in a faithful community. This move is not a Christian one *per se*, as such trajectories are well established within Second Temple Judaism. However, the New Testament, perhaps supremely in the Fourth Gospel, shifts the focus even more sharply onto an individual, Jesus (Jn 2.21). The role of the temple then shifts further onto the community formed and left by Jesus. And there is a further eschatological move that sees the reign of the people of God as entirely obviating the need for all that the temple symbolized, as the symbol itself is fully realized within the people of God (Rev. 21.22). My approach to Haggai is therefore implicitly christological. As I consider what the prophet has to say about the temple, I am also aware of the vision realized in the person of Jesus and maintained through the Christian faith. All the possibilities inherent in the oracles of Haggai therefore help to inform my expectations for the Church in our own day.

Within the Church

I read Haggai as an ordained member of the Anglican Church in New Zealand. This brings with it a whole range of understandings of the nature of the Church. At its most basic level, this constitutes a conscious commitment to the institutional life of the church: its liturgy and hymnody, its authority structures and its hermeneutics. For better or worse, my presupposition is that a pure eschatological vision has not yet been realized and that heaven on earth has not yet been realized. As a result, it is not possible to live out a corporate expression of faith without certain material religious accompaniments to enable that to happen. This is not to say that these are the essence of that faith, nor to deny that they are subject to critique by the very faith which I profess. However, as human beings we cannot sustain any kind of charismatic experience of the divine apart from the temporal contexts in which we find ourselves.

While my Christian context keeps me alert to possibilities beyond the text of Haggai, my temporal context within the institutional Church means that the oracles of Haggai give me much to reflect on about the significance of that institution. In that respect I do not read with any sense that the Old Testament has been surpassed by the existence of the New Testament. Rather, the reading of each is enriched and clarified by the other.

The use to which I am putting my reading of Haggai replicates movements made by Haggai. To a significant extent, the content of his message is fuelled by the work of his predecessors and the memory that makes up the narrative of the people who hear his words. The prophet expects that God will yet again work in a way that has characterized him, but will do so in a manner that is particular to current circumstances. In the same way, my listening for the voice of Yahweh is to a significant extent now fuelled by the work of Haggai and the longer memories which he evokes, while expecting Yahweh to speak and act today in a manner that is both historically characteristic and also contemporaneously particular.

As a Leader

All of the writing prophets set high standards for the leaders of their people—prophets, priests, kings and sages—and most are less optimistic about the value of leaders than Haggai, but Haggai does more than most to load his oracles directly onto particular leaders. As somebody in a leadership role, my reading is captivated by the focus on leaders. I find there another tension between the charismatic and institutional. The narrative begins with expectations on Joshua and Zerubbabel as the leaders of the people and ends with a strong focus on the person of Zerubbabel. In between, what is important and effective is that the people respond directly to the message by the hand of Haggai. That is the key to the success of the rebuilding project. And they do not do so because this message has been further mediated by the leaders; they do so because God is with them and God's spirit abides with them (2.5). There is a place for designated leadership, but the relationship of the people of the covenant with Yahweh is in one sense a highly democratic one. The oracles of Haggai function as a standing rebuke to those within the Church who expect to legislate the relationship between Yahweh and his people, and at the same time to those who would simply vacate the call to leadership.

From within a Western Hermeneutic and Epistemology
So far I have specified a reading from within the church. I now turn from that to consider the consequences of my reading location in the West. Before turning to issues of content, I note tangentially that my reading brings with it certain hermeneutical and epistemological assumptions. At the level of epistemology, I have read Haggai in an essentially linear manner despite my attempts to appreciate the narrative as narrative rather than proposition. I have also privileged the historical-critical method in the sense that my attention to narrative has not eliminated an alertness to that cardinal of historical-critical methodological sins, the anachronism. This has also meant that I am required to argue rather than assume contemporary relevance for the text.

I have also adopted a hermeneutical position that gives credence to the intention of the author while also accepting a responsibility as reader to generate meaning. I have employed categories of relevance and inference in doing so. The self-conscious nature of this enterprise is itself a consequence of my Western context, where I am less free merely to appreciate and appropriate a narrative but must struggle to incorporate the categories of 'fact' and 'fiction' in my reading.

From within 'Panelled Houses'
With respect to the content and setting of the Haggai narrative, my Western context brings two strong points of connection. The first is found in the programmatic statement of Haggai's that those who 'earn wages earn wages to put them into a bag with holes' (1.6). These people are presumably those

who are living in panelled houses while the house of the Lord 'lies in ruins' (1.4). In the body of the commentary I have described this as the failure of adequacy. In that respect it has powerful echoes in the experience of those who live in the West. We enjoy a disproportionate share of the world's physical resources as the well off among us enjoy record levels of personal disposable income. Yet this does not seem to bring a marked increase in general wellbeing; the persistence of mental illness, the incidence of depression and suicide and the high levels of family dysfunction all point to a societal dis-ease. There is also poverty in the West, but we should not think that the Western dis-ease is confined to the materially disadvantaged. We know perhaps better than any other people in history that having enough is not the key to contentment. The words of Haggai, as we relate to this description of ourselves, point us beyond ourselves.

Within the Empire
The second point of connection relates to the place of Judah within the Persian empire of the day. I have explored the fact that after the exile the people of Judah find themselves in a position that they have hitherto not experienced. Since their delivery from slavery in Egypt through the experience of the Exodus they have gradually been formed into an independent people. There were varying degrees of dependence on the pleasure of surrounding states throughout this process, but always they retained a level of autonomy within which to express themselves as God's people. From the time of the conquest onwards, their story was organized around the chronology of their leaders. Of course, there was regular interaction with leaders of other nations, but the story of Israel and Judah was not organized against the chronology of those nations.

Up until the time of the Haggai narrative the people of the covenant have been either slaves or relatively independent nations. There was no middle ground. Now the events in question take place in the 'second year of King Darius's and this marks a sea change. With the restoration and the loss of the monarchy, the people are neither slaves nor an independent nation; they exist at the Persian imperial pleasure. Despite the attempts of some commentators to argue otherwise, the narrative remains paradoxically content to live in this middle ground between slavery and independence. Of course, in real terms it is quite possible that the amount of autonomy enjoyed by the new Judean province within the Persian empire was greater than that available during times when the kings of Israel were essentially vassals of their larger neighbours. Nevertheless, I would argue, a fundamental shift has taken place with the restoration, as the people of God learn to live without a king and to co-exist with the empire. The hopes placed in Zerubbabel and the rebuilt temple point constantly beyond imperial realities but do not of themselves constitute a temporal rebellion against those realities.

In some respects this reflects the Western Church's accommodation with the State. The Church in the West has existed essentially at the pleasure of the State, and has been well used to forming a community within the framework of loyalty to the State. The State is never seen as sufficient, and a Christian eschatology points constantly beyond the State to something greater, yet there is an appreciation of the futility of a frontal temporal rebellion against the State. Positively, this enables the Church to engage with the State in the development of a civil society. But these conditions may also combine to dull the eschatological edge in Western Christianity and to militate against a prophetic function for the Church. Notwithstanding various recent explorations of the theme of exile, it would be fair to say that the Church in Western democracies has little sense of itself as an exiled people, as dwellers in a 'foreign land' (Ps. 137.4). In that respect, the book of Haggai is relevant to our own attempts to live with integrity in an environment in which we exist as a people with the permission of the State, and yet can never give our whole-hearted loyalty to that State. We may live in the reign of Darius (1.1), but always we are a people who have been brought out of Egypt (2.5).

On a Fragile Planet
To look yet wider, in Haggai's view the problem of the purse without holes in it was more than simply a problem of misplaced loyalties, although it was that. It was also a reflection of a land that was at odds with the inhabitants that looked to it for nurture. The prophet draws a link between the state of the land and the state of the temple. Both are desolate, and as

a result the people do not experience prosperity. In the mind of the prophet there is a causal relationship, and once the temple is attended to then the desolation of the land will look after itself, or more accurately, will be looked after by Yahweh. This link between the experience of the land and the priorities of the people resonates strongly with our own day, although in ways that Haggai could scarcely have imagined. We depend on an ecosystem that is increasingly under pressure; species are disappearing, climate change is causing enormous human upheavals in certain places, the consumption of non-renewable energy resources continues unabated, the destruction of deserts and forests is a frightening and evident reality, and the ocean's food stocks continue to be fished out.

These things are not happening merely because the planet is capricious. It is not difficult to draw a link between the pressure faced by our ecosystem and the behaviour of its human inhabitants. At the most basic level, as we maintain our creature comforts much of our behaviour in the West reflects that of Hezekiah when he was confronted with a message of doom by Isaiah: '[at least] there will be peace and security in my days' (Isa. 39.8). Furthermore, we continue to hold to the mantra of growth as the means of progress at a time when the imperative is sustainability. The necessary political will to make adjustments to lifestyle in the name of sustainability simply seems unsustainable. As an additional factor, there are evident inequities between the consumptive West and the rest of the world. At a time when global and international initiatives are required to address some of these issues, it is extraordinarily difficult to gain the necessary accord between competing groups and nations. The Western inability to be self-moderating also means that poorer groups often do not have the wherewithal to behave in sustainable ways. A desolate planet populated by a desolated people is a realistic scenario. In that context, we in the West are especially challenged by the link between the experience of the people and the experience of the environment evident in Haggai.

In a Fractured World

An inescapable aspect of the contemporary reading context is that we live in a world struggling between globalization and tribalization. The most evident and globalized aspect of this phenomenon is what we have come to call 'post-9/11'. As I write, this the morning paper contains stories of panic-stricken passengers, fearing the worst, fleeing a London bus whose engine has caught fire as a result of mechanical breakdown; of seven US marines killed in a suicide attack in Iraq; of the rise of religious hate crimes in Britain; and of the possibility of terrorist cells functioning in Australia. Others will have other perspectives on these things, but from whatever angle we look at the problem, we find radically different worldviews at odds with each other. From my Western and Christian perspective, it is imperative that we learn to share the planet with each other peaceably, lest the fractures destroy us.

A more local phenomenon within my own country is the challenge of immigration. Increasing numbers of New Zealanders look to East and South Asia, the Pacific or the Middle East for their cultures of origin where once most recent arrivals to New Zealand were from Britain or to a lesser extent continental Europe. This leads inevitably to tensions that are not unrelated to events in the wider world such as the West's conflicts with Islam or the emergence of China and India as embryonic super powers. At the time of writing, we in New Zealand are gearing up for a general election, and again fears around immigration are on the agenda. This happens at each election but the fear-mongering hits a different people group each time. On these small islands we experience in microcosm the challenge to live together. In this particular context, the question is sharpened by the presence of an indigenous Maori population and the long attempt to rectify the failure of the largely British settler population to honour the Treaty of Waitangi (1840) between the Maori tribal leaders and the British crown. To whom the land belongs, and at what point somebody may be said to belong on it, remain live questions.

Both the New Zealand and the international contexts of fracture find echoes in the context within which Haggai did his work. He too faced a question of belonging on the land: Was it for those who had returned from Jerusalem or for those who had remained and never gone away? The response of Haggai was to develop a message that spoke to both groups, in that he articulated the loss felt by each and presented a vision that could potentially unite each. The exile had resulted in the destruction of the infrastructure and institutions of the kingdom of Judah, as a result of which a sense of identity and material well-being were significantly diminished both for those who remained in the Judean region and for those who were taken away to exile. Once the exiles had returned to the land, this situation continued to obtain for both groups to a significant degree. For each, Haggai drew a line between the state of the land and the people's own experience. And then he created a common vision, which was the formation of the temple as an offering to God and as a focal point around which the blessing of God could be experienced.

Haggai's contexts and our own are not the same in certain important respects. The cultural divisions are more diverse and much deeper than in that early Second Temple context, and there was a much greater opportunity for Haggai to develop a shared religious vision than is available to us today. Nevertheless, there is something to be learned by noting the commonality of the experience of fracture and the attempt to develop a vision around which people can gather.

Earlier Interpreters

In the light of parallels between the message and context of Haggai and some of the imperatives of the twenty-first century, it is instructive to look at the connections that other interpreters have made during the intervening centuries. Core samples from the 'Recipient Context' section of the Introduction indicate that in some respects the earlier interpreters have been teachers for this reading, and in others they have not quite asked the questions of our own times nor brought the same contextual sensibilities to bear.

Like the earliest Jewish commentators, the translators of the LXX and the collectors of the Qumran material, I have not read the temple building as an end in itself, but rather as a pointer to something greater. Like the slightly later Targums, I have also allowed an eschatological edge to remain in my interpretation. However, I have felt that each lost something by the future orientation of its reading, a reading entirely understandable especially in the case of the Targum, and so I have striven to maintain a link with the oracles' temporal contexts.

The rabbinic material was seen largely to be messianic in its approach, especially with respect to Zerubbabel, despite what to the historical-critical mind are evident problems with that approach. I have been much less confident than the rabbis in that respect, and have been able to give messianic credence to the message of Haggai only in an indirect sense. Zerubbabel can be said to carry messianic hopes only to the extent that he is a torch bearer in the relay of Davidic hope that runs through the Second Temple period.

I noted also that my approach bears some resemblance to the English preacher William Jenkyn during the early stages of the English Civil War. In his reading of Haggai, Jenkyn likened the temple to the people of God in the age of the Church. I too have made a similar move in seeing the temple building as indicative in some sense of the life of the people of God, and also in seeing the hopes centred on the temple ultimately fulfilled in the person of Jesus and the community that he commissioned (see below). However, I part company with Jenkyn's explicit deployment of the story to justify partisan support for one particular side of that conflict. There remains an eschatological angle on Haggai's words which makes such an approach problematic.

Despite that, in a strange way the relevance that emerges from this reading has more in common with the approach of Jenkyn than that of the great reformers, Calvin and Luther. Both of the latter resorted to a messianic reading of the story, and Luther, consistent with his anti-Semitism, was obliged to detach the narrative from its Jewish cultic and temple context in order to be able to read meaning in it. I acknowledge the book of Haggai as a stage in the messianic journey, but again see it as more attached to its context than do either Luther or Calvin.

However, I have not reacted against what might be called the highly fideistic readings of the reformers to the extent that historical-critical consensus of the twentieth century largely has done. In those more recent readings, text-historical and history of religion questions largely predominated, so that the question of contemporary relevance was seldom asked. Such readings tended to be materialist in that they sought for motivations behind the prophetic agenda that was unacknowledged by the text, and were not always highly attuned to narrative-critical categories. As a result, they tended to downplay the religious motivation, and did not explore the eschatological with any expectation that it could apply to today's reader. The value of such readings was in their attention to the huge strides made in understanding the historical, intellectual and literary provenance that produced the oracles of Haggai and their subsequent compilation. I have piggy backed on that work in this commentary, while maintaining an expectation of contemporary divine discourse and a consequent transfer of relevance from Haggai's day to our own. It is in that expectation of relevance chiefly that this reading parts company with much text-historical work.

Although my methodology has been a little different, the outcomes perhaps have most in common with those readers whose various approaches come under the general rubric of 'believing criticism', and which have been examined in the Prolegomena. This commitment to relevance is linked to the point made that the message of Haggai remains earthed in contemporary concerns while looking always just beyond them. I therefore expect that the words of Yahweh by the hand of Haggai will continue to speak to each generation of readers, similarly earthed in contemporary concerns but looking beyond them. That is why it has been important to clarify the context of this present reading of Haggai, to specify what those concerns might be.

Contemporary Relevance

The search for relevance is more than a desire to connect with the great themes of human life contained in a literary classic. The expectation that Yahweh speaks in and through the text lies at the heart of my reading of Haggai. As I discern relevance, I am therefore discerning the voice of Yahweh in my own life and in the days in which I and other readers of this commentary live. I am conscious that this is not a position shared by all readers of this commentary, but it is a defensible epistemological position to adopt and it is the goal of this particular reading.

In considering the context of Haggai as against my own context, the same tension emerges that dogs any attempt to read the Old Testament for relevance today; that is, a tension around the scope of the covenant. I have argued that a covenantal understanding informs the work of Haggai as it does the work of most of his colleagues among the writing prophets. For Haggai, life within the covenant and the life of the society which he was addressing were closely aligned. For those who read from within the Church, for whom the notion of a theocratic society is not an option, this assumption cannot be sustained. Always in our reading a distinction must be maintained between the relevance of the words of Yahweh to those who understand themselves to be the people of God—and hence participants in the covenant—and the relevance of those same words to society as a whole. This distinction is of course not entirely absent from the prophets. Their appeal back to the creation tradition constantly takes them beyond the covenant, and the emerging sense that the 'nations' will in some sense as yet undefined be participants in the benefits of the covenant has the same effect. This sense is present also in Haggai, especially in 2.7. Nevertheless, the distinction between the covenant and the creation mandates is more deeply felt by a Christian reader and especially a Western reader. My sense of the relevance of Haggai to my own times, then, needs to begin with this distinction.

As a caveat, I acknowledge that the distinction between covenant and society in my reading is only valid to the extent that the two contexts of reading are allowed to inform each other. As was Haggai, so must the church be both self-conscious in its common life and aware of its responsibilities to the wider world within which it is situated.

A Vision for Restoration
From within the covenant I find much that speaks into my own times. Perhaps most basically, the message of restoration challenges those who argue that a theology of exile is the necessary default setting for the Church's self-understanding. The vision of restoration earthed in the events of the day continues to encourage the Christian community that a sense of exile need not be a permanent state. This does not deny that there is more yet to come, but it does lead to a strong commitment to read the times and discern the possibilities of restoration among the people of God as we find them.

As we engage in this exercise, we step into a delicate dance with time. While a theology of restoration lives constantly with a sense of the realized future in the face of exile, the fuel for this hope is a remembered past. Just as Haggai constantly draws the remembered story of Yahweh and Yahweh's people into the present, so we are called to do the same. This entails not just the narrative of Scripture but the memory of God at work in the Church and the world ever since. For each of us who makes some kind of confessional commitment, this entails a critical appreciation of our tradition. It also entails a lively sense of God's activity in the world around us bringing forth justice and hope, and a sense that each time we see this happen we glimpse a foretaste of the ultimate restoration of both the church that God has brought into being and the world that God has made. One of the points made above was that Haggai does not engage in theodicy as such, and yet this dynamic perhaps responds to that. The constant hope held out for restoration is a tacit acknowledgment of the existence of evil, and an affirmation that evil is not unanswered.

Discerning Obedience
The path to restoration according to Haggai is that of discerning obedience. There was a time when David discerned that he was not to build a temple and there was a time when Yahweh through Haggai instructed the people to rebuild the temple that had been destroyed. From within a sense of ourselves as inheritors of the covenant, there is never any doubt about our goals, just as there was not for Haggai: to build for the pleasure of Yahweh and for the amelioration of the desolation that we discern around us at any given moment. The challenge is to discover the particular nature of the obedience required to that end. At this point in the hermeneutical process there is inevitably some multivalence and variegation of response among people of faith. Yet there are enough connections between our own day and that of Haggai to make some suggestions as to what this might mean, to be led by scripture in a particular direction.

A Worthy Offering
We undertake the tasks before us with a sense of making an offering to God. While nothing we do is unalloyed or free from

the egotistical realities of human nature, it is nevertheless possible to guard our motivations. The people of Judah were called to rebuild their temple as a pleasing offering to God, not unlike the first fruits of an agricultural offering. Interpreters read between the lines of the prophet occasionally suggest a materialist or self-centred motivation for the project. Whether that was present among the project leaders or not is something that cannot finally be determined, but the text is clear that that would not be the reason for the project being blessed and the desolation being relieved. It is blessed to the extent that it is offered to Yahweh as a type of first fruits.

Whatever it is that we are engaged in, a useful starting point is to guard our motivations. Churches and Christian institutions are as subject to two temptations as any other human organization. The first is the temptation to confuse the mission with the institution. All institutions, and especially institutions of the covenant, need to maintain a lively sense of purpose external to themselves in order to remain healthy; that is their mission or ultimate reason for existence. Once the purpose is reduced to the maintenance of the institution, then eventual desolation, such as that experienced by Haggai's hearers, is inevitable. The temple building was a re-assertion of the mission of God's people. Had it been for its own sake, it would not have been sanctioned by Yahweh just as it was not when David was king. Any project we undertake must pass the test of relevance for mission rather than maintenance of institution.

I have suggested that a materialist hermeneutic of suspicion applied to this brief book does not gain much traction as applicable to the motivation of the prophet. But it does alert us to a second danger inherent in a loss of institutional goal, the loss of a self-critical sense of power dynamics within Churches and Christian institutions. Such organizations have historically been as prone to self-aggrandisement and the marginalization of others, both within and without the organization, as anybody else. Perhaps they/we have even been more prone to such behaviour since unjust behaviours have sometimes been fuelled and justified by a sense of divine accreditation. Again, the call to a worthy offering that honours and pleases God is a significant counter to that tendency. In reading the book of Haggai a trend towards democratization became evident in the gradual uptake of obedience to Haggai's vision on the part of the people. That is a marker that the Church needs to be both alert to in its own sense of mission, and guided by in the way it organizes itself.

It is worth noting also that the democratization of vision and of spirit observed in Haggai incorporated both parties portrayed as in tension with each other in the Ezra–Nehemiah accounts. Together they make up the people who hear and respond to Haggai's message and receive the assurance of God's resident spirit. I have indicated the types of competing interests evident in Churches today in my description of our contemporary Western context. Only to the extent that all may share in the structural life and power dynamics of the Church will the Church have a mandate to speak on these matters to society as a whole. In this and other matters we do well to pay attention to the moat in our own eyes that distorts our constant urge to deal with the specks in others' eyes.

Institution and Charism
And this will be most possible when the Church and the Christian community is fuelled by a genuinely altruistic religious motivation. At this point I take issue with those who assume that all actions can be explained in terms of human self-interest. The book of Haggai points us towards the call to commit ourselves to something bigger than ourselves, and in this case to a project mandated by Yahweh, for it is only in that self-abnegation that human beings are able to discover their true selves. I concede that this possibility creates for us a difficult balancing act, for it is only a short step beyond making this personal risky commitment for ourselves to attempting to recruit others to the same cause to then setting ourselves up in judgment on those who do not participate with us in the righteous cause.

But the balancing act is unavoidable, for in making such a commitment we find ourselves squarely in a couple of other paradoxes of the Christian life that Haggai points us towards. The first is the necessity for the cult. Although I have taken issue with what I have termed materialist readings, which I find to be essentially reductionist in character, it is also the case that Christianity and Judaism both are uncompromisingly interested in the material. God is encountered in the created order and in the fabric of human society. Cultic expressions of faith are therefore inescapable. Engagement in the cult entails the erection of a physical and operational edifice, yet that edifice can never become an end in itself. The prophets constantly point people beyond the cult to the relationship that it is supposed to express while never being able to abandon it. The book of Haggai operates out of a cultic understanding, but only occasionally allows glimpses of the cult itself while pointing people towards the obedience to Yahweh that must form the heartbeat of the cult. The God whose self-revelation is in the cult may never be contained within that cult.

A closely related paradox is that of the institution and the spirit. This emerges most explicitly in the book of Haggai in the promise that God's spirit abides among the people (2.5) as they take courage and engage in the work of rebuilding. From a Christian perspective the spirit of God has been given to all believers in fulfilment of the vision of Joel 2.28-31, and this is often interpreted to mean that this immanent expression of God somehow bypasses the physical instruments of faith such as the cult, the priesthood and the temple. What we have now in the church is a pure community of the spirit for whom all such things are unnecessary, it is said. Yet it is inescapable that the endowment of the spirit in Haggai is in the context of rebuilding the temple and all that that implies. Notwithstanding the message of the book of Hebrews in particular, and the New Testament generally, with its vision of a christological goal for all the institutions of Judaism, the experience of Christianity and of the New Testament is that Jesus is encountered to a significant extent by means of the Church and its embryonic organization discernible within the epistles. To the Christian, working on the assumption that the spirit imbues the people of God, the message of Haggai comes as a challenge not to despise the institutional context within which the faith and mission of the Church are worked out. There is a place for buildings and liturgy and a leadership structure. Such are vital expressions of the people of God, as long as they reflect the imperatives of obedience noted above.

This paradox engages in a complex dance with the mystery of the intimacy and 'otherness' of Yahweh which is also woven through the Haggai narrative. I have noted how the metaphor of 'the Lord's house' set alongside the people's houses functions to draw out the intimacy of the relationship between Yahweh and the people, a sense largely lost in subsequent early Jewish interpretations and indeed in many Christian readings of Haggai. This is reinforced by the notion that God's spirit, almost uniquely in the Old Testament understanding of these things, 'abides among' the builders (2.5). At the same time the Lord's house does eventually emerge as 'temple' in this little book (2.15, 18) and the call to service of Yahweh is encapsulated in the expressed goal of the temple building that the Lord 'may take pleasure in it and be honoured' (1.8). Somehow we are called to live between these two appreciations: of Yahweh as companion and Yahweh as inscrutable master. Our institutional life is called to express this paradox also, of intimacy and trusting obedience, of a common life in which intimacy with God somehow leads to service and service finds its soul in intimacy with God. If we are to take a lead from the narrative of Haggai, the leading partner in this dance is Yahweh's yearning for relationship. This foreshadows the interwoven and counterbalancing metaphors of slavery and marriage used in the New Testament to describe the Christian's and the Church's relationship with Jesus.

Desolation
The link between the desolation of the temple and the desolation of the land, made quite explicit with a Hebrew pun, is also an important feature of the book of Haggai. The fact that the temple is desolate while the people look to other priorities means that the land experiences desolation. That the land experiences desolation means that the people experience a constant nagging sense of shortage or incompleteness which connects the debilitating experience of the people with the fate of the temple. Any contemporary reading of Haggai needs to take account of this interaction between land, temple and human experience. It is an interaction that defies an introverted understanding of faith. From the perspective within the covenant, it indicates that a healthy communal life is likely to contribute to an experience of personal wellbeing, granting the problems of theodicy that recognize the incomprehensible exceptions to these tendencies.

On this reading the current level of disillusionment with the institutional Church in the West must be taken seriously. To respond with the oxymoronic concept of a 'churchless faith' cannot provide a way ahead. To blame those who find shelter in such a faith is unlikely to be productive either, although I suspect that the judgment of history will lay part of the blame for the desolation of the Western Church at the feet of a philosophy that has elevated the doctrine of personal fulfilment to an unsustainable level. Rather, we need to ask whether today's Church has been faithful in its stewardship of the 'temple' that is institutional Christianity. Have we heard the voices of our prophets and leaders as they challenge us to mistrust the goal of physical security and comfort? Have we discerned well the priorities for this age in pursuit of a faith that honours God and speaks to a desolate world? Has our practice reflected the fact that the spirit is among us? Has our common life respected the democratizing impact of that spirit? To the extent that we demur from any of those questions, the book of Haggai is a challenge to the Church. In keeping with the restoration message, it is also an affirmation that the existential Church has a place in the experience and formation of the people of the covenant yet is never the end goal of that experience and formation.

Tangentially, we cannot ignore the concern for purity that also features in Haggai's oracles. In a context-sensitive reading of them, we must remain aware that Haggai is part of a larger canonical project that includes at the very least the message of Zechariah. This wider context points towards a day when purity may be transmitted, where all the limitations of human nature and experience no longer apply, and perfect intimacy is achieved with the Lord of hosts. That possibility both fuels our concern with the institutional expressions of faith and ensures that we sit lightly to them.

So far I have not talked about the intermediate link between the desolation of the temple and the poverty of experience of the people with which the book of Haggai opens. That link is the desolation of the land. More will be said on this below when the societal implications for this reading of the book of Haggai are considered, but the link is also provocative from within the covenant perspective. It invites us to ponder the extent to which the health of the covenant people and the infrastructures that sustain them are linked to the health of the environment and society around them. To draw the link appears to be a bold claim in a Western context witnessing the steady marginalization of the institutional Church. Yet the prophet invites us to do so. Could it not be that the spiritual life of a people makes just as concrete a contribution to their wellbeing as does the economic and political? That disorder in the soul of a nation plays itself out in unanticipated physical ways? That seems to have been part of Haggai's concern for his people. And might it not also be that when those to whom a people look for leadership in the intangibles of wellbeing have themselves lost focus, that the people as a whole suffer? If any of this is possible, then the failures of the Church in the West and its marginalization might in fact be contributory factors to the psychological and emotional, and perhaps even environmental, dis-ease so widely felt in the Western world.

Restoration Vision beyond the Church

This provides a natural link into a different perspective on the message of Haggai, a perspective that asks if Haggai has anything to say beyond the church and to society as a whole. My point immediately above suggests that it does. At a most basic level, it calls the Church to rediscover its ability to model a better way for society as a whole. But there are more specific points that may be made.

The message of restoration is an important one. The created order and society that inhabits it is not caught permanently in exile without hope of a better day. The Old Testament prophetic vision is one of hope for all humanity, and that hope emerges also in Haggai, principally for the prophet's own people but implicitly for any society that succeeds in putting its house in order.

Desolation Again

This is most obvious in the linguistic and conceptual link between the desolation of an unproductive land and the desolation of the unrestored temple. I have suggested that the unhealth of the Church in the West is connected in some way with the general dis-ease in Western societies. A more wide-ranging link can also be made between the priorities of society generally and the desolation of the environment specified above. Everywhere we look we see the planet under pressure. As we ponder this phenomenon, a strong link between human behaviour and the illness of the planet is not hard to draw. In particular, the tension between growth and sustainability as economic goals comes sharply into focus. The Western economies drive a system of resource allocation focused on growth and creation of wealth. The facts are that this path will lead to a situation where the planet can no longer sustain its growing number of inhabitants, and we can foresee a day when intense conflicts could erupt around increasingly scarce resources. It is said that the demand for that most basic of needs, water, will be one such source of conflict. For humanity and the planet itself to survive, we need to shift to an overarching goal of sustainability.

It should not be thought that sustainability and growth are mutually exclusive; they are not. Nevertheless, the shift in focus will not be achieved without some agreement by some people to lower their wealth expectations and to forgo some of the privileges that are now taken for granted. Those who consume the most resources will bear the most responsibility in this regard, and that places the onus squarely on Western societies. Unless we find a way to pollute less, to consume less energy, to create less waste and to resource those whose livelihoods depend on destructive practices, the desolation of our environment will continue to translate into the desolation of human society on a global scale. Sooner or later that will impact the West in cataclysmic ways.

In fact, we are faced with the very dilemma facing Haggai's hearers as they watched their wages slip through holes in the bag and their harvests persistently fail to meet expectation. Like them, in the face of an environmental crisis we hear the call to focus on a project greater than our own interests and to place the imperatives of self-fulfilment to one side. To the extent that we are able to do so, we will discover the same paradox expressed in the Haggai narrative, that when we are able to give allegiance to the interests of a greater good, then we ourselves are better off. But it does not work if the benefits themselves motivate the allegiance. Always we are drawn in some mysterious way to a transcendent reality.

It may be that not many in our world are able to achieve this shift through a Yahwist faith. But increasingly humanity, and particular Western humanity, will need to learn to achieve it through an understanding of creation as something bigger than ourselves, as an entity that calls for our higher service. This will entail an altruism that commits itself to a project whether or not the advantages of that project can immediately be experienced. I can go yet further and suggest that a commitment to the health of the environment and hence to the wellbeing of all those with whom we share the planet can be seen as in the nature of an offering to a greater cause.

The Church and the Material
From the perspective of this particular reader, the Church has an important role to play in calling people in this direction, not least because the call to rebuild the temple and the call for a sustainable approach to the environment are closely related concepts. This is the case in at least four respects. First, and as a preliminary observation, I have commented already that the revelation of Yahweh in the *torah* and in Jesus is fundamentally material. God uses the created matter that God has made in God's self-revelation. So it is right for Christians to be in the vanguard of a call to respect the physical world that God has made and to work for its renewal. Secondly, it is surely on that basis that the call for stewardship of the environment was issued in the creation account (Gen. 2.15). 'Stewardship' is a term out of favour among the practitioners of eco-theology, yet if it is understood as a call to a self-abnegating commitment to the environment as to 'another' who is greater than the one making the commitment, it is still relevant to this conversation.

Thirdly, and somewhat more subtly, a case can be made that the temple as the focal point of worship of Yahweh for the covenant people in fact mimics the ideal of the created environment as the focal point of worship of the creator for all the people that God has made. The eschatological vision of the Second Temple period builds on this possibility. Further, the New Testament focuses these possibilities onto the person of Jesus, and the final apocalyptic vision of the book of Revelation looks to a time when there is no further need for a temple in the new creation. God's dwelling is with humankind and the hopes invested in the original creative activity of Yahweh will have been revealed. Just as Haggai asked the newly returned Judeans to rebuild the temple as an act of worship to Yahweh and as a response to a disjointed world, so all humanity is now being called to rebuild the temple of creation as a response to a similarly disjointed world.

As a corollary to this third point we must acknowledge that a significant component in the current crisis of human suffering and environmental disorder is what one important analyst has called a 'clash of civilizations' between the Western and Islamic worlds. This is not the place to explore the many sides of this complex phenomenon, other than to propose that the vision of Haggai points to the necessity of finding a way to live justly and at peace with all those with whom we share the planet. To deny a stake to anyone on the grounds of culture or religion is a fundamental denial of the vision of which the rebuilt temple is a token. This is a challenge for all peoples in our own day, and to that end the Church is particularly called to a role of peacemaking.

The Temple and Creation
This brings me to the fourth point, the point at which the Christian motivation and a more environmentally focused motivation part company with one another and which I foreshadowed above in not expecting the work of restoring creation to be an act of Yahweh worship for all participants. In the book of Haggai, the restoration of the temple was undertaken to honour Yahweh, and as an offering in which Yahweh could take pleasure. It is in the service of Yahweh that the temple is rebuilt and forms the centre point of a restored creation where the people of God rediscover peace with their environment and consequent blessing. If we think of the created order as the temple of Yahweh within which has been placed humankind as God's priests and stewards, then we cannot remain content simply to concern ourselves with that temple of creation. It is the only context in which we can meet Yahweh, and yet it points us beyond itself to the creator Yahweh who calls us to relationship. It is worthy of the greatest respect, but only as the context in which the creator of humanity meets Yahweh's creatures. Creation itself cannot be the object of worship, for that is idolatry. The Church has common cause with anybody

who relates to the created order in the manner to which these oracles of Haggai beckon us, but always there is a vision of Yahweh beyond it and a sense of a barely imaginable future for the people of God and the world that God has made.

In an age of environmental crisis and religious conflict and unprecedented movements of people groups across national boundaries, the Church must be both a signpost to the future and a working model of possibility for a watching world. This will occur to the extent that the Church is obedient along the lines indicated by this reading of the book of Haggai. As Zerubbabel emerges as the leader of those who task is to rebuild the temple, may our communities of faith truly become the signet rings of God and hence leaders into a better day for all of humankind and for the creation that sustains us.

APPENDIX A: DISCOURSE ANALYSIS OF HAGGAI BASED ON THE SPEECH FORMULAE

What follows is a discourse analysis of the book of Haggai based around the speech formulae in the book. Six oracles are identified based on an analysis of the introduction to each oracle. The beginning of each segment of discourse is identified in the chart below by its speech indicator and by the speaker or agent referred to by the speech indicator. The six level 1 utterances introduce each of the six oracles identified.

Level	1	2	3	4	Speaker [agent]
A1	1.1, *byd hgy hnb'* (*l'mr*) [second year of King Darius, sixth month, first day]				[*dbr-yhwh*]
2		1.2, *kh 'mr*			*yhwh tṣb't*
3			1.2, *'mru*		*'m*
B1	1.3, *byd hgy hnb'* (*l'mr*) [no date]				[*dbr-yhwh*]
2		1.5, *kh 'mr*			*yhwh tṣb't*
2		1.7, *kh 'mr*			*yhwh tṣb't*
2		1.8, *'mr*			*yhwh*
2		1.9b, *n'm*			*yhwh tṣb't*
C1	1.13, *y'mr hgy* (*l'mr*) [second year of King Darius, sixth month, twenty-fourth day]				[*bml'kwt yhwh*]
2		1.13, *n'm*			*yhwh*
D1	2.1, *byd hgy hnb'* (*l'mr*) [second year of King Darius, seventh month, twenty-first day]				[*dbr-yhwh*]
2		2.2, *'mr* (*l'mr*)			imperative, *yhwh* to *hgy*
3			2.4, *n'm*		*yhwh*
3			2.4, *n'm*		*yhwh*
3			2.4, *n'm*		*yhwh tṣb't*
3			2.6, *kh 'mr*		*yhwh tṣb't*

3		2.7, 'mr	*yhwh tṣb't*
3		2.8, n'm	*yhwh tṣb't*
3		2.9, 'mr	*yhwh tṣb't*
3		2.9, n'm	*yhwh tṣb't*
E1	2.10, 'l *ḥgy hnb'* (*l'mr*) [twenty-fourth day, ninth month, second year of Darius]		[*dbr-yhwh*]
2	2.11, *kh 'mr*		*yhwh tṣb't*
3		2.11, *sh'l*	imperative *yhwh* to *ḥgy*
4		2.12, *y'nw* (*wy'mrw*)	*khnym*
4		2.13, *y'mr*	*ḥgy*
3		2.13, *y'nw* (*vy'mru*)	*khnym*
3		2.14, *y'n* (*'mr*)	*ḥgy*
		2.14, *n'm*	*yhwh*
		2.17, *n'm*	*yhwh*
F1	2.20, 'l *ḥgy* [twenty-fourth day]		[*dbr-yhwh*]
2	2.21, *'mr* (*l'mr*)		imperative *yhwh* to *ḥgy*
3		2.23, *n'm*	*yhwh tṣb't*
3		2.23, *n'm*	*yhwh*
3		2.23, *n'm*	*yhwh tṣb't*

Notes on Discourse Analysis

1. The level 1 material more or less coincides with identified narrative (as distinct from oracular) material and with the distribution of the dating formulae.
2. An exception to this is that there are two distinct sections A and B both under the first date.
3. There is a variation of the pattern at section C in both the speech formula and agency.
4. Section E is unique in that the oracle is embedded in a narrative of a conversation between Haggai and the priests.
5. Exceptionally, embedded in level 3 in section A is quoted speech from the people.
6. Following on from that, the interaction of oracle in narrative and narrative in oracle blurs the distinction, and is further argument for the integrity of the Haggai narrative, as against traditional form-critical divisions (seeAppendix B).
7. With the exception of section C noted already, all sections are introduced in level 1 by agency of *dbr-yhwh*.

8. In sections A–D the word of the Lord comes *byd ḥgy* ('by the hand of Haggai') while in sections E and F it comes *'l ḥgy* ('to Haggai').
9. The only divine name used is *yhwh*.
10. It is *yhwh* alone in level 1, and it oscillates in the other levels between *yhwh* and *yhwh tṣb't*, although in no discernible pattern. Thirteen of twenty occurrences of the divine name in levels 2 and below are *yhwh tṣb't*.
11. Every section except section A employs *n'm*, increasing in intensity as the book proceeds.
12. Except for section A, every section concludes with a *n'm*, and in that context it has an emphatic function.
13. Haggai is specified as *hnby'* at the start of each section except section F, thus emphasizing his status.

APPENDIX B:
TRADITIONAL FORM-CRITICAL ANALYSIS OF ORACLES AND NARRATIVE IN HAGGAI

In contrast to the discourse structure expressed in Appendix A and adopted for this reading of the book of Haggai, what follows is the traditional form-critical distinction between oracle and narrative. The coincidence between this pattern and a discourse analysis based on speech formulae is close but not exact.[1]

1	1.1, Narrative *introducing* oracle *to* Joshua and Zerubbabel	
1!		1.2, Oracle *concerning* the people
2	1.3, Narrative *introducing* oracle	
2!		1.4-11, Oracle *concerning* the people
3	1.12-13a, Narrative *describing response* to one oracle, *introducing* the next *response* of Joshua, Zerubbabel and remnant of people/people	
3!		Oracle *to* the people
4	1.14–2.1, Narrative *describing response* to one oracle, *introducing* the next *to* Joshua, Zerubbabel and remnant of the people	
4!		2.2-9, Oracle *to* Joshua, Zerubbabel and people of the land *concerning* 'all the nations'

1. ! indicates oracle connected to the corresponding narrative material.

Appendix B *Traditional Form-Critical Analysis* 247

5 2.10, Narrative *introducing* oracle

5!   2.11-19, Oracle *concerning* the people

6 2.20-21a, Narrative *introducing* oracle *to* Zerubbabel

6!   2.21b-23, Oracle *concerning* nations and Zerubbabel

APPENDIX C:
DATING DETAILS IN HAGGAI

1.1:   In the second year of King Darius in the sixth month on the first day of the month
> 29 August 520 BCE
>> New moon
>>> Harvest season

1.15a   On the twenty-fourth day of the month in the sixth month
> 21 September 520 BCE
>> Harvest season

1.15b–2.1: In the second year of King Darius in the seventh month on the twenty-first day of the month
> 17 October 520 BCE
>> Feast of booths (final day)
>>> Harvest thanksgiving
>>>> Early rains beginning

2.10:   On the twenty-fourth day of the ninth month in the second year
of Darius
> 18 December 520 BCE
>> Ploughing and sowing completed

[2.18:   On the twenty-fourth day of the ninth month]

2.20:   On the twenty-fourth day of the month
> 18 December 520 BCE
>> Ploughing and sowing completed

BIBLIOGRAPHY

Commentaries

Achtemeier, E., *Nahum–Malachi* (Interpretation; Atlanta: John Knox Press, 1986).
Baldwin, J.G., *Haggai, Zechariah, Malachi* (TOTC; London: Tyndale Press, 1972).
Barnes, W.E., *Haggai, Zechariah and Malachi, with Notes and Introduction* (Cambridge: Cambridge University Press, 1934).
Conrad, E.W., *Zechariah* (Readings; Sheffield: Sheffield Academic Press, 1999).
Feinberg, C.L., *Jeremiah: A Commentary* (Grand Rapids: Regency Press, 1982).
Kodell, J., *Lamentations, Haggai, Zechariah, Malachi, Obadiah, Joel, Second Zechariah, Baruch* (Wilmington, GA: Michael Glazier, 1982).
Larsson, G., *Bound for Freedom: The Book of Exodus in Jewish and Christian Traditions* (Peabody, MA: Hendrickson, 1999).
March, W.E., 'The Book of Haggai', in L.E. Keck (ed.), *The New Interpreter's Bible* (12 vols.; Nashville: Abingdon Press, 1996), VII, pp. 707-32.
McKane, W., *Critical and Exegetical Commentary on Jeremiah*, I (ICC; 2 vols.; Edinburgh: T. & T. Clark, 1986).
Meadowcroft, T.J., and N.D. Irwin, *The Book of Daniel* (ABCS; Singapore: Asia Theological Association, 2004).
Merrill, E.H., *An Exegetical Commentary: Haggai, Zechariah, Malachi* (Chicago: Moody Press, 1994).
Meyers, C.L., and E.M. Meyers, *Haggai, Zechariah 1–8: A New Translation with Introduction and Commentary* (AB, 25B; Garden City, NY: Doubleday, 1987).
Mitchell, H.G., 'A Critical and Exegetical Commentary on Haggai and Zechariah', in H.G. Mitchell, J.M.P. Smith and J.A. Bewer, *A Critical and Exegetical Commentary on Haggai, Zechariah, Malachi and Jonah* (ICC; Edinburgh: T. & T. Clark, 1912), pp. 1-362.
Moloney, F.J., *The Gospel of John* (SPS, 4; Collegeville, MN: Liturgical Press, 1998).
Motyer, J.A., 'Haggai', in T.E. McComiskey (ed.), *The Minor Prophets: An Exegetical and Expository Commentary*. III. *Zephaniah, Haggai, Zechariah and Malachi* (Grand Rapids: Baker Books, 1998), pp. 963-1002.
O'Brien, J.M., *Nahum, Habakkuk, Zephaniah, Haggai, Zechariah, Malachi* (AOTC; Nashville: Abingdon Press, 2004).

Petersen, D.L., *Haggai and Zechariah 1–8: A Commentary* (OTL; London: SCM Press, 1984).
Pusey, E.B., *The Minor Prophets with a Commentary Explanatory and Practical, and Introductions to the Several Books*. VII. *Zephaniah and Haggai* (London: James Nisbet & Co., 1907).
Rudolph, W., *Haggai–Sacharja 1–8–Sacharja 9–14–Maleachi* (Gütersloh: Gerd Mohn, 1976).
Skehan, P.W., and A.A. DiLella, *The Wisdom of Ben Sira* (AB, 39; New York: Doubleday, 1987).
Smith, R.L., *Micah–Malachi* (WBC, 32; Waco, TX: Word Books, 1984).
Thomas, D.W., and W.L. Sperry, 'The Book of Haggai', in G.A. Buttrick (ed.), *The Interpreter's Bible* (12 vols.; New York: Abingdon Press, 1956), pp. 1036-49.
Verhoef, P.A., *The Books of Haggai and Malachi* (NICOT; Grand Rapids: Eerdmans, 1987).
Wolff, H.W., *Haggai: A Commentary* (trans. M. Kohl; Minneapolis: Augsburg, 1988).

Other Books and Articles on Haggai

Ackroyd, P., 'The Book of Haggai and Zechariah I–VIII', *JJS* 3 (1952), pp. 151-56.
—'Some Interpretative Glosses in the Book of Haggai', *JJS* 7 (1956), pp. 163-67.
—'Studies in the Book of Haggai', *JJS* 3 (1952), pp. 1-13.
Boda, M., 'Haggai: Master Rhetorician', *TynBul* 51 (2000), pp. 295-304.
Clark, D.J., 'Discourse Structure in Haggai', *JOTT* 5 (1992), pp. 13-24.
Coggins, R.J., *Haggai, Zechariah, Malachi* (OTG; Sheffield; JSOT Press, 1987).
Kessler, J., *The Book of Haggai: Prophecy and Society in Early Persian Yehud* (VTSup, 91; Leiden: E.J. Brill, 2002).
—'Reconstructing Haggai's Jerusalem: Demographic and Sociological Considerations and the Search for an Adequate Methodological Point of Departure', in L.L. Grabbe and R.D. Haak (eds.), *'Every City Shall Be Forsaken': Urbanism and Prophecy in Ancient Israel and the Near East* (JSOTSup, 330; Sheffield: Sheffield Academic Press, 2001), pp. 137-58.
May, H.G., '"This People" and "This Nation" in Haggai', *VT* 18 (1968), pp. 190-97.
Pfeil, R., 'When is a *Goy* a "Goy"? The Interpretation of Haggai 2:10-19', in W.C. Kaiser and R.F. Youngblood (eds.), *A Tribute to Gleeson Archer* (Chicago: Moody Press, 1986), pp. 261-78.
Pierce, R.W., 'Literary Connectors and a Haggai/Zechariah/Malachi Corpus', *JETS* 27 (1984), pp. 277-89.
—'A Thematic Development of the Haggai/Zechariah/Malachi Corpus', *JETS* 27 (1984), pp. 401-11.
Siebeneck, R.T., 'The Messianism of Aggeus and Proto-Zacharias', *CBQ* 19 (1957), pp. 312-28.
Sim, R.J., 'Notes on Haggai 2:10-21', *JOTT* 5 (1992), pp. 25-36.

Tollington, J.E., 'Readings in Haggai: From the Prophet to the Completed Book: A Changing Message in Changing Times', in B. Becking and M.C.A. Korpel (eds.), *The Crisis of Israelite Religion: Transformation of Religious Tradition in Exilic and Post-Exilic Times* (Leiden: E.J. Brill, 1991), pp. 194-208.
—*Tradition and Innovation in Haggai and Zechariah 1–8* (JSOTSup, 150; Sheffield: JSOT Press, 1993).
Tuell, S.S., 'Haggai–Zechariah: Prophecy after the Manner of Ezekiel', in P.L. Redditt and A. Schart (eds.), *Thematic Threads in the Book of the Twelve* (Berlin: W. de Gruyter, 2003), pp. 273-91.
Whedbee, J.W., 'A Question–Answer Schema in Haggai 1: The Form and Function of Haggai 1:9-11', in A. Tuttle (ed.), *Biblical and Near Eastern Studies: Essays in Honor of William Sanford LaSor* (Grand Rapids: Eerdmans, 1978), pp. 184-94.

Books and Articles on the Second Temple Period

Ackroyd, P., *Exile and Restoration: A Study of Hebrew Thought of the Sixth Century BC* (London: SCM Press, 1968).
—'Two Old Testament Historical Problems of the Early Persian Period', *JNES* 17 (1958), pp. 13-27.
Albertz, R., 'The Thwarted Restoration', in R. Albertz and B. Becking (eds.), *Yahwism after the Exile: Perspectives on Israelite Religion in the Persian Era* (STAR, 5; Assen: Van Gorcum, 2003), pp. 1-17.
Barstad, H.M., *The Myth of the Empty Land: A Study in the History and Archaeology of Judah during the 'Exilic' Period* (SOFS, 28; Oslo: Scandinavian University Press, 1996).
Bedford, P.R., *Temple Restoration in Early Achaemenid Judah* (JSJSup, 65; Leiden: E.J. Brill, 2001).
Blenkinsopp, J., 'The Social Roles of Prophets in Early Achaemenid Judah', *JSOT* 93 (2000), pp. 39-58.
Boccaccini, G., *The Roots of Rabbinic Judaism: An Intellectual History, from Ezekiel to Daniel* (Grand Rapids: Eerdmans, 2002).
Carroll, R.P., 'So What Do We *Know* about the Temple? The Temple in the Prophets', in T.C. Eskenazi and K.H. Richards (eds.), *Second Temple Studies. II. Temple and Community in the Persian Period* (JSOTSup, 175; Sheffield: Sheffield Academic Press, 1994), pp. 34-51.
Carter, C.E., *The Emergence of Yehud in the Persian Period: A Social and Demographic Study* (JSOTSup, 294; Sheffield: Sheffield Academic Press, 1999).
Cohen, N.G., 'From *Nabi* to *Mal'ak* to "Ancient Figure"', *JJS* 36 (1985), pp. 12-24.
Dumbrell, W.J., 'Kingship and Temple in the Post-Exilic Period', *RTR* 37 (1978), pp. 33-42.
Fried, L.S., 'The Land Lay Desolate: Conquest and Restoration in the Ancient Near East', in O. Lipschits and J. Blenkinsopp (eds.), *Judah and the Judeans in the Neo-Babylonian Period* (Winona Lake, IN: Eisenbrauns, 2003), pp. 21-54.

Fuller, R., 'The Form and Formation of the Book of the Twelve: The Evidence from the Judean Desert', in J.W. Watts and P.R. House (eds.), *Forming the Prophetic Literature: Essays on Isaiah and the Twelve in Honor of John D.W. Watts* (JSOTSup, 235; Sheffield: Sheffield Academic Press, 1996), pp. 86-101.

Gärtner, B., *The Temple and the Community in Qumran and the New Testament: A Comparative Study in the Temple Symbolism of the Qumran Texts and the New Testament* (SNTS, 1; Cambridge: Cambridge University Press, 1965).

Gelston, A., 'The Foundations of the Second Temple', *VT* 16 (1966), pp. 232-35.

Laato, A., *A Star is Rising: The Historical Development of the Old Testament Royal Ideology and the Rise of Jewish Messianic Expectations* (Atlanta: Scholars Press, 1997).

Petersen, D.L., 'Zerubbabel and Jerusalem Temple Reconstruction', *CBQ* 36 (1974), pp. 366-72.

Rooke, D.W., *Zadok's Heirs: The Role and Development of the High Priesthood in Ancient Israel* (Oxford: Oxford University Press, 2000).

Rose, W.H., *Zemah and Zerubbabel: Messianic Expectations in the Early Postexilic Period* (JSOTSup, 304; Sheffield: Sheffield Academic Press, 2000).

Schiffman, L.H., *Reclaiming the Dead Sea Scrolls: The History of Judaism, the Background of Christianity, and the Lost Library of Qumran* (New York: Doubleday, 1994).

Schmidt, F., *How the Temple Thinks: Identity and Social Cohesion in Ancient Judaism* (trans. J.E. Crowley; BS, 78; Sheffield: Sheffield Academic Press, 2001).

Schniedewind, W.M., *The Word of God in Transition: From Prophet to Exegete in the Second Temple Period* (JSOTSup, 197; Sheffield: Sheffield Academic Press, 1995).

Vanderhooft, D.S., 'New Evidence Pertaining to the Transition from Neo-Babylonian to Achaemenid Administration in Palestine', in R. Albertz and B. Becking (eds.), *Yahwism after the Exile: Perspectives on Israelite Religion in the Persian Era* (STAR, 5; Assen: Van Gorcum, 2003), pp. 219-36.

Books and Articles on Interpretive Methodology

Alter, R., *The Art of Biblical Narrative* (London: George Allen & Unwin, 1981).

Barton, J., *Reading the Old Testament: Method in Biblical Study* (London: Darton, Longman & Todd, 1984).

Barton, S., 'New Testament Interpretation as Performance', *SJT* 52 (1999), pp. 179-208.

Bird, P.A., *Missing Persons and Mistaken Identities: Women and Gender in Ancient Israel* (OBT; Minneapolis: Fortress Press, 1997).

Carston, R., and S. Uchida (eds.), *Relevance Theory: Applications and Implications* (P&B NS, 37; Amsterdam: John Benjamins, 1998).

Clark, W., 'Stylistics and Relevance Theory', *Language and Literature* 5 (1996), pp. 163-78.
Clines, D.J.A., 'Varieties of Indeterminacy', *Semeia* 71 (1995), pp. 17-27.
Cohen, T., 'Metaphor, Feeling, and Narrative', *Philosophy and Literature* 21 (1997), pp. 223-44.
Culler, J., 'Literary Competence', in J.P. Tompkins (ed.), *Reader-Response Criticism: From Formalism to Post-Structuralism* (Baltimore: The Johns Hopkins University Press, 1980), pp. 101-44.
Damrosch, D., *The Narrative Covenant* (Ithaca, NY: Cornell University Press, 1991).
Davies, P.R., *Whose Bible Is It Anyway?* (JSOTSup, 204; Sheffield: Sheffield Academic Press, 1995).
Detweiler, R., 'What Is a Sacred Text?', *Semeia* 31 (1985), pp. 213-30.
Eco, U., *The Limits of Interpretation* (Bloomington: Indiana University Press, 1990).
Fish, S., *Is There a Text in This Class? The Authority of Interpretive Communities* (Cambridge, MA: Harvard University Press, 1980).
Fowler, R.M., 'Who is "The Reader" in Reader Response Criticism?', *Semeia* 31 (1985), pp. 5-23.
Genette, G., *Narrative Discourse* (trans. J.E. Lewin; Oxford: Basil Blackwell, 1980).
Gibbs, R.W., *Intention in the Experience of Meaning* (Cambridge: Cambridge University Press, 1999).
Goldingay, J.E., *Models for Interpretation of Scripture* (Grand Rapids: Eerdmans, 1995).
—*Models for Scripture* (Grand Rapids: Eerdmans, 1994).
Gutt, E.-A., *Relevance Theory: A Guide to Successful Communication in Translation* (Dallas: Summer Institute of Linguistics; New York: United Bible Societies, 1992).
—*Translation and Relevance: Cognition and Context* (Oxford: Basil Blackwell, 1991).
Lanser, S., *The Narrative Act* (Princeton, NJ: Princeton University Press, 1981).
MacMahon, B., 'Indirectness, Rhetoric and Interpretative Use: Communicative Strategies in Browning's *My Last Duchess*', *Language and Literature* 5 (1996), pp. 209-23.
McDonald, J.I.H., 'Rhetorical Criticism', in R.J. Coggins and J.L. Houlden (eds.), *The SCM Dictionary of Biblical Interpretation* (London: SCM Press, 1990), pp. 599-600.
Meadowcroft, T.J., 'Between Authorial Intent and Indeterminacy: The Incarnation as an Invitation to Human–Divine Discourse', *SJT* 58 (2005), pp. 199-218.
—'Narrative, Metaphor, Interpretation and Reader in Daniel 2–5', *Narrative* 8 (2000), pp. 257-78.
—'Relevance as a Mediating Category in the Reading of Biblical Texts: Venturing Beyond the Hermeneutical Circle', *JETS* 45 (2002), pp. 611-27.

Moberly, R.W.L., *The Bible, Theology, and Faith: A Study of Abraham and Jesus* (CSCD, 5; Cambridge: Cambridge University Press, 2000).
Pilkington, A., 'Poetic Effects', *Lingua* 87 (1992), pp. 29-51.
—'Introduction: Relevance Theory and Literary Style', *Language and Literature* 5 (1996), pp. 157-62
Polanyi, M., *Personal Knowledge: Towards a Post-Critical Philosophy* (Chicago: University of Chicago Press, 1962).
Rutledge, D., 'Faithful Reading: Poststructuralism and the Sacred', *BI* 4 (1996), pp. 270-87.
Schneiders, S.M., *The Revelatory Text: Interpreting the New Testament as Sacred Scripture* (New York: Harper Collins, 1991).
Smith, N., and D. Wilson, 'Introduction', *Lingua* 87 (1992), pp. 4-6.
Song Nam Sun, 'Metaphor and Metonymy', in Carston and Uchida (eds.), *Relevance Theory*, pp. 87-104.
Sperber, D., and D. Wilson, *Relevance, Communication and Cognition* (Oxford: Basil Blackwell, 2nd edn, 1995).
Sternberg, M., *The Poetics of Biblical Narrative: Ideological Literature and the Drama of Reading* (Bloomington: Indiana University Press, 1987).
Thiselton, A.C., *New Horizons in Hermeneutics* (Grand Rapids: Zondervan, 1992).
—'On Models and Methods: A Conversation with Robert Morgan', in D.J.A. Clines, S.E. Fowl and S.E. Porter (eds.), *The Bible in Three Dimensions: Essays in Celebration of Forty Years of Biblical Studies in the University of Sheffield* (JSOTSup, 87; Sheffield: JSOT Press, 1990), pp. 337-56.
Trotter, D. 'Analysing Literary Prose: The Relevance of Relevance Theory', *Lingua* 87 (1992), pp. 11-27.
Uchida, S. 'Text and Relevance', in Carston and Uchida (eds.), *Relevance Theory*, pp. 161-78.
Vanhoozer, K.J., 'A Lamp in the Labyrinth: The Hermeneutics of "Aesthetic" Theology', *TriJ* 8 (1987), pp. 25-56.
Verheyden, J., 'The Basic Features of Schleiermacher's Hermeneutics', in D.E. Klemm and T.N. Tice (eds.), *Papers of the Schleiermacher Group and Schleiermacher Society* (San Francisco: AAR, 1997).
Wendland, E.R., 'On the Relevance of "Relevance Theory" for Bible Translation', *BT* 47 (1996), pp. 126-37.
Wolterstorff, N., *Divine Discourse: Philosophical Reflections on the Claim that God Speaks* (Cambridge: Cambridge University Press, 1995).
Wright, N.T., 'How Can the Bible Be Authoritative?', *Vox Evangelica* 21 (1991), pp. 7-32.

Other Books and Articles

Beale, G.K., *The Temple and the Church's Mission: A Biblical Theology of the Dwelling Place of God* (Downers Grove, IL: Apollos, 2004).
Beckwith, R.T., *The Old Testament Canon of the New Testament Church and Its Background in Early Judaism* (London: SPCK, 1985).

Ben Zvi, E., 'Twelve Prophetic Books or "The Twelve": A Few Preliminary Considerations', in Watts and House (eds.), *Forming the Prophetic Literature*, pp. 125-56.

Brueggemann, W., *Theology of the Old Testament: Testimony, Dispute, Advocacy* (Minneapolis: Fortress Press, 1997).

Clines, D.J.A., 'Sacred Space, Holy Places and Suchlike', in *On the Way to the Postmodern: Old Testament Essays 1967–1998*, II (JSOTSup, 292; Sheffield: Sheffield Academic Press, 1998), pp. 542-54.

DeVries, S.J., 'Futurism in the Preexilic Minor Prophets Compared with That of the Postexilic Minor Prophets', in P.L. Redditt and A. Schart (eds.), *Thematic Threads in the Book of the Twelve* (Berlin: W. de Gruyter, 2003), pp. 252-72.

Douglas, M., *Purity and Danger: An Analysis of Concepts of Pollution and Taboo* (Middlesex: Penguin Books, 1966).

Floyd, M.H., *Minor Prophets Part 2* (FOTL, 22; Grand Rapids: Eerdmans, 2000).

Goldingay, J.E., *Old Testament Theology*. I. *Israel's Gospel* (Downers Grove, IL: InterVarsity Press, 2003).

Harrington, D.J., 'Review of Robert Hayward, *Divine Name and Presence: The Memra*', *CBQ* 45 (1983), pp. 133-34.

Hays, R.B., *Echoes of Scripture in the Letters of Paul* (New Haven: Yale University Press, 1989).

Hayward, C.T.R., 'The Holy Name of the God of Moses and the Prologue of St John's Gospel', *NTS* 25 (1979), pp. 16-32.

House, P.R., 'The Character of God in the Book of the Twelve', in *Society of Biblical Literature Seminar Papers, 1998. Part Two* (Atlanta: Scholars Press, 1998), pp. 831-49.

—*The Unity of the Twelve* (JSOTSup, 97; Sheffield: Almond Press, 1990).

Janowski, B., and P. Stuhlmacher (eds.), *The Suffering Servant: Isaiah 53 in Jewish and Christian Sources* (trans. D.P. Bailey; Grand Rapids: Eerdmans, 2004).

Meadowcroft, T.J., *Aramaic Daniel and Greek Daniel: A Literary Comparison* (JSOTSup, 198; Sheffield: Sheffield Academic Press, 1995).

Pattemore, S., *The People of God in the Apocalypse: Discourse, Structure and Exegesis* (SNTSMS, 128; Cambridge: Cambridge University Press, 2004).

Pomykala, K.E., *The Davidic Dynasty Tradition in Early Judaism: Its History and Significance for Messianism* (SBLEJL, 7; Atlanta: Scholars Press, 1995).

Redditt, P.L., ' Zechariah 9–14, Malachi, and the Redaction of the Book of the Twelve', in Watts and House (eds.), *Forming the Prophetic Literature*, pp. 245-68.

Spieckermann, H., 'The Conception and Prehistory of the Idea of Vicarious Suffering in the Old Testament', in Janowski and Stuhlmacher (eds.), *The Suffering Servant*, pp. 1-15.

Stuhlmacher, P., 'Isaiah 53 in the Gospels and Acts', in Janowski and Stuhlmacher (eds.), *The Suffering Servant*, pp. 147-62.

Vischer, W., *The Witness of the Old Testament to Christ*. I. *The Pentateuch* (trans. A.B. Crabtree; London: Lutterworth, 1949).

Watts, J.W., and P.R. House (eds.), *Forming the Prophetic Literature: Essays on Isaiah and the Twelve in Honor of John D.W. Watts* (JSOTSup, 235; Sheffield: Sheffield Academic Press, 1996).

Williamson, H.G.M., *Variations on a Theme: King, Messiah and Servant in the Book of Isaiah* (Carlisle: Paternoster Press, 1998).

Wright, D.P., *The Disposal of Impurity: Elimination Rites in the Bible and in Hittite and Mesopotamian Literature* (SBLDS, 101; Atlanta: Scholars Press, 1987).

Reference Material and Historical Texts

Babylonian Talmud (ed. I. Epstein; London: Soncino, 1938).

Brooke, G.J., *Exegesis at Qumran: 4QFlorilegium in its Jewish Context* (JSOTSup, 29; Sheffield: JSOT Press, 1985).

Calvin, J., *Commentaries on the Twelve Minor Prophets*. IV. *Habakkuk, Zephaniah, Haggai* (trans. J. Owen; Edinburgh: Calvin Translation Society, 1848).

The Dead Sea Scrolls Study Edition (ed. F. García Martínez and E.J.C. Tigchelaar; 2 vols.; Leiden: E.J. Brill, 1997–98).

DiLella, A.A., *The Hebrew Text of Sirach: A Text-Critical Study* (London: Mouton & Co., 1966).

Dimant, D., '4QFlorilegium and the Idea of the Community as Temple', in A. Caquot, M. Hadas-Lebel and J. Riaud (eds.), *Hellenica et Judaica: Hommage à Valentin Nikiprowetzky* (Leuven: Peeters, 1986), pp. 165-89.

Finegan, J., *Handbook of Biblical Chronology: Principles of Time Reckoning in the Ancient World and Problems of Chronology in the Bible* (Princeton, NJ: Princeton University Press, 1964).

Fletcher-Louis, C.H.T., *All the Glory of Adam: Liturgical Anthropology in the Dead Sea Scrolls* (STDJ, 42; Leiden: E.J. Brill, 2002).

Gordon, R.P., *Studies in the Targum to the Twelve Prophets: From Nahum to Malachi* (VTSup, 51; Leiden: E.J. Brill, 1994).

Gordon, R.P., and K.J. Cathcart, *The Targum of the Minor Prophets: Translated, with a Critical Introduction, Apparatus, and Notes* (Aramaic Bible, 14; Edinburgh: T. & T. Clark, 1989).

Harris, R.L., G.L. Archer and B.K. Waltke, *Theological Wordbook of the Old Testament* (2 vols.; Chicago: Moody Press, 1980).

Hayward, C.T.R., *The Jewish Temple: A Non-Biblical Sourcebook* (London: Routledge, 1996).

Jenkyn, W., 'Reformation's Remora; or, Temporizing the Stop of Building the Temple: A Sermon Preached before the Right Honourable the House of Peers, in the Abbey-Church at Westminster, upon the 25th of February, 1645, being the Day Appointed for the Solemne and Pulike Humiliation', in R. Jeffs (ed.), *The English Revolution*. I. *Fast Sermons to Parliament, Volume 22 Feb 1645/6–Mar 1646* (London: Cornmarket Press, 1971), pp. 10-50.

Josephus. VI. *Jewish Antiquities, Books IX–XI* (trans. R. Marcus; Loeb Classical Library; London: Heinemann, 1937).

Luther, Martin, 'Lectures on Haggai', in *Luther's Works*. XVIII. *Lectures on the Minor Prophets* (ed. H.C. Oswald; trans. R.J. Dinda; St Louis, MI: Concordia, 1975), pp. 365-87.

Midrash Rabbah (ed. H. Freedman and M. Simon; London: Soncino Press, 1939).

Philo, IV (trans. F.H.C. Colson and G.H. Whitaker; Loeb Classical Library; London: Heinemann, 1932).

Rainolds, J., *The Prophesie of Haggai: Interpreted and Applyed in Sundry Sermons* (London: William Lee, 1649).

Schleiermacher, F.D., *Hermeneutics: The Handwritten Manuscripts* (ed. H. Himmerli; trans. J. Duke and J. Forstman; Missoula, MT: Scholars Press, 1977).

INDEX OF AUTHORS

Achtemeier, E. 46
Ackroyd, P. 2, 43, 75
Alter, R. 12

Baldwin, J.G. 57, 59, 76, 77
Barnes, W.E. 74
Barstad, H.M. 44, 47
Barton, J. 78
Barton, S. 10, 39
Beale, G.K. 70
Beckwith, R.T. 78
Ben Zvi, E. 60
Bird, P.A. 36
Boccaccini, G. 53, 55
Boda, M. 86
Brooke, G.J. 49
Brueggemann, W. 10

Calvin, J. 71, 72
Cashdan, E. 86
Cathcart, K.J. 65, 67
Clark, D.J. 9
Clark, W. 23
Clines, D.J.A. 5
Coggins, R.J. 43, 44, 74
Cohen, T. 27
Conrad, E.W. 85
Culler, J. 7

Damrosch, D. 12
Davies, P.R. 33, 35
Detweiler, R. 31
DiLella, A.A. 64, 79
Dimant, D. 48, 49
Dumbrell, W.J. 77

Eco, U. 5

Feinberg, C.L. 58
Finegan, J. 42
Fish, S. 15
Fletcher-Louis, C.H.T. 51
Fowler, R.M. 6
Fried, L.S. 47
Fuller, R. 78

Gärtner, B. 49
Genette, G. 17
Gibbs, R.W. 5, 17, 19
Goldingay, J.E. 2, 4, 9, 10, 32, 34-38, 47
Gordon, R.P. 65-67
Gutt, E.-A. 25, 26

Harrington, D.J. 67
Hays, R.B. 28
Hayward, C.T.R. 48, 65, 67
House, P.R. 11, 80-85

Irwin, N.D. 18

Jenkyn, W. 72, 73

Kessler, J. 45, 47
Kodell, J. 74

Laato, A. 44
Lanser, S. 17
Larsson, G. 46
Luther, M. 3, 71

MacMahon, B. 23
May, H.G. 2
McDonald, J.I.H. 9
McKane, W. 58

Meadowcroft, T.J. 4, 11, 18, 28, 38, 52
Merrill, E.H. 76
Meyers, C.L. 42, 44, 54, 55, 57, 76
Meyers, E.M. 42, 44, 54, 55, 57, 76
Mitchell, H.G. 75, 86
Moberly, R.W.L. 29, 33, 37, 39
Moloney, F.J. 12

O'Brien, J.M. 87

Pattemore, S. 16, 19, 25
Petersen, D.L. 53, 76
Pfeil, R. 87
Pierce, R.W. 85
Pilkington, A. 21, 23, 24
Polanyi, M. 4, 13, 35
Pusey, E.B. 70, 74

Rainolds, J. 73
Redditt, P.L. 80
Rooke, D.W. 53, 57
Rudolph, W. 1
Rutledge, D. 31

Schiffman, L.H. 46, 47, 50
Schleiermacher, F.D. 4

Schneiders, S.M. 36, 41
Siebeneck, R.T. 77
Skehan, P.W. 64, 79
Smith, N. 21
Smith, R.L. 82
Song Nam Sun 22, 24
Sperber, D. 16, 20, 22-24, 27
Sperry, W.L. 13, 87
Spieckermann, H. 19
Sternberg, M. 14, 33, 34
Stuhlmacher, P. 18

Thiselton, A.C. 5, 15, 17
Thomas, D.W. 13, 87
Tollington, J.E. 45, 87
Trotter, D. 23

Uchida, S. 23

Vanhoozer, K.J. 9
Verheyden, J. 4
Vischer, W. 37, 38

Wendland, E.R. 25, 26
Williamson, H.G.M. 12
Wilson, D. 16, 20-24, 27
Wolff, H.W. 2, 61, 62, 75
Wolterstorff, N. 33, 34
Wright, N.T. 40

www.ingramcontent.com/pod-product-compliance
Lightning Source LLC
Chambersburg PA
CBHW050134170426
43197CB00011B/1828